SURPRISE ATTACK

Sunday morning, December 7, 1941, was warm and sunny in Hawaii. Aboard the ships in Pearl Harbor the day was just getting under way: morning church services were being held on some; on others, the American flag was being raised.

Meanwhile, in the sky north of Hawaii, Commander Mitsuo Fuchida was leading the first wave of Japanese planes toward the harbor. He grinned, thinking about the destruction of the American Navy.

The first bombs hit Ford Island. As the explosions went off, people panicked and tried to escape the machine-gun fire from the air—but the entire harbor was ablaze. Two hours later, the American fleet lay burning, totally destroyed.

It would be months before the ships could be raised, refitted, and put back into action. The Japanese had won a great victory—this time. But from that day forward, the United States would retaliate heavily—and the history of the world would be greatly changed.

PACIFIC CARRIER

BY RUBEN P. KITCHEN, JR.

ZEBRA BOOKS
KENSINGTON PUBLISHING CORP.

ZEBRA BOOKS

are published by

KENSINGTON PUBLISHING CORP.
21 East 40th Street
New York, N.Y. 10016

Fourth printing: July 1984

Printed in the United States of America

ACKNOWLEDGMENTS

While collecting information for this book I read many books, magazines, and other sources to get the historical facts concerning the *Yorktown* and the years in which she was a commissioned ship in the United States Navy. From these sources I got the background; but it was from the numerous letters, diaries, recorded tapes, phone conversations, and talks with those who served aboard the *Yorktown* that I received many personal glimpses of carrier life, both in wartime and peacetime.

I would like to thank the following people for the interest that they have taken in helping me to compile the stories and facts that have been mentioned in this story about the aircraft carrier *Yorktown,* CV-10.

Joseph R. Kristufek, Richard Eastman, James R. Pfister, Vice Admiral Bernard M. "Smoke" Strean, Joseph H. Huber, Edward Johnson,

Ted Rohrbough, Joe Leathers, Ed Simko, Harland Bickford, Kenneth Parkinson, Ruben P. Kitchen, Sr., Alfred E. Fleener, Donald Seaman, Edward N. Wallace, Richard C. Tripp, Charles McKellar, J. Clifford Huddleston, Boyd Ingram, Melvin L. Bien, Don Lampley, Jack Jones, and George W. Morgan.

These people provided me with numerous human interest stories as well as facts. From them I received letters, diaries, recorded tapes, phone calls, and personal interviews. I am indebted to them, for this is their story and the story of their ship.

The following people also provided me with valuable information about two other ships which operated in the Pacific during World War II.

Jesse A. Clarke, John R. Bates, Harold T. Kunkle, and Mrs. C.E. Mosher

In all the correspondence that I have received concerning the *Yorktown,* I have found one common factor: those served aboard her were all proud of her, and proud to be "Yorktowners". This is their story, and I am proud that they have given me the opportunity to write it.

You yourself can experience the pride that these men have for their ship. She is now a permanent museum berthed in Charlestown, South Carolina. Visit her, and walk the decks that these men walked. After spending several hours aboard her, you too will leave with a little more pride in our country and in those who have made her the greatest country in the world. Because it was thousands of citizens like these who gave us the freedom we enjoy today.

DEDICATION

Men of the sea have always treated their ships as if they were female. The character of each vessel depended upon the type of ship each was. If she was a luxury liner she was considered a delicate and petite lady; a cargo ship or tanker was a robust working girl who could handle the seas, yet still be a lady at heart; a warship was like Joan of Arc: youthful, full of fighting spirit, and willing to challenge the odds and beat them.

In the years following World War I, a new type of warship emerged. This new warship was frail in comparison with the battleship and heavy cruiser. It had only light armament and a long flat deck from which planes took to the air and returned to land. This new type of warship was the aircraft carrier. The attack on Pearl Harbor that put the United States into World War II would come from aircraft carriers, and aircraft carriers would bring the planes that would help defeat the Japanese four years later.

This is the story of one of those aircraft carriers and of the men who fought with her to defeat the Japanese and to help keep the United States safe for over twenty-seven years. The ship is the "Fighting Lady," or, as she was more formally titled, the U.S.S. *Yorktown* CV-10.

The *Yorktown* was born into a wartorn world in 1943 and was a valuable part of the United States Navy until 1970 when she was finally retired. Now she is a museum in Charleston, South Carolina.

The Pre-*Essex* Class Years
And Earlier *Yorktowns*

Chapter I

The Wright Brothers started it all on December 17, 1903. Few people realized the importance of the airplane; to many it seemed just a toy for the rich. As the years passed, the value of the airplane became apparent, and by 1914, fragile planes were going aloft to spy on the enemy. These were the early days of World War I.

During this period, the small, fragile planes were used only for observation. Enemy planes would pass high in the sky above Europe without incident. Then the pilots began taking rifles aloft to shoot at each other. Some even carried small bombs to drop on enemy lines below. The airplane was becoming a weapon of death and destruction. By the time the war was over on November 11, 1918, the airplane had become a specialized weapon of the air.

But even before the start of World War I, men of vision in the Navy had begun to experiment with the new invention. The plane, with its ability to fly high in the air, could scout the horizon for enemy ships in time of war. But to do this most effectively it was necessary to have a ship capable of launching and retrieving the plane. This was the birth of the aircraft carrier.

In the fall of 1910, an eighty-three-foot platform was constructed aboard the cruiser *Birmingham,* reaching from its bridge to its main deck. This deck was inclined downward from the bridge to the main deck toward the bow.

On the morning of November 14, 1910, preparations were made for the first plane to fly from a ship. At 3:16 P.M., Eugene Ely revved up the plane's engine and started down the platform. When the plane left the platform it dropped below the bow. The wheels and propeller struck the water, but the small plane struggled and started to climb into the wind. Sailors on the *Birmingham* cheered as Ely and his small plane flew toward land, two miles away.

The next step was to see if a plane could land aboard a ship. This experiment would take place after Christmas.

By January 11, 1911, a landing deck had been constructed on the stern of the cruiser *Pennsylvania.* A crude arresting gear had been constructed to help stop the plane as it landed. Again, Eugene Ely would be the pilot. He took off from a San Francisco airfield and flew out toward the *Pennsylvania.*

The weather was bad, as it had been in November in Norfolk, and Ely felt excited and nervous. Would it work? Would he crash? Would the arresting gear stop him from ramming into the mast and superstructure of the ship? These were questions that needed to be answered, but could only be answered by landing the plane.

When Ely approached the *Pennsylvania,* he flew over her to inspect the situation, then he turned to make the landing attempt. As he approached the landing deck for the second time, he cut the power; but because of wind currents from the ship's superstructure, he didn't come down onto the deck. Finally, after passing over eleven of the twelve arresting wires, his plane caught the last wire. He was stopped thirty feet past the spot where his plane had been caught by the wire. He had made a successful landing. It had been proven that a plane could land and take off from a ship.

Soon others began to experiment with planes and ships. The United States lost interest and other countries pulled ahead in the search to find a suitable carrier from which to launch and land planes. Great Britain and Japan advanced in carrier technology by leaps and bounds.

The British experimented with different designs, and built the first flush-deck carrier, the *Argus.* They then converted the battleship *Almirante Cochrane,* which had been intended for Chile, into the carrier *Eagle.* The *Eagle* was the first carrier with a modern aspect. She had an offset island with the funnel built into it, and two elevators to carry planes from flight deck to hangar deck. She was named the

Eagle in honor of the American eagle.

The British then built the world's first ship specifically designed as an aircraft carrier. She was the *Hermes*. The British had developed the true carrier, while the United States had all but forgotten about the concept.

The Japanese also leaped ahead of the United States in the building of carriers. They built the world's second ship designed from the keel up as an aircraft carrier. She was the *Hosho*. Years later, the Japanese would teach the Americans some valuable lessons in carrier warfare.

The United States Navy continued to rely on its huge battleships to defend her against aggression on the high seas. For the United States, although first in the field of democracy, is frequently late in other fields, waiting until the need for action arises. This was the case with aircraft carriers. Sometimes men have to be convinced of the need for a new device, either peacefully or with a slap in the face.

The men in the navy who could see that the plane would be the weapon of future wars had to convince older battleship admirals, congressmen, and the general public that a small group of planes with bombs could sink a large battleship. General William "Billy" Mitchell of the army sank the captured battleship *Ostfriesland* using planes alone. Yet the battleship admirals argued that had there been men aboard the ship to fight back and repair the damage, the ship would have remained afloat. Billy Mitchell wasn't trying to help the navy, but he was trying to prove to Congress that the army should have a separate air force. But when General Mitchell did sink the battleship, he inadvertently helped in the development of the aircraft carrier. The navy began looking at the airplane in a more serious manner.

The United States already had one aircraft carrier, the converted collier *Jupiter*. She was the ideal ship to convert. Her large holds could carry planes and spare parts, and house shops to repair the planes. She didn't need a large crew, and therefore had the room for the aircrews. She was commissioned as the aircraft carrier *Langley* on March 30, 1922, her designated number being *CV-1*. The United States now had a carrier, the first of over two hundred to come. The initials "CV" were used to designate this type of ship from others. "C" was for carrier while "V" stood for heavier than air, which the plane was. Thus "CV" meant carrier of heavier-than-air vehicles.

The *Langley* was named after Samuel Pierpoint Langley, a distinguished astronomer and physicist who had experimented with flying machines as early as 1898. The *Langley* was small, only 542 feet long, with an 11,050 ton displacement. She carried thirty-four planes and had only one elevator. She didn't have a superstructure or an island, and her cruising speed was only fifteen knots.

But the *Langley* was valuable to the navy. From her, future naval officers would learn to land and take off from a ship at sea. The navy used her as an experimental ship, learning new techniques and valuable lessons. Because of the *Langley,* the navy decided to build two more carriers. These were the *Lexington* and the *Saratoga*.

Following World War I, it was decided to limit the size of each nation's navy. The Washington Conference led to the United States' conversion of two battlecruisers into aircraft carriers. On July 1, 1922, the two giant battlecruisers that had been authorized for construction prior to the United States' entry into World War I were scheduled to be completed as aircraft carriers. The *Lexington* would be designated as the CV-2, while the *Saratoga* would be designated as the CV-3.

Each ship would displace 33,000 tons and be 888 feet in length. Only the British battlecruiser *Hood* was larger. Both ships could reach thirty-four knots and carry eighty planes. Both ships joined the fleet in 1927. The *Lexington* and *Saratoga* were sister ships of what came to be known as the *Lexington* class. When both carriers travelled together, pilots would get confused as to which ship was which. To help prevent this the *Lexington* had a horizontal stripe painted around her large funnel, while the *Saratoga* had a vertical one.

By 1930, the United States had three carriers: the *Langley,* the *Lexington,* and the *Saratoga*. The latter two were named for famous battles of the American Revolution. But we were still behind Great Britain, with six carriers, and Japan, with three and one more under construction.

Washington was still debating whether carriers were really useful. On February 13, 1929, a bill was passed permitting the construction of fifteen cruisers and one aircraft carrier. Construction was held off until the London Naval Treaty of 1930 was ratified. Finally, on September 26, 1931, the keel was laid for another carrier. She was the *Ranger,* designated as the CV-4, and named after the flagship of John Paul Jones' Navy of 1777.

The *Ranger* was a smaller carrier than both the "Lex" and the "Sara." She displaced 14,500 tons and was 769 feet long. Her speed was only twenty-nine knots, but she carried eighty planes. Even before the *Ranger* was completed, plans were being drawn up for two more carriers.

With funds from the Public Works Administration, the keels for the *Yorktown* and *Enterprise* were laid down in 1934. The United States Navy was growing, and each new class of carrier was built using the experience gained from constructing the previous carriers. The *Yorktown* class would help set the standard for the later, *Essex* class carriers.

The *Yorktown* was named after the battle that ended the American Revolution. She bore the same name as two other ships that had served the United States well in earlier years. She was designated as the CV-5. The carrier *Enterprise* was also named for an earlier ship. The *Enterprise* was designated as the CV-6.

The *Yorktown* was built to take a terrific amount of punishment. She had two catapults to help launch heavy planes into the wind. Both she and the *Enterprise* displaced 19,900 tons and were 809 feet long. Each could reach thirty-four knots.

The *Ranger* was launched shortly after the two *Yorktown* class carriers were laid down. Before the *Yorktown* and *Enterprise* were finished, another carrier was laid down in April of 1936. This ship was small and it combined features found in the other two carriers. She was named the *Wasp,* after a ship that fought well during the American Revolution. She was designated as the CV-7. The *Wasp* could reach a speed of twenty-nine knots and was 769 feet long, with a displacement of 14,700 tons. She could carry eighty-four aircraft and was fitted with a small port-side elevator.

Congress next authorized construction of a modified, *Yorktown* class carrier named the *Hornet* after another ship. The *Hornet* was designated as the CV-8 and was the last carrier built before America's entry into World War II.

Not only were ships being built, but men were learning how to best use this new weapon, men who could see that the day of the battleship would be over in the next war. Most of these men were just sailors who gave their all to the navy. Some were men who would help to shape the outcome of World War II.

The carrier navy of the late thirties was far different from the battleship navy. The battleship navy still demanded the old school of discipline, while the carrier navy was setting new trends. Aboard the *Yorktown* in 1939 was a sailor who had been in the navy since 1924 when he had entered at the age of sixteen. He was a seaman, but later became a chief warrant officer II. His name was C. E. Mosher, and he was one of the first men to see that carriers were to be the warship of the future. Along with Mosher in the carrier navy were men who became household words in the war years of the forties; men like Ernest J. King, William Halsey, Joseph James Clark, Arthur Radford, Gerald F. Bogan and Marc

Mitscher, just to name a few.

As December 7, 1941 approached, the navy had seven carriers. The *Langley* had been converted to a seaplane tender in 1937. The forward half of her flight deck had been removed and a bridge added. She looked more like the experiments of 1911 than the carrier of 1922. The Japanese had ten carriers operating in the Pacific, while the United States had only the *Lexington,* the *Saratoga,* and the *Enterprise. Ranger, Yorktown, Wasp, Hornet,* and CVE *Long Island* were operating in the Atlantic.

The United States not only had a smaller carrier force in the Pacific in the fall of 1941, she also had inferior carrier planes. The navy believed that it took a minimum depth of water of seveny-five feet to successfully drop torpedoes from planes. The average depth of the water in Pearl Harbor was forty feet; thus no torpedo defenses were provided at Pearl Harbor. The navy did not know that the Japanese had developed torpedoes with vanes that could be launched in water more shallow than the water at Pearl. The navy would soon learn that the impossible at times is possible.

In the United States there were two classes of carriers on the drawing board. The smaller CVL, light carrier, or *Independence* class and the larger CV, or *Essex* class. The latter would be built using the lessons learned from the *Yorktown* class. On December 1, 1941, at Newport News, Virginia, the keel was laid down for two *Essex* class carriers. These were the *Bon Homme Richard* CV-10 and the *Intrepid* CV-11. The keel had already been laid down on April 28, 1941, for the *Essex* at Newport

News. At the Bethlehem Company in Quincy, Massachusetts, the keel was laid down for the *Cabot,* CV-16, on July 15, 1941. Also at Quincy, the keel was laid down on September 15, 1941 for the *Bunker Hill* CV-17. So by December 1, 1941, the United States had seven CV's and one CVE, an escort carrier. The keels were laid down for five more CV's, and five more CVL's. Also on the way were five CVE's. These fifteen ships would not be in service until 1943.

The Japanese knew that we would soon have a bigger carrier fleet than they did, and so they decided to attack the American Fleet at Pearl Harbor and destroy it. Under the leadership of Admiral Isoroku Yamamoto they attacked the United States Navy at Pearl Harbor on December 7, 1941. From that day forward the history of the world was greatly changed.

Chapter II

In early December, construction was going along nicely on the five CV's being built in Virginia and Massachusetts. In the Pacific, the fleet was getting ready to return to Pearl Harbor. Although there was war in Europe, the Atlantic Ocean, and parts of Asia, the Pacific was still peaceful. But unknown to the Americans, a strike force of six carriers and 350 planes was making plans to attack Pearl Harbor.

On November 28, 1941 Vice Admiral William F. Halsey, Jr., left Pearl Harbor with the *Enterprise* to take planes to the marines stationed at Wake Island. The *Enterprise* was operating under war conditions, a fact which was unknown to most.

On December 5, 1941, the *Lexington* left Pearl to deliver planes to the marines stationed at Midway Island. Rear Admiral John H. Newton, who was then aboard the *Lexington,* had not been shown Washington's ''war warning'' message. Therefore he

19

did not have the *Lexington* on war alert.

The *Saratoga* was on the Pacific Coast of the United States on December 7.

The Japanese had hoped that all the carriers would be at Pearl, and indeed eight of the nine battleships in the Pacific Fleet were. On Battleship Row were the battlewagons *Nevada, Arizona, Tennessee, West Virginia, Maryland, Oklahoma,* and *California.* In dry dock was the *Pennsylvania,* the flagship of the fleet.

Sunday morning, December 7, was warm and sunny in Hawaii. Aboard the ships in Pearl, the day was just getting under way. Canvas awnings had been placed over the stern of some of the battleships to give protection from the sun. Morning church services were being held aboard some, while aboard others plans were being made for the services. At 8:00 A.M. each ship would raise the American flag, while her band played the "Star Spangled Banner."

Meanwhile, in the sky north of Hawaii, Commander Mitsuo Fuchida was leading the first wave of Japanese planes toward Pearl Harbor. Listening to radio music from the islands, Fuchida grinned as he thought of the destruction soon to be visited upon the American Navy.

Aboard the carrier *Akagi,* Vice Admiral Nagumo waited patiently for the coded signal that would tell whether or not the attack would be a surprise. Admiral Yamamoto was in Japanese waters aboard the flagship *Nagato.*

At 7:49 A.M., Fuchida and his wave of planes reached the islands. Seeing that the attack was going to be a surprise, he shouted into his radio

"Tora . . . Tora . . . Tora." Aboard the *Akagi*, the others knew that the months of waiting and practice were working. Even Yamamoto, aboard the *Nagato*, picked up the code because of unusual atmospheric conditions.

The first bombs hit Ford Island. As the explosions went off, some thought it was an accident. Others thought the low flying planes were hotshot pilots showing off. Then the strafing started. For the people on Ford Island, the war had started at 7:55 A.M.

Aboard the battleships in Battleship Row, the bands were getting ready to play as the flags were hoisted up the masts. The Japanese flew toward the battleships, strafing as they flew. Some bands broke and ran as the explosions flashed all around; others remained and played until the flag was raised. Everyone was surprised and confused.

As the attackers flew toward the battlewagons, some of the gun crews managed to make it to their posts. Aboard the *Nevada*, gun crews kept the attackers away for a while. Even with the steady firing, one plane managed to put a torpedo into the ship, well forward.

The *West Virginia* was hit not once or twice, but six times by torpedoes, and twice by bombs. The *West Virginia* was bellowing smoke that went skyward and drifted over toward the *Tennessee*. Flaming fuel oil poured from ruptured tanks, stopping escape from the ship. Everywhere around the *West Virginia*, the water was covered with flaming oil. With her decks aflame and the surrounding water covered with flaming oil, she sank to the bottom as 105 men aboard her died.

The *Arizona,* seventy-five feet away from the *West Virginia* and the *Tennessee,* then started to take some of the enemy fire. Several torpedoes had already hit the *Arizona* and had caused great damage. Then a bomb fell from the sky and hit beside the B turret, forward. This bomb went into the bowels of the ship and exploded in one of the ammunition magazines. The blast sent flames 500 feet into the air, killing the captain and a rear admiral. Seconds later another bomb went down the ship's funnel. A giant explosion rocked the ship, killing some men with the concussion, cremating others with the flames, and trapping still others below decks to drown, as the *Arizona* too sank to the bottom of the harbor. Before she finally settled to the bottom, she was hit by six more bombs. In the *Arizona* lay the bodies of 1,103 men.

The *Tennessee,* which was berthed beside the *West Virginia,* was threatened by the flames and flying debris from the exploding *Arizona.* Because the *Tennessee* had been berthed inboard the *West Virginia,* she received only two bomb hits, but she couldn't move because she was being wedged against the cement pier by the listing *West Virginia.* Only five men were killed aboard the *Tennessee* that fateful morning.

The *Oklahoma* and the *Maryland* were lying ahead of the *West Virginia* and the *Tennessee. The Maryland,* because she too was inboard, received little damage. Only two bombs struck her and only four men were killed aboard. The *Oklahoma,* on the other hand, received great damage, and many lives were lost aboard her. The outboard *Oklahoma* received five torpedo hits, causing her to capsize almost immediately. As she rolled over and started settling into the mud on the harbor bottom, the men inside her hull fought for their lives.

The world inside the *Oklahoma* turned upside down, confusing many aboard. As she rolled over, men inside slid along the slick decks, the bulkheads, and finally the ceiling itself. All of this took place in total darkness, deep inside.

As the battle raged all around the now capsized *Oklahoma,* the men trapped inside fought for air. It would be hours before any rescue attempt could be made on the men now entombed inside the ship. By the time men with cutting torches managed to cut a hole in the bottom of the hull, many of the men would be dead for lack of air. As the masts of the *Oklahoma* touched the mud on the bottom of Pearl Harbor, the fate of 415 men had been sealed.

The *California* was struck by two torpedoes and began to list immediately because the watertight compartments were not properly sealed. Then two bombs hit, causing a small magazine to explode. Efforts were made to keep her afloat, but she slowly settled to the bottom, and the damage was so great that for three days after the attack she was still settling toward the bottom. She came to rest on the harbor bottom on December 10, taking with her ninety-eight officers and enlisted men.

The *Nevada* was berthed at the northern end of Battleship Row. As the battle progressed, the *Nevada* was able to get up enough steam to start her sortie at around 8:00. She had already been hit well forward by a torpedo, but by 8:25 she was hit by an additional two bombs dropped by "Val" dive-bombers. As she inched out of the harbor, she was attacked by several more Vals. Again she was hit, this time by three bombs. Seeing that she would never make it out of the harbor, her senior officer had her beached. This was to keep her from sinking and blocking the entrance to the harbor. During this small sortie that ended at 9:40, fifty men aboard the *Nevada* were killed.

The flagship of the fleet, the *Pennsylvania,* was not in Battleship Row that morning, but in dry dock along with the destroyers *Cassin* and *Downes,* which were docked directly in front of her. Because of the large amount of antiaircraft fire that these three ships threw up, the *Pennsylvania* sustained only one bomb hit. The two destroyers, though, received heavier damage. An incendiary bomb hit between them, rupturing their fuel tanks. As the fuel spewed out, it caught fire. Within minutes, the two destroyers were engulfed in flames, their magazines exploding. Both ships were total losses.

The destroyer *Shaw* was out of the water in a floating dry dock. A single bomb hit the unlucky ship and blew off her bow. The resulting explosion sank the dock in a spectacular ball of flames and smoke.

The old battleship *Utah* was located on the other side of Ford Island. She had been converted into a target ship. The Japanese mistook the old *Utah* for a carrier and she received more bombs than she was actually worth. Of the one hundred men aboard her, fifty-four were killed.

By 10:00 the American fleet lay burning in the

harbor, a total wreck. It would be months before the ships could be raised, refitted, and put back in action. The Japanese had won a great victory, but in overlooking the fuel tanks and repair facilities at Pearl, they had made a fatal mistake. The damaged warships could be repaired here. And other ships could be repaired in the future at Pearl. This would save costly time, because the ships would not have to be returned to the United States.

Because the Japanese had destroyed or damaged all the battleships in the Pacific Fleet, the United States was forced to use submarines and aircraft carriers as first line defensive weapons. The task fell to several subs and to the carriers *Lexington, Enterprise,* and *Saratoga.* As noted previously, the twenty-nine year old *Langley* had been converted to a seaplane tender a few years earlier.

Since there were only three carriers in the Pacific to stop the Japanese, the United States sent the carrier *Yorktown* to the Pacific. After leaving the Atlantic via the Panama Canal, she arrived at San Diego on December 30, 1941. Now there were four carriers to deal with the Japanese threat. The *Ranger* and the *Wasp* would stay in the Atlantic. The *Hornet* was in Norfolk being readied for her maiden voyage. The *Essex* class carriers were just being started.

But the number would soon go back to three. On January 11, 1942, the *Saratoga* was steaming 500 miles southwest of Oahu when suddenly, and without warning, she was attacked by the Japanese submarine *I-16.* The sub sent a torpedo into the Sara, flooding three of her sixteen firerooms and killing six men. It was decided to send the *Saratoga* to Bremerton, Washington for repairs and modernization. This left the *Lexington, Yorktown,* and *Enterprise* to carry on the war in the Pacific.

It was now decided to make a move against the Japanese. This would help morale and show the Japanese that the U. S. could still challenge them at sea. The raid would take place against the Marshall Islands, where the Japanese had air bases, and against the Japanese-held island of Wake.

The *Lexington* was to attack Wake Island while the *Enterprise* and *Yorktown* attacked the Marshall Islands. The *Lexington,* though, was unable to reach Wake Island. A Japanese submarine had hit and sunk the oiler *Neches* 135 miles west of Oahu. Since on other tanker was available, and because the *Lexington* would need refueling at sea, the mission was called off. This left the Marshall Island raid to be the first offensive against the Japanese.

The *Enterprise* would attack the northern portion of the Marshalls, the *Yorktown* the southern. On February 1, 1942, the raids began. As the *Enterprise* attacked the islands, she herself came under attack. At 1:40 P.M., a "Betty," or Mitsubishi Zero-1, dived on the *Enterprise.* The plane was hit, but her pilot decided to ram the ship with his plane.

Aviation Machinist's Mate Second Class Bruno Gaido saw the plane diving and ran across the flight deck to a parked SBD. He climbed into the rear gunner's seat and started firing at the Betty. As the *Enterprise* tried to maneuver out of the way of the diving plane, Gaido opened fire on the attacker. The wing of the Betty sliced off the tail of the SBD that

Gaido was firing from, and then tumbled into the sea. Gaido was sitting just three feet from where the wing had sliced into the parked SBD.

To the south, the *Yorktown* was carrying out her part of the battle. She launched forty-two planes at the islands in the southern group, but because of bad weather they did little damage. The *Yorktown* lost seven of her planes.

After the attacks, the two carriers returned to Pearl Harbor. The *Enterprise* arrived on February 6, the *Yorktown* the next day. Little damage had been done, but the attacks did raise the morale of the sailors in the fleet.

On February 27, the *Langley* was steaming in the waters around Java. As she was now a seaplane tender, she did not have any air groups aboard, and therefore had no air cover. As she and her two destroyer escorts were steaming toward Tjilatjap, they came under attack by Japanese aircraft. Commander Robert P. McConnell radioed for air cover from the army at Java, but they refused to come. This sealed the fate of the old *Langley*. The Japanese bombs struck and she was disabled. Later in the day, Commander McConnell had the two destroyers sink the *Langley* to keep her from falling into Japanese hands. The *Langley* was the first carrier lost to the Japanese during World War II.

After returning to Pearl from the Marshall Islands raid, the *Enterprise* remained there until April 8. This left only the *Lexington* and the *Yorktown* to cover the broad Pacific. The captain of the *Yorktown* was Captain Elliott Buckmaster, who would later have his career clouded by his decision at Midway.

While the *Lexington* and the *Yorktown* were patrolling the Pacific and making hit-and-run passes at the Japanese, the *Enterprise* and the *Hornet* were making ready a raid that would shock the Japanese and raise the morale of the Americans.

Aboard the *Hornet* for this historic raid against Tokyo was Lieutenant E. T. Stover, or Smokey, as he was called by his friends. Smokey was a young man in his early twenties with a boyish face and grin. He was a man who always thought of his fellows before he thought of himself. He was always willing to help others.

Because of the sixteen B-25's on the flight deck, neither Smokey nor any of the other pilots in the air group could take to the air until after Doolittle's planes had been launched.

Also aboard the *Hornet* was SK3c John R. Bates. Bates remembered hearing that Doolittle and other army pilots wrote messages on the bombs that they would drop on the Japanese in Tokyo.

The *Enterprise* was to give air cover to the aircraft carrier *Hornet*. The *Hornet* needed this cover because on her flight deck were the sixteen Army B-25's. These planes would stay on the flight deck of the *Hornet* until the two carriers came within striking distance of the Japanese homeland itself. Then the B-25's would be launched into the wind to raid Tokyo. The man in charge of this raid was Lieutenant Colonel James Doolittle. The raid would go down in history as the Doolittle Raid.

The planes were launched on April 18, 1942, and the raid was a complete surprise. Doolittle had eighty fliers and nine lost their lives in the raid. After the planes were launched, the *Enterprise* and the *Hornet* headed back to Pearl.

While they were steaming back toward Pearl, it was learned that the Japanese were building up in the Coral Sea area. The Japanese were going to attack Port Morsby and would have to be stopped. But only the *Lexington* and the *Yorktown* were left to stop the invasion forces. The Japanese had the carriers *Shoho, Shokaku,* and *Zuikaku.*

The opposing sides were getting ready for the first naval action in history in which neither side's ships would see each other. The action was carried out entirely by planes.

The planes from the *Lexington* and the *Yorktown* first sighted the carrier *Shoho.* Although the carrier maneuvered to avoid the attacking planes, the pilots were determined to hit the ship. The ninety-three planes came in for the attack. Within minutes the *Shoho* was hit by seven torpedoes and thirteen bombs. The Americans left the *Shoho* a flaming smoking wreck. As the small carrier sank, she took with her 600 of her 800 crew to the bottom.

By the next morning, May 8, the Japanese had located the *Yorktown,* and the *Lexington.* The *Lexington,* under the command of Captain Frederick Sherman, was attacked first. The Japanese came in dropping torpedoes. Eleven torpedoes came toward the *Lexington,* and because of her giant size and slow maneuvering, two torpedoes hit her. These were followed by five bomb hits. The *Lexington* started listing seven degrees. The fires were put out, and the list corrected within an hour. But fate had sealed the *Lexington's* destiny. Because of a faulty design in her fire-fighting equipment, gasoline vapors had leaked into a generator room and ignited. A violent explosion occurred, causing the Lexington to shutter. Explosion after explosion shook the ship and finally the order was given to abandon her. A total of 2,735 men left the *Lexington*. Then the order was given to sink the ship. U.S. destroyers fired five torpedoes at the now disabled *Lexington,* sinking her in the Coral Sea area. The United States had lost its second carrier, this time one of her largest.

Aboard the *Yorktown*, Buckmaster had his hands full. While the Japanese were attacking the *Lexington*, they also went after the *Yorktown*. The enemy aimed eight torpedoes at the *Yorktown*, but because she was smaller and faster than the *Lexington*, all the torpedoes missed. A few minutes, later, however, she was hit by an 800-pound bomb dropped from a dive-bomber. The bomb passed through the flight deck and exploded on the fourth deck. The resulting explosion killed thirty-seven men, and burnt many others seriously. The Japanese thought that they had sunk the *Yorktown*. Later this would prove to be a fatal misconception.

After the battle of Coral Sea, the Japanese had lost one small carrier, while the United States had lost a fleet carrier. But the advance of the Japanese was slowed.

The *Yorktown* was rushed to Pearl, where she was repaired in two and a half days, a record. If the Japanese had destroyed the shipyard at Pearl, the *Yorktown* would have had to be returned to the West

Coast of the U.S. This one mistake on December 7 would cost the Japanese a victory at Midway. Instead of having only the *Enterprise* and the *Hornet*, the U.S. Navy also had the *Yorktown*. This helped decide the outcome of the battle.

The United States broke the Japanese code; thus enabling U.S. Intelligence to learn that the Japanese planned to attack Midway. A small attack against the Aleutians would also be launched in order to draw the American forces there, leaving Midway open. But Midway would not be a surprise as the Japanese had planned.

The *Hornet* and the *Enterprise*, which were now in Pearl, would join up with the repaired *Yorktown*. The Japanese would have the carriers *Akagi*, *Kaga*, *Hiryu*, and *Soryu*. These were four of the six carriers that had attacked Pearl Harbor six months earlier. The *Ryujo* and the *Junyo* would attack Dutch Harbor in the Aleutians.

Admiral Yamamoto knew that the *Enterprise* and the *Hornet* were in the Pacific, but he wasn't sure about the other three carriers. He thought that the *Lexington* had been sunk off Hawaii, and that the *Saratoga* had been sunk at Coral Sea. He wasn't sure about the *Yorktown*. He knew that she had been hit at Coral Sea, but did not know whether she had sunk or not. To be on the safe side, he assumed that she hadn't been sunk. The Admiral was not sure about the *Wasp*, but did know that the *Ranger* was in the Atlantic.

While the *Yorktown* limped into Pearl, Nimitz had only the *Enterprise* and *Hornet* to defend Midway. But within two days the repaired *Yorktown* was again ready for service. The *Saratoga* was on the West Coast awaiting escort vessels, while the *Wasp* was leaving the Atlantic for the Pacific. Both ships would arrive too late for the battle.

On May 28, Admiral Spruance left Pearl with the *Enterprise* and the *Hornet*. He had replaced Halsey, who was in the hospital. On May 30, Admiral Fletcher left Pearl aboard the *Yorktown*. Fletcher was in overall command of the two task forces.

On June 4, the Japanese began their attack of Midway Island. Planes from the four carriers destroyed the command post, mess hall, fuel tanks, and a seaplane hangar. The hospital was set on fire, and the generating plant was damaged. Even with this much damage, a second attack was needed.

At 9:30 A.M. Torpedo Eight, a squadron from the *Hornet*, sighted the *Kaga*. As the planes came in to attack, each was shot down. Fifteen Devastator torpedo-bombers were shot down, all of the planes in Torpedo Eight. Only Ensign George H. Gay survived the attack. None of the torpedoes hit the *Kaga*.

Within minutes, Torpedo Six, a squadron from the *Enterprise* attacked the *Kaga*. This time ten of the fourteen Devastators were shot down, and again not one torpedo hit the *Kaga*.

As the smoke cleared on the *Kaga*, the gunners looked up and saw more torpedo planes. This time it was Torpedo Three from the *Yorktown*. The twelve planes attacked the *Soryu*, but again without success. All twelve were shot down.

Even though three torpedo squadrons were wiped out, their sacrifice was not in vain. The defending

Japanese fighters had to come down from the skies to attack the low-flying torpedo planes, and therefore were not up high enough to intercept the American dive bombers that were now on the scene. Lieutenant Commander Wade McClusky, leading the *Enterprise*-based group, sighted the four carriers.

The group dived between the *Akagi* and the *Kaga*. The first bomb hit the *Akagi*, the flagship of the fleet. Because the planes on board were armed and fueled, they began exploding. Within minutes the *Akagi* was a flaming inferno, and twenty minutes after the first bomb had hit, Admiral Nagumo left the carrier. She was a total loss.

The *Kaga* was hit next. Her luck had run out. She received four direct hits. A small gasoline truck forward of the island was hit, and the resulting fire killed everyone on the bridge. The *Kaga* was now leaderless. She also became a flaming inferno. Men were burned alive where they stood. The *Kaga* too was a total loss.

As the attack planes led by McClusky were pulling out of their dives, others from the *Yorktown* arrived on the scene. Lieutenant Commander Maxwell F. Leslie had flown a nearly direct course to the four carriers. His group picked out the *Soryu* for their target. Twenty minutes after the first bomb had hit, the *Soryu* was abandoned. Fifty minutes after the attack on the three carriers had begun, they were flaming wrecks, waiting to slip beneath the blue Pacific for a long rest.

Only the *Hiryu*, which had been several miles from the other three, was left undamaged. Admiral

Yamaguchi ordered an attack on the American carriers. Lieutenant Michio Kobayashi led his air group toward the carriers. He encountered some U.S. planes and followed them to the *Yorktown* and attacked.

One Japanese Val was hit as it came in for the attack, but its bomb tumbled down and hit the *Yorktown* on its flight deck. Another bomb hit the funnel and exploded, knocking out two boilers and putting the fires out in the others. A third exploded on the fourth deck, starting fires.

At 12:20, the *Yorktown* was dead in the water, but the damage control parties worked furiously to get the ship underway. By 1:40, the *Yorktown* was making twenty knots.

Again the carrier came under attack. This time the *Yorktown* took two torpedo hits in her port side, knocking out communications, breaching fuel tanks, and jamming the rudder. The *Yorktown* listed seventeen degrees, then twenty-six degrees.

Fearing that the ship would capsize, Buckmaster ordered the crew to abandon ship. While the *Yorktown* was being abandoned, the *Hiryu* came under attack by planes from the *Enterprise* and the *Hornet*. The *Enterprise* planes hit the *Hiryu* with four bombs, thus sealing her fate. When the planes from the *Hornet* arrived on the scene, the *Hiryu* was already burning. These planes turned to look for other ships to attack, but found none.

The four Japanese carriers began sinking. The first to go was the *Soryu*, the carrier that the *Yorktown* pilots had found and hit. She carried 718 men to the bottom with her. Next to slip under the waves was the *Kaga*. The *Kaga* had been abandoned, but later a damage control party returned to try to save her. Unable to do anything, they withdrew. The *Kaga* then blew herself up with a gigantic explosion and sank, taking over 800 men with her.

Aboard the *Akagi*, Captain Taijiro Aoki asked for and was given permission to scuttle his ship. Captain Aoki returned to the ship and lashed himself to the anchor. Four destroyers fired torpedoes into the *Akagi*, and seven minutes later she slipped beneath the waves, taking with her 220 bodies as well as her live captain.

Aboard the *Hiryu*, Captain Tomeo Kaku and Admiral Yamaguchi decided to go down with the ship. They lashed themselves to the bridge and ordered two destroyers to fire torpedoes into her. The *Hiryu* sank with 416 men aboard. But the two lashed to the bridge were not the only live men aboard. The men in the engine rooms had not been told to abandon ship, and as the *Hiryu* slipped beneath the waves, thirty-nine of the sixty-seven living men left aboard reached a whaleboat. These men drifted for two weeks in the Pacific before the seaplane tender *Ballard* picked them up. During the two weeks, four men died; another died on board the *Ballard*. Thus ended the four Japanese carriers at Midway.

Meanwhile, the *Yorktown* started to right herself after she had been abandoned by Buckmaster. She was again boarded, and crews worked to save the "Gallant Lady." Most of her 2,300 men were on their way back to Pearl aboard the submarine tender *Fulton*, which had picked the men up from the several smaller ships that had been with the *Yorktown*. BKR3c Harold T. Kunkle, along with 491 others, was picked out of the water by the destroyer *Russell*. Other men were picked up by *Astoria*, *Benham*, *Balch*, *Anderson*, *Morris*, *Hammann*, and *Hughes*.

As Buckmaster and the salvage party worked on board to save the *Yorktown*, beneath the sea the Japanese had a different plan. The *I-168* had slipped through the defense screen set up by the six destroyers around the *Yorktown*. The *Hammann*, which was alongside the carrier to furnish electrical power for the salvage party, suddenly exploded and broke in two. Within four minutes the *Hammann* was gone. Eighty-one men went with her.

Two more torpedoes went beneath the *Hammann* and struck the *Yorktown*, and again Buckmaster gave the order to abandon ship. Again the *Yorktown* remained afloat, so Buckmaster planned to board her yet again the next morning. But during the night the carrier, after being hit by three bombs, two torpedoes delivered by planes, and two torpedoes from a sub, gave up her struggle to live. At 6:00 A.M. on June 7, 1942, she slipped beneath the waves. The *Yorktown* had taken a lot, and would have probably survived Midway if she had not been abandoned so quickly. The navy just didn't realize at the time how much punishment a carrier could take and still live.

After Midway the carrier *Wasp* joined the fleet, as did the *Saratoga*, which had returned from the West Coast ready to take on the Japanese again. With the *Wasp* came the new battleship, the *North Carolina*.

36

The *North Carolina*, with her twenty-seven knot speed, could keep up with the fast carriers, and her antiaircraft guns would help fend off Japanese planes.

After Midway, the Allies decided to take the island of Guadalcanal. With this invasion came the Battle of the Eastern Solomons. This time, Fletcher would have the carriers *Saratoga*, *Enterprise*, and *Wasp*, also the new battleship *North Carolina*. The *Hornet* would stay at Pearl on twenty-four hour notice, to aid the three carriers if needed.

As the American forces moved into the area, they encountered the Japanese carriers *Ryujo*, *Shokaku*, and *Zuikaku*. The Japanese would use the little *Ryujo* as a decoy. She would be in the lead, and if she came under attack the two larger carriers would have time to retaliate. At 9:05 A.M. on August 24, a PBY spotted the *Ryujo*, and by 2:00 P.M. she came under attack from *Enterprise* planes. The pilots did not score any hits, but by this time planes from the *Saratoga* had arrived on the scene. The *Ryujo* was hit by ten bombs and two torpedoes. She sank that night. But the *Ryujo* had done her part well, for she had served as a decoy.

At 3:00 P.M., the *Shokaku* and the *Zuikaku* launched a strike at the American carriers. By 5:00 P.M., the battle in the sky above the *Saratoga* and the *Enterprise* had begun. The American planes tore into the first Japanese strike. Every available plane was in the sky trying to defend the two ships. But even this strong defense could not prevent the inevitable from happening. At 5:14 a bomb crashed into the *Enterprise*. It plunged through the elevator, through the hangar deck, and finally exploded on the third deck. The bomb blast killed thirty-five men and started fires on board ship. It also ruptured side plates, allowing water to pour through.

Within a minute, another bomb hit, this one only ten feet from where the first had hit. This bomb exploded in a gun gallery, killing thirty-nine men, exploding ammunition, and putting one-fourth of the *Enterprise's* guns out of commission.

A few minutes later, a third bomb hit, but this did little damage. The *Enterprise* had been hit for the first time during the war.

The *Enterprise* made her way back to Pearl for repairs. The Battle of the Eastern Solomons was over, with another victory for the Americans. The next few days were quiet for the *Saratoga*, the *Wasp*, and the newly arrived *Hornet*. But this was soon to change.

On the morning of August 31, the Japanese sub *I-26* spotted the *Saratoga* and fired six torpedoes at the ship. Only one hit the *Saratoga*, but it was enough. Although she wasn't badly damaged she was put out of action. Her speed had been reduced, and she would have to put into a shipyard for repairs. For the second time in eight months the *Saratoga* had been hit by torpedoes fired from a submarine. With the *Enterprise* and the *Saratoga* hit, only the *Hornet* and the *Wasp* were left to defend the "Slot," a narrow strip of water near Guadalcanal.

On September 15, the *Hornet* and the *Wasp* headed toward Guadalcanal in separate task groups to cover U.S. transports bringing in reinforcements.

At 2:42 P.M., while the *Wasp* was recovering planes, the sub *I-19* fired six torpedoes at her. The torpedoes came at the ship, which eluded only three; the other three hit the carrier. Because fuel lines were open in order to refuel the newly recovered planes, uncontrollable fires broke out. Within minutes the *Wasp* was pouring out grayish-black smoke.

While the fires were raging aboard the *Wasp*, the Japanese sub *I-15* fired six torpedoes at the *Hornet*. But the *Hornet* was luckier, and managed to dodge the torpedoes. One of the torpedoes fired at the *Hornet* did hit the new battleship *North Carolina*, while another hit the destroyer *O'Brien*.

The *Wasp* was now a hopeless, smoking wreck. Fires raged throughout the ship, and at 3:00 P.M. an explosion shook the carrier. At 3:20 P.M. she was abandoned. A destroyer pulled in close and finished her off. The *Wasp* lost 193 of her crew. The navy had lost her fourth carrier, including the old *Langley*.

Now the *Hornet* was the only operational carrier the Americans had in the Pacific. With the *Wasp* sunk, and the *Enterprise* and *Saratoga* in shipyards, the *Hornet* would get all the attention of the Japanese Navy. Also in shipyards were the battleships *North Carolina* and *South Dakota*. The only capital ships left now were the *Hornet* and the *Washington*.

It was decided to hold back the *Hornet* until she could be joined by other carriers. On October 16, 1942, the *Enterprise* rejoined the *Hornet* for the upcoming Battle of Santa Cruz.

For the Battle of Santa Cruz, the Japanese had the carriers *Junyo, Shokaku, Zuiho*, and *Zuikaku*. The Americans had only the *Enterprise* and the *Hornet*.

On October 26, 1942, Japanese search planes spotted the *Hornet*. At 7:00 A.M., the *Shokaku,* the *Zuikaku*, and the *Zuiho* launched their planes. At 7:30, the *Enterprise* and the *Hornet* launched theirs. The stage was now set.

At 9:00 A.M., the Japanese planes sighted the *Hornet*. The *Enterprise* had gone undetected for awhile. The Japanese, however, were confused because they expected to find the *Saratoga* instead of the *Hornet*. But, confused or not, they attacked, inflicting great damage. One bomb hit the side of the flight deck. A damaged Japanese plane crashed into the *Hornet's* funnel. From there the plane plunged into the flight deck. Two bombs on the plane exploded. Next, two torpedoes hit the ship, then three more bombs. Again, a pilot flew his plane into the *Hornet's* flight deck. The carrier was now ablaze from stem to stern. She listed 8 degrees, and was almost dead in the water.

While the *Hornet* was undergoing her fatal attack, the Japanese carriers *Shokaku* and *Zuikaku* were about to undergo attack themselves. The *Shokaku* was hit by five 1000-pound bombs. Her flight deck was now useless, and she was burning. She withdrew from the battle.

Before the *Shokaku* was hit, she launched her planes. They found both the damaged *Hornet* and the newly discovered *Enterprise*. Seeing that the former was badly damaged, the pilots concentrated on the latter.

One bomb tore through the flight deck and exploded just above the water line in the bow. Then another bomb hit the *Enterprise*. This bomb broke in two. Part of it exploded on the hangar deck, while the other part exploded on the fourth deck. Here it killed forty men. A third bomb exploded close to the carrier and opened a fuel tank to the sea. The *Enterprise* began to leak oil.

Forty minutes later, the two ships came under attack again. This time the two carriers were not hit, but several escort ships were.

In the early afternoon, it looked as if the *Hornet* could be saved. She had been hit by six bombs, two torpedoes, and two flaming planes; and she still stayed afloat.

But the Japanese had other plans. At 3:00 P.M., on October 26, the *Hornet* came under attack again. This time a torpedo hit the engine room. The carrier began listing 14 degrees. Then a bomb hit the flight deck and she was abandoned. Later the Japanese hit the *Hornet* with another bomb.

A Japanese destroyer fired eight torpedoes at the *Hornet*. Three of these hit the ship. Then another destroyer fired eight more, and six of these hit her. But she still remained afloat.

Seeing that the *Hornet* was not sinking, the destroyers fired over 400 rounds of five-inch shells into the ship. In total, the *Hornet* had been hit by eight bombs, twelve torpedoes, two planes, and over 400 rounds of five-inch shells. Still the *Hornet* remained afloat. The Japanese were determined to sink this carrier, and two Japanese destroyers closed

41

in to finish her. They put four more torpedoes into the *Hornet*. Finally on October 27, 1942, she slipped beneath the waves.

Aboard one of the American destroyers, SK3c John R. Bates, who had served aboard the *Hornet* since her commissioning, wondered about the fate of the American fight in the Pacific. All that was left in that ocean was the battle-damaged *Enterprise*. Could she hold out until the *Saratoga* was repaired and new carriers arrived on the scene?

The United States had lost the old CV-1, *Langley*; the CV-2, *Lexington*; the CV-5, *Yorktown*; the CV-7, *Wasp*; and the CV-8, *Hornet*. The CV-3, *Saratoga*, was in a shipyard undergoing repairs, and the CV-4, *Ranger*, was too slow for the Pacific war. She would remain in the Atlantic. This left only the CV-6, *Enterprise*, until more carriers could be built. Back in the United States, the shipyards were working full time to build the new *Essex* class carriers. It would be these ships that would take over the brunt of the Pacific War, and finally defeat the Japanese Navy.

CV-10
1941–1952

Chapter III

During the last months of 1942 and the first half of 1943, there was a lull in the carrier war in the Pacific. The British had sent the carrier *Victorious* to the Pacific to help strengthen the carrier forces there. The *Victorious* joined up with the repaired *Saratoga* to monitor Japanese activities in the Southwest Pacific.

Back in the United States, work progressed since early 1941 on the building of the new *Essex* class carriers. The *Essex* would be the CV-9. The ships that followed it would have larger numbers. Before the end of the war, twenty-six of these carriers would have their keels laid; seventeen would actually see action in the Pacific; two would be cancelled; and one would not be completed until 1950.

The second ship of the *Essex* class, the CV-10, had her keel laid down on December 1, 1941, just six days before Pearl Harbor. Also on that day the keel was laid down for the CV-11. Keels had already been laid down for the CV-16 and the CV-17, as well as the CV-9.

The CV-10's keel was laid down at Newport News, Virginia, on that pre-war day in December. She would be called the *Bon Homme Richard* in honor of the ship that John Paul Jones had used to defeat the British ship *Serapis* in the Revolutionary War. Work was scheduled to be finished in January, 1945. The attack on Pearl Harbor changed that schedule. Now she was to be finished as quickly as possible. Work preceeded into the Christmas season. As the winter of 1941–42 turned into spring, the hull began to take shape. The hull had a bulbous bow to reduce resistance at high speed. The bilge was nearly square to provide more volume for the anti-torpedo system. The stern was of cruiser design with a single rudder.

During the Battle of Midway, the United States had lost the carrier *Yorktown*. It was decided that to confuse the Japanese, the CV-10 would have her named changed. On September 26, 1942, the name for the CV-10 was changed from the *Bon Homme Richard* to *Yorktown*. The name *Bon Homme Richard* would honor another carrier, the CV-31.

Changing the name of the CV-10 to *Yorktown* was the first step in a series of events that would link the two *Yorktowns* together. The first coincidence the series concerned the ships' numbers. The old *Yorktown* had been the CV-5, while the new one would be the CV-10. Both ships had a number that was a multiple of five.

Progress advanced on the *Yorktown*, and she was beginning to take the appearance of a carrier. Bulkheads were put in place, and the flight deck was added. Utmost speed was essential in the completion of the ship. The crews at Newport News did a fine job in this stage of the *Yorktown's* life.

The *Essex* had already been launched at Quincy, Massachusetts, on July 31, 1942, but the keel for that ship had been laid almost eight months before the keel for the *Yorktown* had been laid. Finally on January 21, 1943, the *Yorktown* was ready for launching. It had taken thirteen months from the keel laying to the launching of the *Essex*. The *Yorktown* was completed in thirteen months also. The *Essex* was commissioned on December 31, 1942. It had taken twenty months from keel laying to commissioning. The *Yorktown* was out to beat this time.

Numerous personalities were present for the ceremonies on that cold January day in 1943. Among them was the former captain of the CV-5, Captain Elliot Buckmaster, now a rear admiral. It was Buckmaster who had been skipper of the old *Yorktown* when she went down at Midway. Again the old *Yorktown* was linked with the new *Yorktown*.

The person who would christen the *Yorktown* was none other than the first lady, Mrs. Eleanor Roosevelt. She too was a part of the old *Yorktown's* history. She had christened the old CV-5, and would now christen the CV-10.

As the dignitaries made their speeches, the excitement mounted. Mrs. Roosevelt stepped up to the small platform to christen the CV-10. Suddenly the ship started to move, several minutes ahead of schedule. Quickly Mrs. Roosevelt swung the bottle of champagne against the ship's bow. The bottle of champagne burst against the bow with a crash, spewing forth its foaming wine. The *Yorktown* was launched, and because of the slight mix-up in the launching time she was dubbed ''An Eager Ship,'' a name that was to stick.

At this point in the *Yorktown's* career, she was the fourth *Essex* class carrier to be launched. The *Lexington*, the *Bunker Hill* and the *Essex* had already been launched in the order listed above.

In the early months of 1943 work progressed on the *Yorktown*. Even though she had been launched, she still had to be finished at the fitting-out dock. The island had to be completed on the ship, guns had to be added, and a hundred other things needed to be done to make a floating hull a fighting ship. By mid-May she was ready to be completed and commissioned. She had gained time on one of her sisters, the *Bunker Hill*, which would not be commissioned until nine days after the *Yorktown*. The *Intrepid*, whose keel had been laid on the same day as the *Yorktown's*, would not be commissioned for three months. The *Yorktown* had begun to live up to the title of An Eager Ship.

While the *Yorktown* was being fitted out she took on a small crew: these were the plank owners, the original crew. Among these men were Martin "Tadpole" Tauber, James A. McNally, R. Knowlton Stuart, Stanley M. Abramczyk, and Ted Rohrbough. Ted, in his own words, was "a hick boy just learning about the ways of the navy." He had enlisted at the age of seventeen, and been assigned to a ship larger than any he had ever dreamed about.

He was put into the Fourth Division, and for the first few weeks he and several others slept in the compartment forward the torpedo room. He had never seen a torpedo before, and until someone explained that they had to be armed before they would go off, he had a few sleepless nights.

For Ted and the others, that few weeks before commissioning were hectic. Scores of box cars and flat cars were brought to the pier where their contents had to be unloaded into compartments and stowed aboard the *Yorktown*. Food, clothing, ammunition, bombs, torpedoes, construction materials, tools, and dozens of other types of articles were loaded aboard. The *Yorktown* was a floating city, because now just about anything which could be found in a city was aboard.

On May 15, 1943, the *Yorktown* was commissioned into the United States Navy to join her two sisters, the *Essex* and the *Lexington*. It had taken the *Essex* and the *Lexington* twenty months to go from keel laying to commissioning. The Yorktown had taken the same route in a little over seventeen months, a record that still stands for the building of a fleet carrier.

Again, fate played a part in the careers of the two

Yorktowns. The first captain of the new *Yorktown* was a former executive officer of the old *Yorktown*: his name was Joseph James Clark, known by his fellow seaman as Jocko.

Jocko was a colorful person. He was out to get Tojo's scalp. Since Jocko was part Cherokee, he probably had the skill. Jocko had been in aviation for several years; in fact, he was one of the old hands of naval aviation. He had been involved in several plane mishaps, and had a limp because of one. He had loved the old *Yorktown*, and he was out to avenge his former ship. He would help the new crew of the *Yorktown* to learn all there was to know about running a carrier successfully.

After Jocko had been promoted to the rank of captain, in February, 1942, he left the old *Yorktown* to go to the Atlantic, where he found himself skipper of the CVE-27, the *Suwannee*. The *Suwannee* was built around an oiler's hull. It had been active against German submarines. But now the "Patton of the Pacific," Captain Jocko Clark, was back where he wanted to be, aboard another *Yorktown* bound for Japanese waters.

Jocko sailed the *Yorktown* out of Newport News, Virginia for its shakedown cruise. Aboard were many new and inexperienced men. Steaming in the Atlantic, Jocko was not content just to give orders. He was down on the flight deck with a bullhorn in his hands shouting and showing how to spot the planes. Speed was of the utmost importance on a carrier flight deck in battle. Jocko was constantly on the flight deck showing the "Airdales" where he wanted the planes.

One day, while off the coast of Trinidad, air defense was blown on the bugle to signal the gunners to man the guns. Ted Rohrbough and the others of his gun crew thought that the bugle was blowing flight quarters; therefore they did not man their guns. This made Jocko furious, and he let them know about how he felt, using characteristically colorful language to express his feelings. Needless to say, the crews got a well-earned chewing-out. The next time the crews knew what the bugle meant.

Also, while on the shakedown cruise, the *Yorktown* was selected as the carrier which would give qualifying tests to the newly developed SB2C-1, better known as the Helldiver.

The Helldiver was the United States' newest dive-bomber. The Helldiver would later replace the SBD *Dauntless*. In May, 1943, it was the Helldivers planes which were placed aboard the *Yorktown*. When the tests were carried out in the Atlantic, off the coast of Virginia, the planes behaved badly.

The planes, upon landing, would sometimes miss the hook because of "hook bouncing." This created some tense moments as the planes skidded forward along the flight deck. The landing signal officers, Lieutenant (jg) Ed Volz and Ensign Richard C. Tripp were good landing officers, but even they could not control hook bounce. At other times the tail wheel would collapse on impact, and the plane would skid into parked planes. Some of the SB2C-1's even had structural failure while in the air. It was these incidents that led Jocko to recommend that the order for the Helldiver be cancelled, but because production was already in the planning, the navy did not listen to his advice. Later improvements would make the Helldiver a workable warplane.

After the qualifying tests on the SB2C-1 were completed, the *Yorktown* set sail for the Panama Canal. The 872-foot ship eased through, barely clearing the sides of the locks. The small elevator on the port side had to be raised as the ship passed through the locks. Finally on July 11, 1943, the *Yorktown* cleared the Panama Canal and steamed toward Pearl Harbor.

While in the Pacific, the men of the *Yorktown* drilled under the watchful eye of Jocko. He was a man who would settle for nothing less than 4.0. He was rough on the men, but he knew that only the best would survive; and he, his ship, and crew were going to survive.

His voice bellowed through his bullhorn almost hourly. He was everywhere: helping, showing, commending, and criticizing when necessary. The men feared his wrath, but seemed to like him. The men of the *Yorktown* were becoming as one. This spirit of unity would never leave the *Yorktown*, but would endure from year to year, and from crew to crew.

Aboard the new *Yorktown* were men who had served aboard the old *Yorktown*, including part of the marine detachment. It would be these men as well as veterans of other ships who would hlep mold the new, green crew into fighting men. Most of the crew were men fresh from the States with no combat experience whatsoever. It seemed that the spirit of the CV-5 was trying desperately to renew itself in the CV-10.

As the crew of the *Yorktown* entered Pearl Harbor, they experienced an atmosphere different from that which the crew of the old CV-5 had found. The war was beginning to go in our favor. The arrival of the new *Essex* class carriers helped to build new confidence.

The *Yorktown* drew past Battleship Row, where the *Arizona* now lay at rest with most of her crew still aboard. By August, 1943, except for the *Arizona*, there was little left to show that the harbor had once been the site of the United States' greatest defeat during World War II, and quite possibly during her entire history.

Also aboard the *Yorktown* was a movie crew under the direction of Lieutenant Dwight Long, who was supervising the production of a film. This film would enable the folks back home to get a look at carrier warfare in the Pacific. The movie was shot in color. It was filmed by both naval photographers and professional civilian photographers.

While the ship was in Pearl, the two LSO's, Ed Volz and Dick Tripp, were sent ashore to give "bounce drill," or field carrier landing drill, as it was more properly called. Dick and "Red" hit all the various naval air stations: Barbers Point, Kaneohe Punune and Kaialua in Maui, and Hilo in Hawaii. At times the Air Group CO would let them fly with one of the squadrons during practice flights.

Bounce drill taught the newer pilots that landing aboard a carrier was quite different from landing on a mile-long airstrip. A small portion of the field, the size of a carrier, would be marked off. As the pilot approached he would watch Dick or Red, because it was these two men who would be his eyes. As each pilot approached, he would observe the paddles in the hands of the LSO, and react according to the position of these paddles. As he eased his plane in at a slow eighty knots, the pilot watched carefully for the kill signal. If he received it, he would kill his engine and settle to the field; if not, he would gun the engine and come in for another pass. Both LSO's were good at what they did.

Also aboard the *Yorktown* was a young, stocky fellow who had a boyish grin and was liked by everyone. He was from Dallas, Texas, and his name was Elisha Terril Stover, nicknamed Smokey. Smokey Stover had been aboard the old *Hornet* during the Doolittle Raid on Tokyo. He had also been aboard the *Hornet* during the Battle of Midway. From the *Hornet* he was transferred to the *Saratoga* for the Guadalcanal campaign. After we had taken Guadalcanal, he flew with old VF-5, as the air group was now land-based for lack of carriers. While flying from Guadalcanal he shot down three Japanese planes, and crashed head-on into another.

After leaving Guadalcanal, he was sent back to the States where he was assigned to the *Yorktown*, not as a pilot, but as a fighter director controller. This was a job he disliked, but did well. With Smokey in the Radar Plot was Lieutenant (jg) C. D. "Charlie" Ridgway.

The air group aboard the *Yorktown* was Air Group Five. This group had been formed on February 15, 1943, at Norfolk, Virginia, under the command of Commander James H. Flatley. Commander Flatley had been aboard the old *Lexington*,

CV-2, at the Battle of Coral Sea. It was during this battle that he and his gunner, John Liska, had won the Navy Cross. After the loss of the *Lexington*, Jim went aboard the *Enterprise*, where he formed Air Group Ten. During this period Air Group Ten became known as the "Grim Reapers." As new *Essex* class carriers were commissioned, new air groups needed to be formed. For this reason, Jim was sent back to the States on February 13, 1943, where he formed Air Group Five.

Within thirty days after the air group was formed, the squadrons started training. On May 21, 1943, Air Group Five came aboard the *Yorktown* for flight training off the East Coast. It was Air Group Five that gave the qualifying test to the SB2C, or the "Beast," as it was called. The air group then reembarked for the Central Pacific on July 6, 1943.

As Air Group Five flew from the deck of the *Yorktown*, now steaming in the Pacific, the pilots had a look at the blue waters where the Japanese had hoped to prove victorious in the early months of the war. As the pilots returned to the carrier, they were brought in for a safe landing by Ed "Red" Volz. As each plane approached the *Yorktown* the pilot could see the red stripe painted on its flight deck. She was the only carrier to have this red stripe, making it easy to distinguish her from the other *Essex* class carriers from the air.

Among the pilots were Lieutenant Raymond F. Kilrain, Lieutenant Fred H. Bozard, Jr., Lieutenant J. W. "Pop" Condit, and Ensign Thomas E. McGrath. It was these men who would carry the war from the *Yorktown* to the Japanese.

Now that the *Yorktown* had her air group, she was ready for "Indian Country." Jocko turned the ship back toward Pearl to join up with the *Essex*. These two ships, under the command of Rear Admiral Charles A. Pownall, were going to raid Marcus Island. This island was only 1,000 miles from Tokyo, and the first step toward the island of Japan.

Pownall had been commanding officer of the *Enterprise* from 1938 until April, 1941. He was now the commander of Task Force Fifteen, and was flying his flag from the *Yorktown*, the first *Essex* class carrier to be a flag ship. The date was August 22, 1943.

As the *Yorktown* steamed into enemy waters with the *Essex* and the light carrier *Independence*, all eyes were on the alert for the Japanese. Air Group Five flew patrol overhead, searching for any enemy planes that might happen upon them. As for most of the crew, they knew that in the coming days they would experience something they had never experienced before. They were going to kill or be killed. This was a new feeling that each man kept to himself. They all dreaded the coming days. But each man knew he must do his best to help keep the ship and his fellow shipmates safe.

Finally, the day arrived. On August 31, 1943, all the planning, training, and waiting were over, and the crew would learn whether they were fit for the job at hand. In the predawn air the engines of the new F6F Hellcats were warmed up. Crews also started up the Dauntless SBD's and the TBF Avengers. After the pilots were briefed on the day's events in the ready rooms beneath the flight deck, they walked briskly to their waiting planes. Lieutenant Commander Richard Upson, Ensign Owen H. Ramey, Lieutenant J. W. Dondit, and others climbed into their planes in the darkness of early morning.

The planes were launched into the wind, and the pilots, although they did not realize it, were making history. The *Yorktown* had launched her planes before the *Essex*. These men were the first men ever to fly from an *Essex* class carrier into combat. The *Yorktown*, although she was the fourth *Essex* class carrier to have her keel laid, was the first to fly her planes into combat. It had taken the *Essex* twenty-eight months to fly her planes into combat; the *Yorktown* had done the same in only twenty-one months. She truly was An Eager Ship.

The three carriers sent a total of six strikes against the Japanese at Marcus. With the brightly colored smoke from the exploding flack bursting all around Lieutenant Woodrow McVay and the others, they succeeded in destroying the installations on the ground, which included the radio station, barracks, sundry antiaircraft defenses, and the airfield. The men of Air Group Five, under the command of Commander James Flatley, also destroyed eight enemy planes on the ground.

Although the men of Air Group Five flattened eighty percent of Marcus Island, they also had their losses. While making a run in his TBF Avenger, Lieutenant J. W. Condit's plane was hit. As Pop tried to get the plane back to the *Yorktown*, his luck ran out. He made a crash landing in the Pacific, off

Marcus. With him were Machinist Kahlbert and Machinist Marshall. All three men were picked up shortly by a Japanese submarine, and taken to a POW camp. Since Pop Condit was a flyer he got special treatment. He was beaten to try to force information from him. Though badly beaten and half starved, he did not give them any vital information. He and his crew were the first pilot losses for the *Yorktown*.

Alone in his F6F, Ensign Oren C. Morgan was making a run on the island when his plane was hit by enemy antiaircraft fire. His plane burst into flames and crashed. Ensign Morgan was the first fatality aboard the *Yorktown*. Later that evening, crew members would miss Ensign Morgan, Lieutenant Condit, Machinist Kahlbert, and Machinist Marshall. These men had met the enemy, and had given the most of themselves.

After the raid on Marcus, Pownall, aboard the *Yorktown*, led the other two carriers back to Pearl to join up with the new *Lexington* CV-16, and with the light carriers *Princeton* and *Belleau Wood*. While joining up with these three carriers of Task Force Fourteen, Jocko gave Pownall the ride of his life.

Jocko was rather daring and flamboyant in his tactics. As the *Yorktown* approached the other ships, Pownall needed to have the *Yorktown* in the key position. After all, she was the flagship. Jocko wanted to show the men of the other carriers that the *Yorktown* deserved to be the flagship. This he did in a most daring way.

As the 27,100-ton *Yorktown* approached the formation, Jocko, instead of slowing down and proceeding with caution, slid the carrier in between a half dozen lesser ships and slapped the ship into formation. This distressed Pownall; but because of Jocko's keen sense of timing, and the fact that he knew what the *Yorktown* was capable of doing, the maneuver was not as reckless as it looked. It was, however, impressive.

By now the film crews aboard the *Yorktown* were getting some fine footage for the movie *The Fighting Lady*. Also, they were impressed by the fact that one of the LSO's could "cut," or have the tail hook grab, a plane on the wire that he called out. Ensign Dick Tripp soon started making bets with members of the movie crew, and was consistently taking their money. He would call wires two through six, passing the first wire. Since there were ten wires in the arresting cables, the movie people were quite impressed that he could cut the cable he called out.

After the raid on Marcus Island, Task Force Fourteen joined up with the *Yorktown*. She then set sail for Wake Island. This time the *Essex* would be the flagship, and the task force commander would be Rear Admiral Alfred E. Montgomery. The *Essex*, along with *Yorktown*, *Lexington, Cowpens, Independence*, and *Belleau Wood*, set sail on September 29, 1943, to hit the enemy defenses at Wake Island.

Sailing again into Indian Country, Jocko had the crew of the *Yorktown* on their toes. Once again Jocko was everywhere: drilling, getting the men and the ship into fighting shape. Jocko was lucky in one sense: he had one of the best ordnance officers in the business. James T. Bryan, Jr., saw to it that the planes were armed and ready to go at almost a moment's notice. With Jim were some of the most dedicated men in the navy, among them were Chief Warrant Officer Second Class T. W. "Gunner" Pepper, AOM2c Martin "Tadpole" Tauber, and AOM2c Joseph Coppi. These men, and others like them, handled each bomb, torpedo, rocket, and round of ammunition that went into the planes flying from the *Yorktown*'s deck. Without them the *Yorktown* would have no sting.

Now that the Marcus raid was over, Commander James H. Flatley was relieved as commander of Air Group Five and returned to the *Enterprise*. Commander Charles L. Crommelin was now its leader. Commander Crommelin was a tough and rugged man. He would lead the group during the attack on Wake Island.

On October 5, the *Yorktown* and the other carriers hit Wake Island. Wake had been in U.S. hands at the start of the war, but had been lost to the Japanese on December 22, 1941, after a heroic fight waged by a force of slightly over 500 army, navy, and marine personnel. The October attack was to show the Japanese that they were now the ones in trouble.

As the planes took off that day, Crommelin had men like Lieutenant Joseph R. Kristufek and Lieutenant Raymond F. Kilrain flying with him to make the attack on Wake. The planes came in over Wake to drop their bombs at an altitude of between 3,000 and 1,000 feet. With pin-point accuracy, the pilots of Air Group Five bombed the island, doing considerable damage to the Japanese installations on Wake. After bombing, the pilots would come in flying at angles of forty-five to sixty degrees for strafing runs. They would level off at 500 feet.

During the raids, Lieutenant Kicker and Ensign Tyler were shot down. Cromelin spotted them in the water, and stayed over them until a submarine, the *Skate*, surfaced and picked them up. All this was going on right underneath the eyes and guns of the Japanese on the island. As shell blasts straddled the *Skate*, she picked up the two flyers. Several shells came so close that they splashed water onto the conning tower of the submarine. The pilots were later returned to the *Lexington*.

During the Wake Island raids, the *Yorktown* had dropped eighty-nine tons of bombs on the island, and the pilots and gunners on the carrier had fired 155,000 rounds of ammunition.

The men of the *Yorktown* had finished their first two raids, and they had been quite successful. A few friends had been lost in the action, which was regrettable, but their sacrifice had not been in vain. The Japanese had paid dearly for the American lives. Also, the *Yorktown* had earned her first battle star. This star was a memorial to the men who had given their lives so that some day the threat of war might be wiped from the face of the earth.

After the attack on Wake Island, the *Yorktown* returned to the United States, where Jocko gave state side liberty to the crew top priority on his agenda. The *Yorktown* was a fighting ship, however, and she was soon heading back to Indian Country.

Even though the *Yorktown* was not involved in

any battles at this time, the drilling went on. Jocko was a man who still demanded perfection, and drilling was the only way it could be achieved. The gun crews practiced by firing on target-sleeves towed behind planes. They would train on the long sleeve with a short burst of fire. The next time they fired the sleeve would fall to the ocean, the result of a direct hit. The gunnery aboard the *Yorktown* was the finest of any ship in the navy.

The film *The Fighting Lady* was progressing nicely under the direction of Lieutenant Dwight Long. Dwight had made friends with Smokey and had filmed him often in the Radar Plot, now called the Combat Information Center, or CIC. Smokey had even loaned Dwight a leather flight jacket which he wore when the *Yorktown* operated in cooler climates.

The film included several good shots of the *Yorktown*'s planes flying through the multi-colored burst of antiaircraft fire on Marcus and Wake Islands. The film was incomplete, but it looked as if it was going to be a classic war documentary.

The crew of the *Yorktown* began to notice that their ship did not have a nickname like the other ships in the navy. They decided to look for one. The *Enterprise* was the "Big E," but "Big Y" seemed too obvious. "Yorky" would serve to confuse her with the old *Yorktown*. "The Lucky Y" sounded good, but she had not seen enough combat to earn a nickname like that yet. A few even called her "The Old So and So," but this was not the nickname for a lady. It would be months before she would finally get a nickname, but it would be one which would become a classic in the annals of naval warfare.

The *Yorktown*, like all American warships, had chaplains aboard to give men the comfort they needed when facing possible death at the hands of an enemy. The *Yorktown* had two chaplains. The Protestant chaplain was Robert L. Alexander, and the Catholic chaplain was Father Joseph W. Moody. Both men were always there when they were needed.

By mid-November, it had been decided to invade the Gilbert Islands. The *Yorktown* joined up with the new Fast Carrier Task Force designated as Task Force Fifty. Early in 1943 it had been decided to designate task forces according to number of the fleet in which they operated. The Atlantic Fleets were even-numbered, while the Pacific Fleets were odd-numbered. Throughout the rest of the war the Fleet would be called either the Third or the Fifth, depending on whether Halsey or Spruance was in overall command.

For the Gilbert Island invasion the *Yorktown* was again the flagship of Admiral A. C. Pownall. There were four carrier task groups with the *Yorktown*. These were in TG 50.1; they included the carriers *Lexington* and *Cowpens* It would be the *Yorktown's* task during the invastion to guard a sector of the sea and air from the Japanese.

Since the *Yorktown* was the flagship of a task force comprising eleven attack carriers, several battleships, cruisers, and a number of destroyers, the men aboard the carrier in CIC would have their hands full. Charlie Ridgway, Smokey Stover, Lieutenant Alex Wilding and a few others, had become the heart not only of the *Yorktown*'s air defenses, but of the entire fleet's air defenses. Even though the job was demanding, Smokey still wanted to fly, where he felt he could do more good. Jocko, though, believed that Smokey could do the best job were he was, and so Smokey remained in CIC.

On the morning of November 19, 1943, the Gilbert Island operation began. The marines landed on Tarawa on the morning of November 20th. This was the first amphibious landing of the war, and a lot still had to be learned, as the casualities at Tarawa showed.

At the same time the marines were landing on Tarawa, the army was landing on Makin. It had been decided that these islands had to be taken before the Marshalls could be captured. After the two atolls were captured, planes would fly from them to help support the Marshall Island invasion. This looked simple on paper, but proved to be quite difficult. Some of the bloodiest fighting in the entire Pacific War occurred on these two islands. Before the marines finally captured Tarawa, over 3,000 of them were killed trying to take a piece of rock less than half the size of New York City's Central Park.

Meanwhile, back on the *Yorktown*, Smokey had been doing a fine job of keeping the fighter defenses up around the ships of the fleet. The *Yorktown*, with the *Lexington* and the *Cowpens*, was patrolling the area north of Makin Island watching for enemy planes that might attack from the Marshalls. The ships did not have to wait long. At dusk on November 20, long range torpedo-carrying Bettys from Kwajalein attacked the fleet. Because United States ships had no equipment for night fighting, the

Japanese had the advantage. Nine of the Bettys were shot down, but not before one of them put a "fish" into the light carrier *Independence*. She had to withdraw to safer waters.

By now the *Yorktown* was working around-the-clock, defending herself and getting ready to attack during daylight hours. On November 23, the *Yorktown* sent her planes aloft to intercept more planes coming in from the Marshalls.

Commander Crommelin led his air group into the sky over the blue Pacific between the *Yorktown* and the Marshall Islands. Air Group Five intercepted and shot down several enemy planes, and it became obvious that if the army did not capture Makin soon, so that the fleet could leave, something disastrous was going to happen. The army was not used to operating with the navy, as the marines were, and so the army was cautious in securing Makin, taking a great deal of time and endangering the valuable fleet offshore.

On the evening of November 23, four fighters from the *Liscome Bay* lost their ship and asked for permission to land on the *Yorktown*. The first three Wildcats made a safe landing, and while the plane handlers were taking them out of the way, the fourth made his approach. On deck was AOM2c Joseph Coppi of V1A Division. He was a rearming crew chief, and was standing on the flight deck with several other men. He watched as Dick Tripp tried to bring the pilot in safely. The pilot had forgotten to lower his arresting hook. When his plane touched down, instead of cutting his engine, he gunned it. This caused the F4F to slam down onto the deck and bounce over the safety net that had been set up to stop planes from crashing into the parked planes forward. As the F4F slammed into the net, men ran for their lives. But the resulting crash and explosion trapped five men and they were killed. One of these men was Joe Coppi. As the flames spread, six planes were destroyed. The pilot was lucky. He was thrown clear and escaped with minor injuries. Joe's division officer, Jim Bryan, Jr., was deeply saddened by the accident.

The next morning Commander Crommelin took Air Group Five aloft again to search out the enemy and destroy him before he could damage the ships of the fleet. While Commander Charles Crommelin was leading Air Group Five toward the island of Mili in the Marshalls, his brother, Captain John Crommelin, was fighting for his life aboard the *Liscome Bay*.

Silently running in the Pacific beneath the fleet, was the Japanese submarine *I-175*. The *I-175* slipped close to the carrier *Liscome Bay* and launched one torpedo. Because the *Liscome Bay* was scheduled to send her planes aloft at dawn, she was a sitting duck. When the fish hit the ship a chain reaction went off. The entire ship exploded. Apparently the fish hit the bomb storage, setting off the bombs, which in turn set off the fueled and armed planes on the flight deck. Within minutes the carrier was a furnace. Captain Crommelin had been taking a shower at the time of the explosion. He had to help get men out of the inferno while stark naked, and then jump into the Pacific to save himself. The *Liscome Bay* sank in twenty-three minutes, taking over 600 sailors with her to a watery grave. On the atoll only sixty soldiers had been killed. The capture of Makin had cost the navy more than ten times the number of lives it had the army. Had the army been accustomed to operating with the navy, as the marines were, the *Liscome Bay* would have been gone from the atoll.

While Captain John Crommelin was fighting for his life aboard the burning *Liscome Bay*, his brother Commander Charles Crommelin, was leading Air Group Five for the attack on Mili Island. While Charles was making a low-level strafing run, his Hellcat was hit by a Japanese cannon shell. The shell shattered, "frosted" his "greenhouse," or windshield, destroyed his instruments, and wounded him in several places. One eye was blinded by the flying glass and the other was hurt; his right wrist was broken, and bleeding.

The *Yorktown* was over 120 miles away, but he knew that if he was going to live he had to make it back to the ship. If he ditched near Mili Island it would be suicide, because if the sea did not get him the Japs would. By sticking his head out of the cockpit he could see with his partially good eye. The slipstream helped to keep him from passing out. A blackout at this point meant certain death.

Flying like this for 120 miles, Charles sighted the *Yorktown*. When he approached the *Yorktown*, Red Volz brought him in for a safe landing. Charles then taxied his plane away from the arresting wire, parked it, and climbed out of it. Only after knowing he had safely landed his plane aboard the *Yorktown* did Charles allow himself to collapse from loss of blood. He was then rushed to sick bay, where he recovered from his wounds. Since Charles would be unable to fly until he was fully recovered, Lieutenant Commander Edgar E. Stebbins was given command of Air Group Five.

As more raids came from the Marshall Islands, it was decided to launch air attacks on the airfields there. On December 4, the *Yorktown* led six carriers toward Kwajalein and the other Marshall airfields. The carrier came under attack from four torpedo planes. As the planes came in from the starboard side, they were attacked in turn by the *Yorktown's* gunners. Four planes came in low, armed with torpedoes, ready to sink the *Yorktown*. As they approached, one was shot down by some excellent gunnery from the *San Francisco*. But still the other three came on, threatening and deadly. Although shells exploded around the three planes, they held their course and came closer. Two of the planes began smoking from hits, but the third continued to fly close to the water. Closer and closer the two smoking planes came, while the undamaged one followed closely behind. For some reason, unknown even today, the two damaged planes flew a few feet over the flight deck without releasing their fish. One of these Kates was hit by a five-inch shell as she passed over the *Yorktown*. She burst into flames. A photographer caught the flaming plane on film. It was developed and given to Jocko who called it "The Flaming Kate."

Two of the planes crashed into the sea in flames. The last passed over the flight deck and was shot down as it made its attempt to escape. The *Yorktown* had come under attack by four Kates and had shot down three of them. The *San Francisco* had got the other one.

If the planes had dropped their fish, the *Yorktown* would have been in great trouble, because there were armed and fueled planes on the flight deck. The *Yorktown* might have been lost, like the *Liscome Bay* only days before. Some started calling the *Yorktown* the Lucky Y, because she had been quite lucky. Nothing should have stopped the three planes that had already completed their runs from dropping their fish, but they did not. No one has ever figured out why the fish weren't dropped.

After Jocko received the picture of the flaming Kate he had the ship's photographer make a print for every man aboard. He then presented the photos to the crew members as Christmas presents. For Ted Rohrbough, the photo was also a birthday present. The Kate was shot down on his birthday, December 4, 1943. On that day he became eighteen.

That night the *Lexington* was hit, but not badly. The *Yorktown*, who was seeing more action than her sisters, was still unscratched.

Finally the moon set and the attacking Betty vanished. Aboard the *Yorktown*, Jocko had the quartermaster inscribe the following in the log at 1:27 A.M.: "The moon set—thank God." The remainder of the trip to Pearl was peaceful.

The Kwajalein raid cost Pownall his job as the officer in tactical command. He had not been aggressive enough and had passed up opportunities to strike. His successor, picked by Admiral Nimitz, was Admiral Marc A. Mitscher. Mitscher would replace Pownall and carry his flag aboard the *Yorktown* for his first venture as OTC.

After the raids on the Marshall Islands the *Yorktown* returned to Pearl Harbor. As she sailed into Pearl, there was an air of confidence aboard the ship. Jocko had helped to inspire this feeling and was justly proud of his ship and crew. Not only had the *Yorktown* crew been first on several occasions, but they had also beaten off several aggressive Japanese pilots in a death duel. The green crew of only three months before had now become battle-hardened veterans.

After tying up in Pearl, replacements were brought aboard the ship. It was the plank owners job to mold these new men into a unified, fighting team.

One of these new replacements was Seaman Third Class Don Seaman. Don had joined the Navy at the age of eighteen in January, 1943. After getting to Ford Island, Don had run into some friends. They told him he was going to be transferred to a carrier. There were two that were going to be taking replacements, the *Intrepid* and the *Yorktown*. Don picked the *Yorktown* because it had been overseas longer, and he felt it would have a more experienced crew. In later years Don would realize that this had been a lucky choice.

The *Intrepid* had been built close beside the *Yorktown* at Newport News, Virginia. They were more like sisters than the other *Essex* class carriers because they had their keels laid the same day. But the *Yorktown* was now a proven veteran, while the *Intrepid* was still green.

While the *Yorktown* was in Pearl, Dick Tripp and

Ed Volz went ashore to give more bounce drill to the pilots. Smokey also went ashore. He wanted to fly so that he could keep his flight status. Smokey still badgered Jocko to let him fly. After Commander Crommelin was hospitalized for wounds incurred during the Gilbert Island campaign, Lieutenant Commander Edgar E. Stebbins had been taken out of Air Plot and given command of Air Group Five. Because of this, Smokey felt that he might still have a chance to fly again.

The *Yorktown* had lost several experienced pilots to the Japanese, and these men had to be replaced. Smokey argued that since he had already served aboard the *Hornet* and the *Saratoga*, as well as old Air Group Five off Guadalcanal, there was no one aboard better qualified than he to fly with the air group. Still Jocko kept him in Combat Information Center.

On December 15, 1943, Air Group Five lost an Avenger piloted by Lieutenant Raymond F. Kilrain. With Kilrain were ARM2c Donald W. Wellman and ARM2c Edward H. Smith. After the loss of these men, Smokey again went to ask to be returned to flight status. Jocko liked men who fought and who were brave, willing leaders. He knew that soon he would probably give in to Smokey.

The *Yorktown* was in Pearl Harbor on December 24, 1943. The crew spent a peaceful Christmas in Hawaii. On the hangar deck was a large Christmas tree, and presents were passed out to the men. For Christmas dinner there was turkey with all the trimmings.

In a war-torn world, men still took time to honor

one born almost 2,000 years before, who had done more for men than all the kings, lawmakers, armies and navies of the world combined. It was His birthday; and His wish for peace on earth was shared by everyone aboard the *Yorktown*. Church services were being held on the hangar deck by Chaplains Alexander and Moody.

The next day, December 26, Smokey got his Christmas present. Orders arrived detaching him from the ship's company, and assigning him to "Fighting Five" as a pilot. He quickly checked out on the F6F Hellcat. Fighting Five went to Kaneohe on Oahu Island to train. While the *Yorktown* was at sea, they flew her flight deck. By mid-January Smokey was ready to go get the enemy. His dreams had come true.

On December 31, 1943, James W. Sands left the *Yorktown*. He had been the yeoman to the carrier's first executive officer, Raoul Waller. Also leaving the *Yorktown* on that day was James A. McNally. He had been the first engineering officer on the ship. Like Sands, he came on in April 15, 1943, and was a plank owner of the *Yorktown*. The abilities of these two men would be missed, but duty called them elsewhere.

Chapter IV

By January, 1944, the Gilbert Islands were under American control. Bloody Tarawa had been costly to the United States. The marines, under Major General Holland M. "Howlin' Mad" Smith, had lost 1,056 men taking the island from the Japanese. But because of the victory at Tarawa, other islands would be won more easily. Much had been learned from the operation. Certainly, more intensive bombing would be used in the future.

The Marshall Islands would be the next target. The pilots of Air Group Five had already bombed Kwajalein and several of the other islands in the Marshall chain. This had been done in early December, 1943, because the Japanese were harassing our troops at the Gilberts. The bombing was haphazard during the Gilbert operation, but now the entire task force was going to give the islands a going over.

As the *Yorktown* left Pearl Harbor she was once again the flagship. This time the task force was called Task Force Fifty-eight, under the command of Rear Admiral M. A. Mitscher. At various times until the end of the war this task force would be numbered either Fifty-eight or Thirty-eight, depending upon which fleet they were operating in at the time. Admiral Mitscher had under his command twelve carriers holding over 650 planes. The *Yorktown* spearheaded the fleet.

Smokey was delighted that he could now fly. Mitscher had been the skipper of the *Hornet* while Smokey had been aboard.

On January 29, the pilots of Air Group Five took off from the *Yorktown* to "soften up" the islands for the invasion forces. In the early morning, the pilots climbed aboard their planes. As each plane roared down the flight deck and the large number "10" passed beneath it, each pilot wondered what the day would bring.

Aboard the ship VIA Division, under the leadership of Division Officer Jim Bryan, was getting ready for the next strike. These men were the ones responsible for arming each plane with ammunition; bombs or torpedoes. As each man performed his duty, it appeared to be a rehearsal or drill rather than the real thing. Each man had been well-rehearsed for his part. As the ammunition was handed from one man to the other, no verbal contact was needed. Swiftly, silently, and efficiently these men worked, arming each plane for the task ahead.

While the men of VIA were going about this task,

Lieutenant Joe Kristufek, Lieutenant William Meehan, Ensign Donald R. Simenson, and others were attacking airfields on the islands. Luckily there were not many Japanese planes in the air, but the antiaircraft fire was murderous to American planes.

When they reached their targets the SBD's would dive. As the planes screamed out of the air toward the ground below, the pilots could see the deadly ack-ack coming toward them. The puffs of brightly colored smoke slipped by the wing tip, and the tracers from the guns spiraled up toward them. It took nerves of steel to hold on course and drop the payload. After dropping the bomb, the pilot would climb back into the air out of reach of the ack-ack.

The pilots in the Avengers also came in for bombing runs, and they too had to run the gauntlet of murderous fire to drop their bombs.

The pilots of the F6F Hellcats, after protecting the SBD's and TBF's from enemy planes during their runs, would swing out of the blue sky for strafing runs. As the pilots brought the nimble fighters out of the sky, at diving angles of forty to fifty degrees, they would pick out a target. When a target was spotted, the pilot would press the firing button on the joy stick. A steady stream of bullets would spit out of the six wing-guns toward the ground below. As the bullets kicked up the dust their trail could be followed toward the target. Finally whatever the pilot was shooting at would be hit. By this time the plane was within 1,500 to 500 feet of the ground. Pulling back on the joy stick, the pilot would then climb back to the safety of the sky.

Smokey was in command of a four-plane division

which included Lieutenant Robert W. Duncan, Smokey's wingman, Lieutenant Denzil Merrill, and Ensign D. O. Kenney. These men flew F6F's and were responsible for the protection of the SBD's and TBF's.

Although Smokey was lucky on January 29, other pilots were not so fortunate. While making their bomb runs at the targets on the islands, several of the planes could not find a safe path through the deadly puffs of brightly colored smoke and the bullets thrown up by the Japanese defenders on the islands. Lieutenant William Meehan's plane was hit by the deadly fire. It exploded and crashed to the ground, and he was killed along with his two crewmen, ARM2c R. H. Olds and ARM2c G. D. Haigh. Still the brave crews continued to attack the targets below. Another plane was hit. This time Ensign Donald R. Simenson died along with his crewmen, ARM2c R. L. Parks and ARM2c P. W. Atwater.

The planes returned to be fueled and rearmed. As each plane approached the carrier in a landing pattern, the LSO would direct it in or wave it off to ditch in the ocean beside the *Yorktown*. Some of these planes were badly hit and damaged by ack-ack. Several had close calls, but all landed safely.

After the deck was cleared of damaged planes by the men of VIT Division, the rearmed and refueled planes were spotted for the next strike. Again each plane roared down the flight deck to hit the enemy. More damage was sustained by the Japanese, and the Americans lost another plane and crew. By nightfall on January 29, another TBF Avenger had been plucked out of the air. This time Ensign

Thomas E. McGrath and his crewmen ARM2c R. C. Robinson and ARM2c Edwin W. Haselgard had given their full measure in this war against the Japanese. All these men were sadly missed by their squadron mates that night.

By February 3, 1944, the pilots of Air Group Five had made over 468 sorties over the target, dropping 121 tons of bombs. Several troop-carrying barges had been sunk, and fourteen Japanese planes had been destroyed on the ground before they had a chance to take off. By supporting the army with their deadly concentration of fire, Air Group Five had helped ease the troop landings. By February 4, 1944, the Marshall Islands were under American control.

After the actions of Air Group Five against the Marshall Islands, Jocko Clark issued the following statement:

"Pilots of all types indicated a complete knowledge of their particular jobs. The state of their training cannot be surpassed. The high degree of morale, skill, and unwavering determination effected by all pilots in the numerous attacks was impressive."

On February 4, the ships of Task Force Fifty-eight, with the *Yorktown* in the lead, entered the lagoon at Majuro. Majuro Lagoon was twenty-six miles long and six miles wide. Admiral Mitscher now had an advanced base for his carriers where they could be safe from the whims of the wide Pacific Ocean. Along with the *Yorktown* in Majuro were the CV's *Enterprise, Saratoga, Essex, Intrepid* and *Bunker Hill*. There were also six CVL's: *Belleau*

Wood, Cabor, Monterey, Cowpens, Princeton, and a new ship, *Langley*, named after the first American aircraft carrier, built in the 1920's and sunk during the first months of the war.

Aboard the *Yorktown*, Smokey made his normal patrol flights watching for enemy planes along with the other pilots. It was Smokey who made the 7,000th landing aboard the carrier. As Smokey climbed out of his F6F, he was greeted on the flight deck by Jocko himself. Jocko was grinning from ear to ear as he presented a cake representing the 7,000th landing to Smokey. Just months earlier, Smokey had been badgering Jocko to let him fly, and now Jocko was presenting him with a cake. The cake came at the right time, because on February 9, Smokey celebrated his twenty-fourth birthday.

Since the fleet had encountered little opposition in the invasion of the Marshall Islands, it was decided to attack the Japanese fleet at Truk. Truk was in the Caroline Islands, and it was the Japanese "Pearl Harbor." The Japanese had been building up defenses for years in the area. To capture Truk would be a great victory for our side. As the *Yorktown* steamed toward Truk with Admiral Mitscher directing the operations from the bridge, Smokey was beginning to behave differently. One day he walked across the hangar deck to the place where Chaplain Alexander was leaning on a rail. As the two men talked, Smokey pulled from his wallet a poem he had clipped from a magazine. It was titled *High Flight*. The poem was an inspiring one about a pilot flying high in the sky. The last line of the poem was: "Put out my hand and touched the face of God."

Smokey carried the poem and showed it to Chaplain Alexander because he had a premonition that he too would soon touch the face of God. Smokey and Chaplain Alexander talked a while longer, and then Smokey walked off carrying his poem in his wallet.

That night as Smokey and his wingman, Bob Duncan, were talking about various things, Bob noticed that a brand new pair of shoes was laid out with Smokey's flight gear. Confused, Bob asked Smokey why he had a new pair of shoes beside his flight suit. Smokey calmly replied that when he got shot down he would need a new pair of shoes, because the Japanese would not give him any.

That night few of the pilots slept. The thought of the next day's fighting kept them from doing anything but catnapping.

By 4:00 A.M. on the 16th of February, Ordnance Officer Jim Bryan had risen from his bunk to get the planes armed for the day's event. The Japanese would put up a tough fight and everything had to be ready for the returning planes. Before going about his duties, he noticed a light on in Smokey's small compartment. As he stuck his head in, he noticed that Smokey was waterproofing his pistol. Jim wished Smokey luck, and then went about his duties.

At 6:30 A.M., after a hearty breakfast of steak and eggs, the pilots climbed into their planes. As each plane shot down the flight deck and into the air, each pilot wondered what would happen to him that day. Only Smokey did not. He knew what would happen to him on this date.

77

As *VF-5* approached Truk, it joined up with fighters from other carriers. There were seventy-two F6F's in the air over Truk Lagoon. Suddenly the air was filled with Japanese planes and antiaircraft fire. This was the most concentrated firepower the pilots of Air Group Five had encountered to date. As Smokey and his wingman engaged the enemy planes, a burst of flack hit Bob Duncan's engine, forcing him to return back to the *Yorktown*. Without a wingman Smokey was more vulnerable to attack. As he pressed on through the antiaircraft fire, his plane was hit by a burst of flak. Denzil Merrill flew up next to Smokey and looked at the damage. He radioed Smokey that he was hit bad. Seeing that he could not make it back to the ship, Smokey decided to jump while he still had sufficient altitude. As he drifted toward the water, Denzil flew overhead, watching to see if he made a safe landing.

Smokey hit the water, opened his life raft, and climbed into it. Seeing that he was safe, Denzil buzzed him to let him know that he saw him. Finally Denzil had to return to the *Yorktown* because of lack of fuel. Denzil tried to radio the submarine *Searaven* just a few miles to the northwest, but could not get through. The *Searaven* was in the area specifically to pick up downed fliers.

Later in the day, as Air Group Five made more attacks on the Japanese at Truk, they would pass over the spot where Smokey had gone down, but they never did see him again.

Word about Smokey was never received. What happened to him is anybody's guess. The next day, seven captured airmen were executed on Dublon

Island in retaliation for the raid on Truk. Smokey may have been one of those airmen, or he may have used the pistol that he was waterproofing on the morning of February 16. He had always said that he would never be taken alive. A dry pistol would insure that. In any case, Smokey had "put out [his] hand and touched the face of God."

That night the men aboard the *Yorktown* were depressed. Smokey had touched a lot of lives aboard the ship, and would be sadly missed. Because he had been part of the ship's company and also of the air group, he was known by both pilots and crew members.

While the loss of Smokey was a terrible blow to the men of the *Yorktown*, the damage that the fleet had inflicted upon the Japanese was great in terms of both morale and material. The Japanese had lost forty-one ships. Over 200 of their planes had been destroyed on the ground. The myth of Japanese impregnability had been exploded.

While Smokey and Air Group Five were facing death in the sky, the *Yorktown* came under attack from the Japanese. Several times the *Yorktown* had come under attack, but men on her guns had shot down the attackers.

In one instance, a "Nick" dived on the *Yorktown*. The gunners managed to flame the plane, but not before the pilot dropped his bomb. As the instrument of death fell from the sky toward the carrier, the helmsman quickly maneuvered the ship out from under the path of the falling bomb. The bomb fell harmlessly, one hundred yards astern of the ship.

Twenty-five minutes later, the *Yorktown* came under torpedo-plane attack. Four of the planes dropped their fish, but none hit. The *Yorktown* might merit the nickname of the Lucky Y, because she was indeed lucky.

After the raid on Truk, the *Yorktown* proceeded on to the Marianas Islands. After attacking these islands she proceeded to Pearl Harbor.

Another man had also been killed during the raid on Truk. ARM2c Jack Hancock had died from wounds received on the 16th of February. He had been aboard a TBF Avenger at the time.

While the *Yorktown* was in Pearl, the crew took liberty and went ashore. Like sailors of every nation, the crew liked to sightsee and spend money while ashore. In order for the men to get this money on payday, the staff in the payroll office had to work efficiently and hard. One of these men in payroll was Don Seaman. Don and the other men would work into the late hours of the night to see to it that the men were paid on payday. This may seem like an unimportant job, but try to tell a sailor on payday that his pay is not ready. Then you will see how important the job really is! In 1944, the pay ranged from $50.000 a month for a seaman, Third Class, to $175.00 a month for a chief warrant officer. With over 3,000 men aboard, the task of seeing that each man got his pay in the correct amount and on time was a rather large one.

On one of these paydays, Don had the risky task of giving Jocko his money. Jocko, as has already been established, was a man of many words; and he did not care how he used them. Whenever something did not suit him, he let the person involved know about it.

It seemed that Jocko had been married several times. On this payday one of his wives had, through red tape, taken her share of his check. Jocko was to be paid $3,000, but his ex-wife had taken $2,000 of it. The officers in the payroll office knew that Jocko was going to raise the roof when he found this out. They were all afraid to take the money to Jocko. Finally it was decided that Don would be the "lucky" one. Don proceeded to Jocko's quarters and presented him with the money. When Jocko discovered what had happened, he exploded; but, of course, there was nothing he could do about the money. Everything was legal, but it probably did hurt to have two-thirds of his pay taken from him. Don always remembered that day.

By mid-March the *Yorktown* had a new Captain. Captain Joseph James "Jocko" Clark had been promoted to the rank of rear admiral, and had left the *Yorktown* on February 10, 1944, just six days before the first raid on Truk, the raid in which Smokey had been shot down. His replacement was Captain Ralph Edward Jennings. Captain Jennings, unlike Jocko, was a quiet man who never lost his cool. He was efficient and calm, and he possessed the rare ability to tolerate error. He knew how to counsel those who committed errors to prevent their reoccurring. Captain Jennings was lucky, because he had in his command a well trained crew. The Patton of the Pacific had seen to that. Although the *Yorktown* retained Jocko's spirit, she would become a "lady" under Captain Jennings.

After a brief visit to Espirito Santos, the *Yorktown* set sail with Task Force Fifty-eight on March 23, for the raid against the Palau Islands. At 5:30 A.M. on March 29, the *Yorktown*, along with the *Lexington* began launching its planes. For two days the planes from Task Force Fifty-eight hit the islands, destroying the Japanese installations there. These islands lay on the path to the Philippines. Destruction of the Japanese here and at other islands would make the return to the Philippines a little easier.

After hitting these islands for two days, the *Yorktown*, turned due east and hit Woleai Island on April 1, April Fool's Day. The Japanese had become uncertain about where our forces would hit next. On April 21, they found out.

A Japanese summary had listed Woleai as the last place the American forces would strike. "Island hopping" was helping to win the war, by confusing the Japanese as to where we would hit next. When the Japanese finally figured out that we were going to hit Hollandia, for example, our transports were already in the harbor.

On the morning of April 21, Captain Jennings watched the F6F's, SBD's, and TBF's roar down the flight deck and climb into the early morning air off the bow of the *Yorktown*. This would be his first large engagement of his new command. Questions were running through his mind, yet he showed the cool, calm leadership that he was noted for. Luckily for the ships of Task Force Fifty-eight, the B-25's under the command of General George C. Kenney had destroyed most of the 300 enemy planes in New

Guinea that were in the Hollandia area. The *Yorktown*, along with the other ships, gave air cover and bombed the airstrips for three days before the ground troops landed. The carrier then supported the amphibious landings at Humbolt Bay. With the help of the Fifth Fleet, General MacArthur was starting his return to the Philippines.

During the first day of the air strikes against Hollandia, the TBF Avengers in Air Group Five ran into some antiaircraft fire. As the pilots flew their planes in toward the targets, the ack-ack was murderous. The deadly fire came at the planes steadily, trying to burn them out of the sky.

As Ensign Owen H. Ramey was making his run against his assigned target, the ack-ack tore into his Avenger. His plane was hit badly. Losing control, either because he had been hit himself, or because of damage to the plane, the pilot crashed the smoking plane into the jungle. Killed with Ensign Ramey were his two crew members, J. M. Russell and D. D. Parker.

After hitting Hollandia, New Guinea, the *Yorktown* started toward Pearl, but first there was some unfinished business to attend to at Truk. The Japanese considered this to be their most formidable island stronghold in the far reaches of the Pacific. This raid was an attempt to show them that the American forces could attack anywhere they pleased. Since Smokey had been lost here during the raid on February 16, the pilots of Air Group Five would take special pleasure in hitting Truk again.

On April 29, the pilots of Air Group Five once again flew toward the island and its large harbor where they had lost one of their members to the Japanese on Dublon Island. At the end of the first day there was smoke and fire everywhere. This time, though, the Japanese had pulled most of their ships out of the harbor.

The next day, while attacking Truk, another Avenger was lost. This time Lieutenant Commander Richard Upson was shot down with his crew, Lieutenant (jg) Paul Searless and AMM2c R. E. Wertman. These were the last men from Air Group Five to die while serving aboard the *Yorktown*. By midday the *Yorktown* was proceeding to Pearl Harbor for rest, recreation, supplies, replacements, and a new air group.

As the *Yorktown* pulled into Pearl Harbor a few days later, Air Group Five, under the command of Lieutenant Commander Edgar E. Stebbins, left its first ship for duty aboard another ship. These men had helped to start a list of victories against the enemy that would grow into one of the most impressive records that any ship could ever hope to achieve.

Air Group Five had set a record by fighting in more operations than had any other air group before them. They had been engaged in every operation in the Pacific except one, the Rabaul raids. No other air group could say the same.

The pilots and their crew members had shot down ninety-five Japanese planes which were seen to crash. They had destroyed 195 planes on the ground and had strafed 117 more. The F6F Hellcat squadron had shot down ninety-three Japanese planes while losing only one to enemy air attack. This was a new record.

As for shipping destroyed, Air Group Five sank over 57,500 tons of enemy shipping and damaged 234,500 additional tons. The men under the leaderships of Commander Flately, Commander Crommelin, and Lieutenant Commander Stebbins were proud of the fact that no American dive- or torpedo-bomber was ever shot down by enemy aircraft, and only one American fighter was lost to enemy aircraft. The other planes had been downed by antiaircraft fire or lost due to operational accidents. The men of Air Group Five left with a feeling of satisfaction with a job well done.

The *Yorktown* got some replacements. Some of the new men were officers, but most were enlisted men. One of the men who came aboard was a new Assistant LSO. He was Lieutenant (jg) James E. Cozzens. He would eventually replace Lieutenant Ed Volz, but first he would act as a relief man.

Also coming aboard was Seaman First Class Ruben Kitchen. Ruben was from Pike County, Kentucky, where his father, James, was employed in the coal mines. He had joined the navy soon after reaching his eighteenth birthday. After going to boot camp in the Great Lakes region, he was put aboard a transport, the *Storm King*, and sent through the Panama Canal to Pearl Harbor. After reaching Pearl, he and the other men from the *Storm King* lived in tents for a couple of weeks before being assigned to different ships. Ruben was lucky enough to get assigned to a carrier, the *Yorktown*. He had wanted to be assigned to a submarine, but later would be thankful that he had been put aboard a carrier.

Another man to be assigned to the *Yorktown* on May 18, 1944, was Seaman First Class Kenneth Parkinson. "Parky" was from Illinois, and he and Ruben were assigned to the R-1 Division as damage-control men. This was the start of a friendship that would last for years.

When the two went aboard the *Yorktown*, they reported to their division officer, Lieutenant Fred Weatherford. Fred would show them the ropes. They learned to respect him because he was a fine officer and a gentleman.

While the new replacements were getting accustomed to the *Yorktown*, she was taking on supplies. Bombs, torpedoes, and other kinds of ammunition were carefully taken aboard by the men in the VIA Division under Jim Bryan, and stowed below decks in a safe place in the magazines.

In the payroll office, Don Seaman was getting the names of the new men and their divisions, so that they could be paid on payday.

Although duty called for everyone, there was still time to read, engage in hobbies and sports, or just lie around. One man, Seaman First Class Edward Johnson, liked to practice his boxing. He was the lightweight champion aboard the ship, and practiced to stay in shape whenever he got the chance. While in Pearl, he would practice whenever possible.

At night on the hangar deck, the curtain would be raised to let fresh air pass through that large floating garage while members of the crew watched a movie. Movies were a great pastime; new movies were anticipated with as much pleasure as mail from home.

It was the job of the men in the K-Y Division to

see to it that the mail reached every sailor aboard the ship. One of the men responsible for getting the mail to the men was Mailman Third Class Joseph H. Huber. He had come aboard the *Yorktown* on May 18.

Another man to come aboard the *Yorktown* on May 18 was Gunnersmate First Class Edward N. Wallace. Ed had been serving aboard the U.S.S. *Takanis Bay*, CVE-89. On Friday, May 13, he was transferred from the "Kaiser Coffin," as the CVE's were called, and told to report to Ford Island for further assignment. Like the others, he came to the *Yorktown* and was assigned to the First Division which operated the five-inch guns.

Also in May, the *Yorktown* received her second air group, Air Group One. When Air Group One came aboard, the man in command was Lieutenant Commander Bernard Max Strean. Strean was from Oklahoma and had graduated from Annapolis in 1933. He then went aboard the battleship *Pennsylvania*. But in 1935, he became a naval aviator, serving with Air Groups Six, Three, Eleven, and Twenty-three. His first command would be Air Group One aboard the *Yorktown*.

Strean, upon being admitted to Annapolis in 1929, was given a nickname by an upperclassman. Strean is a Scottish name and is pronounced "Strain." Rather than explain this to everyone, Bernard said his name was pronounced "Strean." One upperclassman thought he had said "screen," so he called him "Smoke Screen." The nickname Smoke stayed with Bernard, and everyone began to call him Smoke. He is not to be confused with Smokey.

Some people do get the two confused because they were both pilots serving on the *Yorktown* within just a few months of each other. Smoke was destined for greater heights in the navy, while the memory of Smokey would also soar. Both men would be associated with the *Yorktown* in years to come.

With a new air group, replacements, supplies and new orders, the *Yorktown* was ready to sail for Indian Country. At 3:10 P.M. on May 29, 1944, the *Yorktown* hoisted her anchor and steamed out of Pearl Harbor. Her destination was Majuro Lagoon, or Sleepy Lagoon, as it was called.

While the *Yorktown* was at sea, Captain Jennings had the gun crews practice for at least two hours a day. This included actual firing time as well as learning to load the guns quickly and safely. For instance, if the loader on a 40-mm gun put the clip in incorrectly, the clip, containing four shells, would explode. This happened once and two men were killed. Knowing this made loaders like Edward Johnson want to be certain that they knew what they were doing. By practicing daily these men could load the 40-mm's by rote memory. This would be helpful in battle because when a plane is boring down on you it has a way of interrupting your concentration.

Don Seaman also practiced with the 20-mm guns. Don had held various positions on the 20's, each one as important as the next. It was the 20's that fired at the enemy from extremely close quarters.

Also on one of the 20's was Joseph Huber. He had just come aboard the *Yorktown* and had been assigned, with the Marine Division, as a loader on a 20-mm gun just forward of the number two elevator. Joe would learn quickly what it was like to be in the thick of the action.

Chapter V

On June 3, the *Yorktown* anchored in Majuro Lagoon. Task Force Fifty-eight under the overall command of Admiral Raymond A. Spruance, was the largest fleet to ever sail the seas. Under Spruance was Admiral Mitscher who was carrying his flag aboard the *Lexington*. Within the next few weeks, the Japanese and Americans were going to be at each other's throats. Not since the Battle of Midway had the Japanese been as ready to engage the American Fleet as they were now.

One June 6, 1944, the *Yorktown*, with the rest of Task Force Fifty-eight, pulled out of Majuro Lagoon in the Marshall Islands. The time was 1:00 P.M. History was being made then on the beaches of France in the European Theater. It was D-Day for thousands of Allied troops attacking Omaha Beach, Utah Beach, and the other beaches in Normandy,

France. General Eisenhower had made his move. For the first time in the war the Germans were going to be on the defensive in Europe, as the Japanese had been in the Pacific since August, 1943.

Meanwhile, back on the *Yorktown*, F6F's were being launched to scout for Japanese planes. It did not take long to find one of the enemy. Fifty-four miles from Majuro a Japanese plane was spotted and shot down. The upcoming storm was gathering quickly.

Early in the morning on June 11, the pilots of Air Group One arose to a breakfast of steak, eggs, buttered toast, and hot coffee. On that day, men were going to fly a strike against Guam, which was in the Marianas Island chain. While Smoke Strean, Richard T. Eastmond, Lieutenant Norman Merrell, Jr., Lieutenant James R. Pfister, and others ate their breakfasts and then went to the ready rooms beneath the flight deck for briefing, other men were getting their planes ready for action.

The ordnance men in the VIA Division under Jim Bryan, Jr., were arming the various types of aircraft with the needed bombs, torpedoes, and other kinds of ammunition. Other men gassed the planes up and spotted them on the flight deck. Near the stern were the TBF Avengers, next in line were the SBD Dauntlesses, and nearest the bow were the F6F Hellcats. This left only a little over 400 feet for the planes to take off. After the planes were spotted, the radio engineers would make the final adjustments on the planes' radios.

To avoid confusion on the flight deck, each division had its own color. The men in the various divisions would wear colored shirts to distinguish themselves. "Tadpole" Tauber and the other ordnance men wore red shirts, as did the fire fighters. The men who handled the catapault and arresting gear wore green, while the men who slid the chocks under the wheels wore purple. From the bridge, the shirts gave a colorful, circus-like appearance to the ship that contrasted curiously with the serious nature of the ship's work. After the pilots emerged from the island structure, they walked confidently to their planes. When Lieutenant Norman Merrell climbed into the cockpit of his Avenger, his two crewmen were already waiting for him. ARM1c Harold E. Mongraw and AOM2c Stanley E. Carr were ready to give the Japanese a rough day. As each plane awaited its turn to run down the flight deck, the men gave the equipment one last checking-over.

A live flight deck can be as dangerous to the crew as enemy fire, and the Airdales, the plane handlers, watched carefully for whirling propellers. Ted Johnson had already seen a friend of his walk into the propeller of a plane that was running almost full speed. His friend was cut to pieces, killed instantly. Any pilot revving his plane could blow an incautious Airdale into the propeller of the plane behind him. A live flight deck could and did kill crew members.

Captain Jennings leaned on the bridge railing watching the men work below him. Finally the plane director started giving the pilots the take-off signal. The F6F's roared down the flight deck, followed by the SBD's and the TBF's. Once these planes were in the air, preparations were begun for the landings.

Guam had been in American hands before the

war, but the Japanese had taken the island on December 9, 1941. This would be the first attempt to recapture an American possession from the Japanese. To recapture Guam would be a morale boost to the military as well as to the folks back home. Moreover, Guam had excellent airfields and the best deepwater harbor in the Marianas.

Air Group One took off into the sky over Guam. As the bursts of ack-ack exploded around the planes, each pilot courageously flew his plane into the deadly fire and hit his target. Experience had taught the pilots to hit the installations first, then the guns, buildings, and supplies. Only at the end of the last strike would they hit the fuel dumps. The exploding fuel dumps hid other targets with their thick black smoke, so these were the last hit during a strike. The SBD's and TBF's bombed the airfields at dusk just before the fuel dumps were hit. The oncoming darkness made repairing the bombed-out runways difficult. Spruance had learned every little trick in the book.

As the planes began returning from Guam, Captain Jennings watched with keen interest. These men had just gone out to fight the enemy, and he was interested in their safe return. As the planes landed, they were taken forward out of the way. The *Yorktown* has a reputation for being able to launch and recover her aircraft faster than any other carrier in the fleet.

As a F6F Hellcat approached, the LSO saw that only one landing gear was down. Looking the situation over carefully, he gave the pilot permission to land. The F6F touched down perfectly, but its tail hook missed the arresting wire. The plane then skidded sideways down the flight deck toward the island structure and several men standing in that area.

Seeing that the plane was coming toward them, the men started running to get out of the way. Violently, the plane struck the structure near a five-inch gun mount. This knocked the plane 270 degrees around, and in the process the F6F broke in two. Finally, it came to a stop in the center of the flight deck about midway down. The pilot climbed from the plane unhurt but shaken.

As the planes landed Captain Jennings counted them. One Avenger was missing. Lieutenant Norman Merrell, Jr's. plane would not land. He and his two crewmen, ARM1c Harold E. Mongraw and AOM2c Stanley E. Carr were killed over Guam. The Americans lost one plane, but shot down thirty of the Japanese defenders at Guam.

By this time the Japanese, under Vice Admiral Jisaburo Ozawa, were getting ready to attack and destroy the American Fleet. This would be the decisive battle that the Japanese admirals had been waiting for. The plan was to lure the Fifth Fleet into the waters between Palau, Yap, and Waleai. Once in these waters, Admiral Ozawa hoped to destroy the Fifth Fleet, and bring victory to Japan.

The Japanese brought in 5 fleet carriers, 4 light carriers, 28 destroyers, 11 heavy cruisers, 2 light cruisers, 5 battleships, and 473 planes to hit the Fifth Fleet. This confrontation became known as the Battle of the Philippine Sea. With Ozawa was the worlds's largest battleship, the *Yamato,* and her sister, the *Musashi.* The *Yamato* was a legend among the sailors of the American Fleet, with her eighteen-inch guns and 72,809 ton displacement. The *Yorktown* had a displacement of 27,100 tons and five-inch guns. If the *Yamato* were allowed to hit the carriers of the Fifth Fleet she could do a lot of damage. The largest American battleship was the *Iowa*, with a displacement of 48,500 tons and sixteen-inch guns. The Japanese naval officers hoped that the *Yamato* would turn the tide of the war.

On June 11, the Japanese Combined Fleet defense lines consisted of the following:

1. Admiral Soemu Toyoda, Commander in Chief of the Combined Fleet, was aboard his flagship *Oyodo* in Hiroshima Bay.

2. Vice Admiral Kakuji Kakuda, commander of the First Air fleet (land-based aircraft) controlled over 1,000 planes. He operated from headquarters on Tinian Island, and assigned planes to the Marianas, Carolines, Iwo Jima, and Truk.

3. Vice Admiral Jisaburo Ozawa, commander of the First Task Fleet and the Third Fleet, had under his command the largest number of aircraft carriers since the attack on Pearl Harbor. His fleet consisted of seventy-three ships at Tawitawi anchorage in the southwest area of the Sulu Sea which was west of the Philippines. They were there awaiting the upcoming battle.

4. Vice Admiral Chuichi Nagumo controlled the marines and other naval units which were to defend the Marianas against amphibious operations.

On June 13, after seeing that the Americans were going to attack the Marianas, Admiral Toyoda ordered Vice Admiral Ozawa to attack the Fifth Fleet and destroy it. He would lure the Fifth Fleet into waters between Palau, Yap, and Woleai. The Japanese would also fly planes from the homeland to the Bonin Islands. From here they would attack the Fifth Fleet.

Luckily, Admiral Spruance learned of both of the plans. His strategy was to avoid the waters between Palau, Yap, and Woleai and to neutralize the threat from the Bonin Islands. Admiral Spruance told Admiral Marc Mitscher about the planes on the Bonins. Mitscher replied, "I want those planes."

Mitscher, who was in command of Task Force Fifty-eight, called upon Admiral J. J. "Jocko" Clark, who was commanding Task Group 58.1, to sail north and destroy the planes on the Bonin Islands. Jocko was to take with him Rear Admiral William K. Harrill, who commanded Task Group 58.4. Jocko was to be in tactical command of both task groups. Mitscher, who was aboard the *Lexington,* would keep the rest of the task force on standby duty while Task Groups 58.1 and 58.4 attacked the islands.

Jocko, who was carrying his flag aboard the new *Hornet*, would have in his task group the *Bataan,* the *Belleau Wood*, and his old ship, the *Yorktown*. Harrill would have in his task group the *Langley, Cowpens,* and *Essex*. Together the two task groups steamed north at twenty-five knots, directly into Japanese-held waters and a typhoon.

While the *Yorktown* steamed north, Captain Jennings put the carrier on full alert, and sent patrol planes ahead of the ship to search for any enemy activity. Throughout the day on June 14, patrol planes scanned the seas below, while aboard the ship, eyes watched the skies for enemy planes.

On board the *Yorktown*, men were stationed at the guns. High upon the superstructure on quad seven was Edward A. Johnson. He was a loader on gun number three in quad seven. Here, ninety feet above the water, he would have a good view of the activity below. Just a few feet away and a little higher up on the island, next to the smoke stack, was Theodore H. Rohrbough. He was on battery six, a 20-mm gun battery, which overhung the flight deck. He too would see plenty of action.

During the day, patrols from the two task groups spotted the *Tatsutakawa Maru* and attacked her. After leaving her burning in the water, Jocko dispatched the destroyers *Boyd* and *Charrette* to sink her and to pick up survivors.

One June 13, Air Group One, under the leadership of Commander Bernard M. "Smoke" Strean, flew toward Iwo Jima. With Smoke were dedicated pilots like Lieutenant (jg) John H. Keeler, Lieutenant Charles W. Nelson, Lieutenant (jg) Carl H. Sanborn, Jr., and many others. At 2:30 P.M. these men and their crews roared over Iwo Jima. The Japanese were expecting the Americans and were in the air waiting for them. Soon the sky became filled with dog-fights as the F6F Hellcats fought it out with the "Zeros," while the TBF Avengers and SBD Dauntlesses bombed the island.

Soon most of the enemy planes had been shot out

of the air, and then the bombers attacked. Flying through the colorful display of antiaircraft fire, the pilots rained death and destruction upon the island. Flames and smoke shot high into the air. Buildings were blown apart, airfields were damaged, planes caught on the ground turned into flaming wrecks, and several small ships burned in the harbor. In all, the Japanese had twenty-four planes shot out of the air. Their base on Iwo Jima was wrecked.

After the attack on Iwo Jima was over, the pilots turned their attention toward Chichi Jima. By now the seas were starting to kick up, but Jocko figured there was still time for the attack. As the planes flew over this island, the Japanese did not put up any defense planes, but relied upon their antiaircraft fire to knock the Americans out of the air. As Lieutenant John H. Keeler swooped down upon the Japanese, his plane was hit by the colorful but murderous antiaircraft fire. The flack tore into the plane, wounding him and damaging his Avenger. The pilot lost control of the plane and crashed into the sea. Killed with Keeler were ARM2c Edward R. Webster and AOM2c Alfred P. Normandin. These men, too, had given their lives while fighting for freedom. Ensign James Spivey was also killed in the line of duty when his Hellcat, hit by antiaircraft fire, spun into the sea.

When the others from Air Group One returned to the *Yorktown*, the ship was rolling slightly in a white, foaming sea. Carefully, Red Volz brought the pilots in for safe landings. As soon as one plane landed, the Airdales would push the plane out of the way, making room for the next plane to land. By late afternoon all the planes were safely back aboard. Jocko decided to stop operations until the weather cleared.

That night the *Yorktown* rolled somewhat, but not as bad as the small destroyers. In water like this the men aboard them were buffeted all night.

That night a few night fighters managed to get into the air. They flew over the islands, warning the Japanese of the continued American presence.

The next morning, as dawn approached, rain was still coming down, and the wind was blowing quite heavily. Aboard the *Hornet*, Jocko paced the deck of the bridge. There were still Japanese planes on the islands and he knew that they had to be destroyed to insure the success of the Marianas invasion. He monitored the weather and the clock closely, because he had orders to rendezvous with the rest of Task Force Fifty-eight on June 18. If the weather did not clear soon his mission would be a failure.

By noon there was a lull in the weather, and Captain Jennings received orders from the *Hornet* to turn into the wind and launch his planes. The *Yorktown* became alive with ordnance men arming planes, while others fueled them. The Airdales spotted the planes on the flight deck, while the pilots were briefed on the mission. Finally the *Yorktown* was in position, and the air officer bellowed over the intercom, "Pilots, man your planes." Smoke and the others rushed toward their planes. The weather was still on the windy side, making speed was of the utmost importance. Quickly the planes went aloft and the pilots headed toward Iwo Jima.

Meanwhile on Iwo Jima, the Japanese were also

waiting for a break in the weather so that they could attack the carriers in the two task groups. The Japanese officers were confident that a strike could not be made against them, and so were completely surprised when the first F6F appeared over the island.

Surprised by Jocko's fifty-four Helldivers and Hellcats, the Japanese ran around confused and startled. When the Americans left Iwo Jima, sixty-three Japanese planes were left burning or destroyed. The mission had been easy, because the planes were lined up and loaded with fuel and ammunition. They had been waiting for the weather to get a little better. The Americans had been more aggressive than the enemy had figured, and so the Japanese lost the planes they were going to use against the Americans at the Marianas.

As the planes returned to the carriers, the wind kicked up again and the rain came down again. The *Yorktown*, as well as the other carriers, had slick, pitching decks upon which the pilots would have to land. Recovery seemed almost impossible.

As the planes from Air Group One came aboard the *Yorktown*, it looked as if some would crash. If the LSO read the plane wrong, or if the aft section of the flight deck pitched at the wrong time, a crash would probably occur. Also, if the plane landed, but missed the arresting cable, the pilot would not be able to stop on the rain-slick deck. With each plane-landing, disaster threatened, but in the end all the planes were safely aboard. Only one crash occurred in the two task groups. That was aboard the CVL *Belleau Wood*. Jocko had gambled with the weather and the enemy, and he had won. After all the planes were safely aboard the carriers, Jocko turned the ships around and headed for his rendezvous, 160 miles west of Tiniara. The invasion forces would not have to worry about planes from the Bonin Islands. Part One of Admiral Toyoda's plan had been shattered. Jocko had left the island a wreck and had destroyed 108 Japanese planes while losing only four American planes.

As the *Yorktown* and the other carriers proceeded south for the rendezvous with the rest of Task Force Fifty-eight, Admiral Spruance was confronted with an important decision. Should he move west after Ozawa and his ships, and try to destroy them before they reached the Marianas, or should he stay and give protective cover to the landing forces? Since the Japanese controlled the islands, they had a larger range than did Spruance. Spruance had only a 350-mile range because his planes had to return back to the ships. Ozawa had a 600-mile range because his planes could land on the islands, refuel, and then attack the Americans again on their way back to their carriers. Spruance decided to stay near the Marianas. Toyoda failed to lure the Americans out.

Back aboard the *Yorktown*, the gun crews practiced for at least two hours each day in anticipation of the upcoming action. The *Yorktown* had sixty 40-mm guns. These guns could fire so rapidly that the Japanese thought they were machine guns. Most of the guns were in twin mounts, and each gun had its own loader. Therefore, in a Quad there were four loaders putting in four shell clips at a steady pace. This enabled sixteen 40-mm shells to be fired almost as fast as four 40-mm shells in a single mount. That was why the Japanese thought that the Americans had a machine gun that could fire 40-mm shells. When several of these Quads fired at a single plane, it was almost suicide to attack the ship from the air. In fact, until this point in the war; every plane that had attacked the *Yorktown* had been shot down. But every man on those guns wondered if the *Yorktown* could continue to hold that record.

Jim Bryan's VIA Division was quite busy. More ammunition, including bombs and torpedoes was brought up from below to storage closer to the hangar deck. This would save valuable minutes in arming the planes if the ship should come under attack. AOM2c Martin "Tadpole" Tauber and the others were always ready to arm the planes for the fly boys, because, without the planes, the *Yorktown* was only a defensive ship. You don't win wars with defense alone.

The men in Damage Control checked the pumps and lines that carried CO_2 and foam for fire fighting. They also inspected hundreds of pieces of equipment needed to repair damage. At various stations all around the ship, men worked the maze of lines carrying the CO_2, foam, and water to where it would be needed. Each man was in charge of his "frame," or area, of the ship. Ruben Kitchen, Kenneth Parkinson, Harland Bickford, and the others had all been well trained in the few weeks since they had been put aboard the *Yorktown* at Pearl. They were still green, but they knew their jobs.

Topside on the flight deck, the men in the VIT Division or Airdales as they were called, were constantly spotting the planes for takeoff and landing. Patrols were in the air constantly, and it kept Carl Tobias and the others busy pulling these planes all around the flight deck. Even though the planes sent out were only patrols, there was still danger on a live flight deck from the whirling propellers.

Occasionally you could see Scrappy walk between the planes spotted on the flight deck. Scrappy was the ship's mascot. Unlike the large dogs sometimes seen on other ships, Scrappy was just a small dog. There was a reason that the crew picked a small dog as the mascot. The reason was that a large dog would not stand a chance on a live flight deck. Scrappy was small enough to walk under the whirling propellers. He would jump at a plane, prance around it, and then walk off looking victorious. He had challenged the roaring, fire-spitting monster, and it just sat there, afraid to attack him.

The crew topside always brought bits of food to Scrappy from the mess halls. With Scrappy around, the tensions of war were sometimes eased.

On the signal bridge were the men in the K-S Division. It was the duty of Signalman Joe Leathers and the others to receive messages from the *Hornet*. When the *Yorktown* was the flagship, they sent messages to the other ships in the task group informing them what the plans were next.

The man who was responsible for all the others leaned on the railing of the bridge looking down at the activity of a well-trained ship. The man was Captain Jennings.

Lieutenant Dwight Long was still making his movie about carrier warfare. He had taken scenes in the bakery, laundry room, and other areas of the ship to show that a carrier is a floating city capable of supporting itself while at sea. He also saw to it that many interesting and valuable shots were taken of the combat in which the *Yorktown* was engaged. Little did he realize that the upcoming action would be one of the heaviest air operations that the *Yorktown* had been engaged in since her commissioning.

On June 18, the *Yorktown* and the others made their rendezvous with the rest of Task Force Fifty-eight. Again Admiral Mitscher had under his command five task groups. Four of the task groups were fast carrier groups, while the fifth consisted of battleships under Admiral Willis A. Lee. Lee was to form a battle line fifteen miles south of the carriers to assist with antiaircraft fire.

Early on June 19, the sun rose over the blue Pacific, while the Fifth Fleet rode the gentle swells. Mitscher had already received the following battle plan from Spruance. From the bridge of the *Lexington* Mitscher read the following:

"Our air forces will first knock out enemy carriers, then will attack enemy battleships and cruisers to slow or disable them. Battle line will destroy enemy fleet either by fleet action if the enemy elects to fight, or by sinking slowed or crippled ships if enemy retreats. Action against the enemy must be pushed vigorously by all hands to ensure complete destruction of his fleet."

The four task groups formed in four circles, each about four miles in diameter, with their centers twelve miles apart. The Fifth Fleet encompassed an area of the ocean twenty-five miles long by thirty-five miles wide. The gunners on the superstructure of the *Yorktown* could see for forty miles. From there the ocean was covered with ships.

Suddenly, aboard the *Yorktown*, "General Quarters" was sounded. A Japanese Zero had attacked the destroyers on the picket line. It had come out of nowhere, catching the ships in the battle line by surprise. The Zero dove toward the *Stockham* and dropped his bomb. Luckily, the bomb missed, and before the Japanese pilot could make his getaway, he was shot down by the *Yarnall*. The Battle of the Philippine Sea had begun.

Tense eyes watched the radar in the CIC aboard the *Yorktown*. Where were the rest of the planes? No "bogeys" appeared on the screen; all was quiet again. The men at the guns rested, but stayed close to the guns, while below decks, some of the watertight hatches were opened to allow air to flow into the compartments.

Task Group 58.1, under Jocko, was the nearest group to Guam. At 7:05 A.M., a combat air patrol was dispatched from the *Belleau Wood* to investigate a bogey over Guam. Upon reaching Guam, the patrol was surrounded by enemy fighters. Immediately, the American pilots called for help. Again "General Quarters" was sounded, and Jocko sent twenty-four fighters to aid the air group from the *Belleau Wood*.

Mitscher sent help from the other carriers to Guam, but by the time they got there the fighting was over. Soon more Japanese planes showed up on the radar, as other planes were being sent from other bases to Guam. Immediately Jocko sent F6F's from his carriers to intercept and destroy these planes. Soon the sky became full of twisting, turning planes. In the action which followed, Lieutenant Russell Reiserer from the *Hornet* shot down five planes himself, while the rest of the pilots shot down another thirty of the enemy. Later Reiserer would receive the Navy Cross for his action over Orote Field.

While the patrol which discovered the Japanese planes over Orote Field, was taking off, one of Ozawa's reconnaissance planes spotted the *Yorktown* and the other ships of Task Group 58.1. Ozawa was delighted. He was where he wanted to be, about 400 miles from Task Force Fifty-eight, and out of its range. Because he was able to use Guam to land and refuel his planes, he would be able to pull off a "Midway" in reverse. Spruance's planes simply would not be able to carry the fuel for the two-way flight. He had Guam to refuel his planes. Success seemed imminent.

Aboard the *Taiho* at 8:30 A.M., Ozawa ordered the first strike against the Fifth Fleet. As the planes began taking off from the Japanese carriers, Warrant Officer Sakio Komatsu from the *Taiho* performed a brave act. As he took off on a flight from the *Taiho*, he saw a torpedo streaking toward his ship. Immediately he directed his plane into the deadly missile and exploded it before it could hit the *Taiho*. He was killed instantly. Then another torpedo hit the *Taiho*, but the damage was light.

Where did the torpedo come from? It came from the U.S.S. *Albacore*, an American submarine. The sub had sneaked into the middle of the Japanese Fleet and launched its six fish; only one hit. Soon after the hit, Japanese destroyers began depth-charging the *Albacore*, but without success. The *Albacore* slipped to safety. But greater damage was done to the *Taiho* than had at first been thought.

Back aboard the *Taiho*, damage-control gangs repaired the minor damage. But they had left a broken gasoline line unrepaired. Slowly, the dangerous vapors drifted down into the *Taiho*.

As Ozawa's planes were heading toward Task Force Fifty-eight, Mitscher sent more fighters to Guam to intercept the planes trying to land at Orote Field. Suddenly the *Alabama's* radar picked up incoming Japanese planes. From the *Lexington* the code signal "Hey Rube!" was sent to the fighters over Guam. This informed them that their ships were about to come under attack. They broke off and headed back to the fleet.

Aboard the *Yorktown*, "General Quarters" was sounded. Hatches were sealeld, which, in that heat, made the compartments below decks hot and stuffy. Gunners manned their guns, while lookouts scanned the sky for any bogeys.

In the ready rooms, Smoke Strean briefed his pilots. Lieutenant James Pfister, Lieutenant Richard T. Eastmond, and other fighter pilots of Air Group One checked over the reports. When "Pappy" Harshman called over the intercom: "man your planes," they quickly walked from the ready rooms on the gallery deck beneath the flight deck to their planes.

The Airdales already had the planes spotted, and they were ready for takeoff. The first pilot off was Smoke, followed by the rest of the pilots from Air Group One.

Mitscher had put a total of 450 Hellcats into the air to stop the Japanese before they could reach the Fifth Fleet. Pilots from the *Cowpens, Bunker Hill*, and *Princeton* intercepted the first wave of Japanese planes. These pilots shot down twenty-five of this first wave before it finally broke through them. A few minutes after they had broken through this group of Hellcats, the enemy was attacked by other pilots. This time sixteen Japanese planes hit the water. Finally a few remaining planes reached the battle line, and one made a direct hit on the *South Dakota*. Aboard the *South Dakota*, twenty-seven men were killed. The Japanese planes did not reach the carriers.

Some of Lee's picket-destroyers reported they could see planes falling like plums. The Americans were giving the Japanese a rough time. Shortly after this first wave had been knocked out of the sky, a second wave approached. Again these planes were cut to ribbons by patrolling aircraft, although six did manage to get through to the carriers. But the *Yorktown* was not damaged by any of them.

Then a third wave had reached the fleet. However, it was flying way off course so that only a few planes came in contact with our Hellcats.

During these dogfights Smoke and the pilots of Air Group One did their part in destroying the Japanese planes. Lieutenant James Pfister had engaged the enemy twice and scored both times.

Pfister intercepted the enemy and engaged a Japanese Zero. Twisting and turning, the Zero tried to evade Pfister; but because of Pfister's superior flying skill, the Zero could not get away. Finally

Pfister managed to put a burst of fire into the Zero, and it burst into flames. Because Zeroes did not have self-sealing fuel tanks, they would explode quite easily when hit in the right spot. Next Pfister managed to knock a torpedo plane out of the sky.

Meanwhile, Lieutenant Richard T. Eastmond had engaged several planes. Flying with the skill of an ace, Eastmond managed to knock five planes out of the air on this one day. He was awarded the Navy Cross for his actions of June 19. Before the war was over he would have shot down nine planes, most of them while he was stationed aboard the *Yorktown*.

Spruance had his pilots into the air from 10:30 A.M., alternating them with different air groups. Now, late in the day, the fleet came under the fourth and final attack. The Japanese had finally managed to break through to the carriers.

Don Seaman, Joseph Huber, Ted Rohrbough, and others on the 20-mm guns scanned the sky for enemy planes, while Ed Johnson, Joe Leathers, and others on the 40-mm guns did likewise. In the five-inch gun turrets, men like Ed Simko used the latest electronic equipment to locate targets at great distances. They could not see these with the naked eye.

Tension mounted as the enemy planes began their attacks. All that training paid off again. Ed Johnson slapped one clip after another into the 40-mm gun on quad seven. Because of the excellent gunnery aboard the *Yorktown*, she managed to fend off all attacks and came through unharmed. Her sister carriers were not so lucky.

The *Wasp* came under attack and just barely

missed being hit. The bomb dropped by the plane hit the water close enough to cause some minor damage from the concussion.

At the same time that the *Wasp* came under attack, so did the *Bunker Hill*. She too had a near miss. Shrapnel from the bomb caused some minor damage.

Because these two carriers had been damaged, added pressure was put on Spruance. His critics had wanted him to search out and attack the enemy carriers, but he felt he should stay behind to protect the amphibious fleet. Now he had to make a decision. Since he was certain the airfields at Guam had been neutralized and that the safety of the landing was assured, he decided to go after the Japanese Fleet. His planes had knocked out over 352 enemy planes. Task Group 58.1, got 109 of these, while the *Yorktown*, got 52, a better-than-average number.

Back with the Japanese Fleet, Ozawa was having his troubles. While most of Ozawa's planes were being blown out of the air by the brilliant piloting of Smoke, Eastmond, Pfister, and the other pilots of Task Force Fifty-eight, he was about to undergo an ordeal himself. As the huge *Taiho* was steaming through the sea, an inexperienced damage-control officer opened ventilation ducts throughout the ship to help rid it of deadly gasoline vapors. Instead of disappearing, the vapors settled deeper into the hull of the *Taiho*. Commander James W. Blanchard, skipper of the *Albacore*, had done more damage than he realized. In his report he wrote, "probable damage to a Japanese carrier."

Beneath the Japanese Fleet was the submarine

U.S.S. *Cavalla*, skippered by Commander Herman J. Kossler. With quiet skill he maneuvered the *Cavalla* into position to launch its six fish. At 12:20 P.M. three of these torpedoes exploded against the hull of the carrier *Shokaku*. Immediately she fell out of line. Her fuel lines were ruptured, and the deadly fuel spread throughout the ship. The damage-control gangs aboard could not cope with the spreading fuel. Deadly fumes seeped deep into the ship. Unlike the American carriers, the Japanese carriers could do little to control deadly fuel vapors. This was their weak spot.

As the damage-control gangs on the *Shokaku* worked hard to stifle the deadly fumes, the fleet destroyers dropped depth charges on the *Cavalla*. For three hours they hunted the sub, but Kossler managed to evade the deadly "ash-cans."

On the surface, the *Shokaku* was listing, and salvage looked impossible. Suddenly at 3:00 P.M. the huge carrier blew apart. The deadly vapors had penetrated the ship, causing it to expode. Quickly the *Shokaku* settled by the bow, her hulk engulfed in flames. Men were cremated alive as the fireball covered the ship. As she settled deeper by the bow, water poured in through the hangar deck. Silently, the *Shokaku* disappeared beneath the waves. With her went the bodies of 1,263 men. Ozawa had lost one of his fleet carriers, and still he had no word from his planes. Were they destroying the American fleet? Had they landed on Guam? Where were they?

Ozawa watched with horror as the *Shokaku* blew apart and sank. He could not know that the *Taiho* was about to meet the same fate. At 3:32 P.M. the deadly gasoline vapors on the *Taiho* were ignited by a spark. The huge *Taiho* was enveloped in flames. A cruiser managed to get close to the stricken carrier, and Ozawa and his staff, as well as the emperor's picture, were taken aboard. Because the flames spread so rapidly, the rest of the men could not be taken off the burning carrier. When the *Taiho* slipped under the surface, she took with her the bodies of 1,650 men. In just a few minutes Ozawa had lost two of his nine carriers, including the *Taiho*, which was the largest carrier in the Japanese Navy.

At about the time the *Shokaku* was hit by the torpedo, the *Yorktown's* radar picked up a flight of planes. These planes turned southwest. Then the *Yorktown's* radar picked up the planes again at a distance of 100 miles. Several Hellcats were sent to intercept, but no contact was made.

As June 19 finally drew to a close, Ozawa realized that his planes were not going to return. He decided to withdraw to the northwest and reorganize. He would attack the Fifth Fleet on June 21 and destroy it. Ozawa had taken quite a beating, but he still believed he could at least damage the Fifth Fleet enough to prevent them from advancing for a while. By the time night fell on June 19, Ozawa had lost two of his carriers and 300 of his planes along with their pilots.

Spruance had not acted as Ozawa hoped he might. Ozawa tried to draw the planes of the Fifth Fleet into the waters of the Pacific in order to destroy them. He thought that any he did not destroy would run out of fuel before they could return to their carriers and would crash into the sea. Instead, Spruance had elected to keep his planes near the fleet in order to protect his carriers. Because Ozawa's pilots had to go against the deadly American pilots, as well as the heavy antiaircraft fire put up by the Fifth Fleet, they did not have a chance. Ozawa's plan had failed. He had managed to destroy only twenty-three American planes that day. As far as the American ships were concerned, he had caused only slight damage. The "Marianas Turkey Shoot" had been costly, but Ozawa still had hopes for a victory. On June 21, he would make the score more even.

On the morning of June 20, Mitscher, with approval from Spruance, went after Ozawa's fleet. Spruance decided to let Task Group 58.4 stay at Saipan to cover the amphibious landings from there. The other three task groups raced westward after the Japanese Fleet.

Throughout the morning and the afternoon, search planes scanned the ocean for the Japanese Fleet. Finally, at about 4:00 P.M., a search plane from the *Enterprise* spotted the fleet. Mitscher knew it was too late in the afternoon for a daylight attack, and he hated night flying. Finally, after careful thought, Mitscher decided this was a chance to deal a staggering blow to the Japanese Fleet. He gave the OK to launch the attack.

The signal was sent to the *Yorktown* to launch planes. At 4:30 P.M., Commander Bernard M. Smoke Strean led his planes toward the Japanese Fleet. Spearheading the attack, Smoke had eighty-five Hellcats, seventy-seven Helldivers, and fifty-four Avengers with him. He had planes from the *Lexington, Yorktown, Hornet, Bunker Hill, Wasp, Enterprise, Belleau Wood, Cabot, Monterey, Bataan,* and *San Jacinto* behind him. A second group was preparing to launch when it was discovered that Ozawa was sixty miles farther west than had been thought at first. This meant that the planes already in the air would have to land after dark, and many would be low on fuel. The extra 120 miles would drain their tanks. The second flight was called off.

With Smoke were many pilots from the *Yorktown.* In the Avengers were Lieutenants Charles W. Nelson and Robert T. Carlson, Jr. These two pilots talked with their crew members, trying to relieve the tension. They knew as well as the others, that they would be short of fuel for the return trip.

Smoke was in overall command of the plane flights from all the carriers. The *Yorktown's* Helldivers were under the leadership of Lieutenant Commander J. W. Runyon, while Commander James M. Peters led the Hellcats. As the planes from the *Yorktown* flew through the Pacific sky toward the Japanese Fleet, Captain Jennings, aboard the *Yorktown,* was quietly wondering about the night landings that were going to take place in a few hours. Most of the pilots had never landed at night. What would happen?

After the *Taiho* was sunk, Ozawa finally transferred from the *Haguro* to the carrier *Zuikaku.* It was from there that he would fight the final battle in the First Battle of the Philippine Sea.

At 6:25 P.M. on June 20, lookouts from the

Zuikaku spotted planes from the Fifth Fleet approaching for an attack. Ozawa looked up and saw the Americans flying toward his flagship.

Almost immediately after the planes from the *Hornet* attacked the *Zuikaku*, Lieutenant Commander J. W. Runyon led his *Yorktown*-based Helldivers in for the kill. As his planes dived on the Japanese flagship, they put three bombs into the carrier. Flames shot out from one of the holes; so the last two pilots thought the carrier was finished. They dropped their bombs on a heavy cruiser.

After hitting the *Zuikaku*, the other *Yorktown* planes turned a few miles south to hit the carriers in Carrier Division Two. Smoke scanned the sky for enemy planes, but he did not see any. Looking down he did see the carrier *Hiyo*. He led his group down toward the ship. Flying through intense antiaircraft fire, Smoke dropped his bomb. The others followed. They scored three hits and five near-misses. One bomb had passed through the flight deck before exploding in the water.

One of the *Yorktown* pilots, while pulling out, made a head-on pass at a Val. As Ensign Reinert pulled out of his bomb attack, he was met face to face with the Val. He fired at the plane. This was the only aerial combat for VF-1 that evening.

Another *Yorktown* group began its attack. This time the target was the carrier *Ryuho*. Leading the attack was Lieutenant Charles W. Nelson in an Avenger. As Nelson dived through the deadly antiaircraft fire sent up by the *Ryuho*, he dropped his bomb. Instantly, he began his pullout to escape the deadly fire. At 220 knots, 300 feet above the sea, his

Avenger was hit in the fuel tank by a stream of bullets. The Avenger exploded and crashed into the sea. Killed with Nelson were ARM2c Conrad A. Lantron and AOM2c Lyle L. Young.

Flying high in the sky in an F6F Hellcat was Commander James M. Peters from the *Yorktown*. He had seen Nelson's plane take the hit, and reported later that none of the pilots had scored a hit on the carrier. Finally darkness was starting to fall, and the *Yorktown* planes, as well as the others, headed back toward the Fifth Fleet. Below them was the Japanese Fleet, damaged and burning. Ozawa's flagship was burning, but it would be repaired later. The *Hiyo* was sinking, and several other ships were badly damaged. Ozawa's attack of June 21 would never materialize. He had lost the battle. Badly hurt, he limped off to lick his wounds.

As Smoke led the planes back to Task Force Fifty-eight, each pilot watched his fuel gauge. Some knew they would run out of fuel before they reached the carriers. Below them the ocean was dark and forbidding. To go down in the ocean at night would mean almost certain death. They hoped their sacrifice would be worth it.

Back aboard the *Yorktown*, Captain Jennings sat looking out at the darkness in front of the bow. He wanted to help the pilots, but knew of no way. Quietly he sat thinking, looking for a way. Dick Tripp was now on duty as the LSO, and he knew that, in this darkness, a disaster might occur. Aboard the *Lexington*, Mitscher was smoking on a cigarette. He, too, was concerned with the darkness. He was steaming his carriers toward the incoming planes, trying to give them a better chance, but knew that once the planes were spotted, he would have to head east for the landings.

First one plane and then another dropped into the sea from lack of fuel. At last the planes approached the carriers. But in the darkness, the pilots could not make out which ships were carriers and which were not. Mitscher knew as well as others that unless something was done many good men were going to be killed trying to land in the darkness. Slowly he got up from his seat and gave the order, "Turn on the lights!" These four words were as deadly in meaning as Farragut's "Damn the torpedoes, full speed ahead!" Lighting up the fleet would enable the American pilots to find their way back home, but it would also help Japanese pilots and submarines to find the fleet. Still, Mitscher believed that it was worth the risk. He had promised he would get the pilots home safe, and he was going to keep his word.

The *Yorktown* quickly turned on all her lights. As she did so, a lump came to each man's throat as he thought: To hell with the Japs! Our pilots are not expendable. If there is a chance, they will be saved.

High in the air, pilots could not believe their eyes. Here below them were dozens of ships with thousands of men aboard endangering their lives to save slightly over two hundred men and planes. Incredulous, but grateful for the lights, the pilots looked for their carriers, but it was confusing. This time Mitscher broke another rule. He sent the message, "Land on any carrier."

Quickly, pilots jockeyed for landing position.

Dick Tripp seemed to be landing planes quicker than it was possible to do so. Still planes had to ditch in the sea for lack of fuel. Smoke approached the *Yorktown*, and was given the OK by Dick. As his plane caught the arresting cable and came to a stop, it died from lack of fuel. Quickly the Airdales pushed the plane forward.

A few minutes later, Lieutenant M. M. Tomme landed on the *Yorktown*. He made a good landing, and taxied his plane forward. When he was preparing to get out of the plane, another plane came in for a landing. This plane bounced over the barrier and hit the top of Tomme's plane. Tomme was killed instantly by the whirling propeller. Ted Rohrbough, whose general quarters station was gun battery six on the superstructue, had a clear view of the drama that unfolded next.

After the plane hit Tomme and killed him, the crash started a fire on the flight deck. The Airdales scattered out of the way of the fire, but not before a few had been killed. Quickly the damage-control gang put out the fire. The damaged planes were shoved overboard to make room for more landings.

Dick brought in more planes, and when he was through, he had landed fourteen *Yorktown* planes and fourteen planes from other carriers.

While spotting planes the Airdales saw a sight which horrified them. Near the bow was the blackened body of a man. Apparently, he had been in the fire just a few minutes before. He had been badly burned, yet he had managed to crawl through the parked planes to within a few feet of the forward edge of the flight deck. He must have lived for several minutes since he had managed to crawl that far, but in the confusion no one had seen him. He died on the flight deck, alone.

Thirteen of the *Yorktown's* planes landed on other carriers, while eleven made water landings. The crews were picked up safely. Of the forty planes the *Yorktown* had sent out on June 20, thirty-eight had made it back to the ship. Two Avengers were lost. Lieutenant Nelson, his plane, and his crew were lost, as was the plane piloted by Lieutenant (jg) Robert T. Carlson, Jr. Killed with Lieutenant Carlson were his crew members ARM2c Charles A. Trau, Jr., and AOM2c Michael V. Shea.

That night, after all the pilots were aboard, the lights were again turned off. Mitscher had gambled and won. Ozawa was the disheartened loser.

The next morning funeral services were held aboard the *Yorktown* for the two Avenger crews and the men killed in the flight-deck crash. Within a few days, things were back to normal aboard the *Yorktown*.

After the defeat of the Japanese in the First Battle of the Philippine Sea, Admiral Mitscher sent three of his task groups back to Eniwetok for a brief rest. The fourth task group, Task Group 58.1, would be sent on a special mission. Jocko, who had attacked the Jimas during the previous week, felt his work was unfinished. He asked Mitscher if he could strike the islands while returning to Eniwetok. Mitscher agreed to let the Patton of the Pacific have the chance to destroy more Japanese planes based on those islands.

After refueling his carriers, Jocko left for the

Jimas. Mitscher referred to the operation as Operation Jocko. By 6:00 A.M. on the morning of June 24, the *Hornet, Yorktown, Bataan*, and *Belleau Wood* had launched their Hellcats. Aboard the *Yorktown* Lieutenant Richard T. Eastman, Lieutenant James Pfister, and the other F6F pilots manned their durable, little Hellcats. The seas were almost as rough as they had been during the previous attack. As the little Hellcats rose into the gray sky, Captain Jennings watched from the bridge. Once again, he and the former skipper of the *Yorktown* would be the Americans nearest to Japan, spearheading the operations.

Captain Jennings and Jocko were spotted by a Japanese patrol plane. Admiral Sadaichi Matsunaga, the commander of the Twenty-seventh Air Flotilla based at Iwo Jima, sent all of his fighters and a few bombers to intercept the fifty-one Hellcats approaching the islands.

At 8:15 A.M. the two sides met half-way between the islands and the carriers. The Hellcats jettisoned their bombs and lit into the oncoming Japanese planes. Within minutes the gray sky was filled with twisting, turning planes. Back aboard the *Yorktown*, the men in CIC could hear the battle over the planes' radios. Listening quietly, the men could hear familiar voices over the squawk box located on the bulkhead. The air battle proceeded and the Japanese lost planes at an alarming rate. When it was finished, the Japanese had lost sixty-nine planes. They had shot down only six of Task Group 58.1's Hellcats.

After the fierce but brief air battle, the remaining

Hellcats returned to the carriers. Arriving near the carriers, they intercepted more planes and destroyed seventeen of these. Dogfights continued until 6:30 P.M.. By that time Jocko was heading his carriers back to Eniwetok for a well-deserved rest.

Jocko's interest in the Jimas had become so great that the pilots of the various air groups on the four carriers had certificates printed granting membership in the Jocko Jima Development Corporation. These certificates offered "choice locations of all types in Iwo, Chichi, Haha, and Muko Jima. Only 500 miles from downtown Tokyo." These were signed by Admiral Clark, as president of the corporation. Every participant in the strikes was given a certificate.

On June 27, the *Yorktown* and the other ships of Task Group 58.1 arrived at Eniwetok for the rest they had earned. There the officers had a chance to watch some boxing matches between the enlisted men. One of these boxers was Ed Johnson. He had been the Golden Gloves champion in 1938, and had a trophy for the fastest knockout, forty-one seconds. Ed was also the lightweight champion on the *Yorktown*. The officers enjoyed watching him because he was a winner, just like their ship.

Before each bout, the boxers were given special meals and time to work out. Each boxer was given twenty dollars for the bout. The winner received a wallet. Ed always won the wallet.

In the shipfitter's shop, the men worked on their special projects when time allowed. Ruben Kitchen made knives for himself and his brother, Woodrow, who was in Europe fighting the Germans. He also worked on a large knife for his father, James, and

121

on a smaller one for his nephew, James Henry, both of whom were living at Turkey Creek, Kentucky. Other men were working on watch bands, jewelry boxes, and other personal items, to help pass their free time while aboard the ship.

Knives were quite useful aboard a ship for performing routine tasks; but they were mostly carried for protection against sharks, in case a man fell overboard. Sharks trailed behind ships eating the garbage that was tossed overboard. One day while on lookout duty, Ted Rohrbough noticed a fifty-caliber machine gun ammunition box made of wood floating about 6,000 yards from the stern of the ship. Every now and then the box would shoot ten or fifteen feet into the air, and then land back in the water. Air Defense was notified of this strange happening. Observers from Air Defense decided that a shark was playing with the wooden box. That was why most of the men carried knives; so a shark would not play with them if they were lost overboard.

While at Eniwetok, the *Yorktown* also took on supplies: spare parts, ammunition, and other items essential for the running of a carrier. Jim Bryan's men stored the bombs and torpedoes, and other ammuniton while other ordnance men repaired the systems on the planes.

But all good things finally come to an end, and on June 30 the *Yorktown* pulled up anchor and headed back toward the Marianas to give aircover to the troops still trying to take the islands.

Now that Saipan was in American hands, the task force anchored in the harbor just off the island. The sun beat down on the flight deck, making it quite miserable for the men manning gun-watch along the flight deck. After a few hours, someone noticed several large flies flying around their heads. Soon there were more flies. Within a few minutes the *Yorktown* and the other ships were being attacked by swarms of large flies coming from Saipan. Mitscher was getting worried that these flies might be carrying diseases that could affect the men. It was then decided to pull the fleet out of the harbor for open sea. Only at sea would they be safe from the flies.

Meanwhile, on Saipan, the soldiers watched the ships pull out. Some of the men had hoped to visit friends aboard other ships. Ted Rohrbough's brother, who had been aboard the *Yorktown* once for dinner, looked forward to going aboard and visit Ted again.

The soldiers on Saipan watched the ships pull out and then continued their gruesome task of burying the hundreds of Japanese dead. It was from these bodies that the swarms of flies had come. Until the dead were buried the flies were a threat to the health of the soldiers on the island. Luckily for the sailors, they could escape the flies by going to the open sea. The soldiers had to put up with the pesty insects.

On July 4, Independence Day, Jocko sent his planes to strike the Jimas again. This time he caught the Japanese as they were about to attack the American Fleet. Many of the planes were destroyed on the ground. Only seventeen planes were left to attack TG 58.1. Japanese Navy Captain Kanzo Miura instructed these pilots to dive at the American ships with their torpedoes, their lives, and their souls. This would be the first planned suicide attack in the Pacific War. The Kamikaze units were formed four months later, but these seventeen pilots would kill themselves in an attempt to destroy the U.S. carriers.

As the planes approached the ships of TG 58.1, they were cut to ribbons by intercepting Hellcats. The planned suicide mission was a failure. Only five of the seventeen planes were able to return back to Iwo Jima.

Jocko then turned his ships toward Guam, and on the morning of July 9, the *Yorktown* launched planes to raid Guam. Flying on a low-level bombing mission over the island was Lieutenant (jg) Carl H. Sanborn, Jr. As he was bringing his plane into the slot for the run, it was hit by ground fire. He crashed into the island. Killed with him were ARM2c James S. Buchanan and AOM2c Earl J. Steffen. The other planes returned to the *Yorktown* after doing considerable damage.

Still undamaged, the *Yorktown* avenged her namesake. On July 18, her planes struck Rota. The *Yorktown* was so close that the gunners on the superstructure of the ship could see the island. On July 20, while blasting the island by way of getting ready for the invasion on July 21, the *Yorktown* lost another Avenger. This time Lieutenant Leonard E. Wood was shot down with his crew members, ARM3c Edward C. Donahue and AOM3c Albert J. Sabol. None survived.

From July 25 through July 28, the *Yorktown* attacked Yap Island, Ngulu Atoll, and Ulithi Atoll.

This was her last combat before being sent back to the United States for refitting. The *Yorktown* had earned six battlestars; her Hellcats had been the first to fly into combat; planes from the *Yorktown* were the first to fly into combat from an *Essex* class carrier; and she had been used as a flagship most of the time while in the Pacific. She had been in more combat than any other *Essex* class carrier up to that date, had ventured closer to Japan than any *Essex* class carrier, and had been chosen as the carrier for the movie *The Fighting Lady*.

The *Yorktown* had left her mark. On July 29, 1944, she sailed for the Bremerton Navy Yards, in Bremerton, Washington. Her first voyage was over. The movie *The Fighting Lady* was finished. The carrier *Ticonderoga* would be used for some follow-up scenes, but the *Yorktown* was the star of the movie. The *Ticonderoga* was not commissioned until May 8, 1944. Most of the action in the movie was over before she ever reached the Pacific. In fact, she was the *Yorktown's* replacement.

Before the *Yorktown* left for the states, Dick and the other LSOs held a party for Red Volz. He was leaving the *Yorktown* for other duty. This made Dick the senior LSO aboard the *Yorktown*. He was now a Lieutenant (jg).

Many friends had been lost on this first voyage; but, in a few months, the *Yorktown* would be back in the thick of the action, avenging those fallen comrades who had given their lives for the final victory.

Chapter VI

For the *Yorktown* and her crew, the war was over for a few months. She had hit the enemy hard for twelve months, and she was worn and weary. Newer *Essex* class carriers appeared in the Pacific, giving the *Yorktown* a chance to rest. She was homeward bound!

Air Group One left the *Yorktown* on July 28, leaving behind quite an impressive record. Smoke and his group had destroyed 205 enemy planes, sunk 11 ships, damaged 15 ships, and made hits on 4 enemy aircraft carriers. In addition Air Group Five had destroyed 180 planes, sunk 15 ships, and damaged 45 ships.

Indeed, the *Yorktown* had achieved great fame throughout the fleet as a hard-fighting ship with uncanny skill and luck. Throughout the war, she had never been damaged by the Japanese. Several of her younger sisters were not so fortunate. The *Bunker*

Hill and *Wasp* had received near misses, while the *Lexington* and *Intrepid* had received battle damage. On some of these carriers the *Yorktown* was known as The Lucky Y, a nickname well earned. But still the crew was looking for a better name.

On August 4, the *Yorktown* left the forward area for Hawaii. From Pearl Harbor she sailed for Bremerton, Washington, for an extensive overhaul. Some of her younger sisters had been improved during construction, and she would get these improvements.

Sailing east through the blue Pacific, the rigors of war were left behind. Although still on alert for stray Japanese submarines, she was now in peaceful waters. The crew had time for the pleasures of an ocean voyage. Parts of the flight deck became a sunning deck. Men white from the lack of sun while serving below decks had a chance to come up into the sunlight. A few got minor sunburns, but they enjoyed the chance to feel the warming rays of the sun.

Edward Johnson and some of his fellow boxers could now put on boxing matches, called smokers, for the crew. For this purpose one of the elevators would be lowered to within a few feet of the hangar deck. Upon this elevator a boxing ring would be constructed. Ted and the others would take turns boxing in this ring while members of the crew would watch from seats placed on the hangar deck. Some of the crew would be more daring and sit on the edge of the flight deck with their feet dangling into the elevator well. From here, these bold men had a bird's-eye view of the matches.

Other sports were also played while the ship was sailing toward Bremerton. Basketball nets were erected on the hangar deck, and teams from the different divisions competed for the championship.

But the crew enjoyed the movies most of all. A huge screen was placed at one end of the hangar deck and movies were shown on it nightly.

The hangar deck also served as a church on Sundays. Here Chaplains Moody and Alexander held church services for members of the crew. It was now noticed that fewer attended than when the *Yorktown* was about to go into battle. The fear of possible death always brought larger crowds; this was just human nature. It happened on all ships of war.

Captain Jennings was quite proud of his ship and crew as he sailed through the Pacific. On August 17, as the *Yorktown* sailed into the Bremerton Naval Yards, all the available crew were topside on the flight deck in full uniform. They, like Captain Jennings, were also proud of their ship and of each other. Now they were safe at home, the home they had just been fighting to defend. They hoped that they would get to visit family and friends sometime while in the States. They did not have to wait long. Almost as soon as the *Yorktown* was tied up, Captain Jennings began issuing leaves. He was going to let his men have those visits. He had indeed created a happy ship.

While some of the men took turns going home, others were left aboard as a skeleton crew. These men would eventually go home, but a partial crew was needed aboard at all times. Because the ship-builders were all over the *Yorktown* with their torches, tools, and other construction needs, the ship had lost her neat appearance. Hundreds of torch hoses lay across the flight deck; some stretched through elevators and into hatches throughout the ship. Construction workers intermingled with the crew and some became friends.

Ruben Kitchen and Kenneth Parkinson of the R-1 Division, got to know one of the construction workers fairly well. One night he invited them to his home for dinner. Gladly they accepted. This was their first home-cooked meal in months. They enjoyed the meal and appreciated the thought. One of the workers gave Ruben a fiberglass hard hat to send home to his father, James, to use while he worked in the mines in Pike County, Kentucky. This was how friendships were formed while the *Yorktown* was undergoing her refitting.

The crew were now better trained than they had been when Jocko had taken them on their shakedown cruise off Trinidad. Once the alarm for battle stations was set off accidentally, while the *Yorktown* was in the naval yard in Washington. To the amazement of the construction workers, the crew rushed to their battle stations. Within a few minutes the ship was in combat readiness. Even though it was probably a false alarm, the crew were so well trained that they treated it as if it were the real thing. Up on the bridge, Captain Jennings' head was held high. Here was the proof that his crew was the best.

Throughout the month of September, the crews at the Navy Yard outfitted the *Yorktown* with new electronic devices to help the men fight more efficiently. The stack on the superstructure was now hardly visible behind all the antennas and radar screens. Many improvements had been made in the field of electronics since the *Yorktown* had been built, and now she would have the benefit of these improvements.

On the starboard side of the ship, crews had erected new 40-mm gun mounts located in sponsons that were built onto the side of the ship. These new Forties would give added firepower to help fight off Japanese planes.

Next the *Yorktown* was camouflaged with the measure Thirty-two paint scheme. This included pale gray, haze gray, and navy blue colors arranged in an erratic pattern. The decks were painted deck blue. Finally on October 5, 1944, the *Yorktown* built up steam and headed out of Puget Sound.

As she slipped out into the blue Pacific, she was watched with admiration by the people who happened to be along the coast. Here was another gallant ship heading out into the Pacific to fight the Japanese. Some wondered if she would still be as elegant in a few months. But before she headed toward the war zone, she had to make a stop in San Francisco. Here she would pick up new replacements to go with her new captain.

Captain Jennings, like Captain Clark, had been promoted to the rank of rear admiral. When he left the ship, many felt a deep sense of personal loss. Captain Jennings had created a happy ship. He had also carried on the tradition of efficiency aboard ship. His replacement was Captain Thomas Selby Combs. He took command of the *Yorktown* on September 29, 1944.

Down the west coast Captain Combs took the *Yorktown*, until she was off the coast of San Francisco. Here he turned east and entered the Golden Gate. As the ship steamed through the bay and approached the Golden Gate Bridge, the crew decided that someone should have the honor of being first under the bridge. That honor came to the catapult officer, Lieutenant Blaha.

The *Yorktown* entered her mooring place; the date was October 8. Again the crew received passes to tour the city. For several days the crew looked over the city, but on Friday, October 13, the *Yorktown* weighed anchor and sailed out of the harbor. She would not return to the States until after the war. For some, this would be their last look at the home they loved, America.

The *Yorktown* sailed toward Hawaii with Captain Combs now at the helm. Captain Combs had been a commodore, but was dropped back one rank to captain so that he could command a ship. He had been in the navy for several years, and had once served aboard the U.S.S. *Arizona*. It was on the *Arizona* that he had earned the nickname of "Theda." While on the *Arizona*, he was going to the shower one day, wrapped only in a towel. One of his shipmates yelled, "There goes Theda Bara than ever!" From then on he had the nickname Theda.

Before Captain Combs came aboard the *Yorktown*, he had been the chief of staff of COMAIRSOWESPAC, and had become one of the most popular officers in the entire navy. The *Yorktown* had been fortunate indeed to get such a fine officer as skipper.

Also aboard was a new chaplain. George A. Wright had replaced Robert Alexander as the Protestant chaplain on September 3, 1944. Chaplain Joseph W. Moody, a plank owner or original crew member, was still aboard as the Catholic chaplain. Many sailors would turn to these two men in moments of personal troubles.

While the *Yorktown* was in the States, the Japanese had invented a new and deadly weapon. It was the kamikaze. These were men dedicated to killing themselves in attacks on American ships. They hoped to stop with their lives the American victory which had begun to look certain. It was against these pilots that the *Yorktown* would fight her most fierce battles. The kamikazes had already done great damage to the U.S.S. *Suwannee*, one of Jocko Clark's former ships. Would the *Yorktown* be dealt the same fate?

On November 3, 1944, the *Yorktown* rejoined Task Force Thirty-eight at Ulithi. She was chosen as the flagship of Task Group 38.1. Task Force Fifty-eight had become Task Force Thirty-eight.

Admiral Spruance went ashore in August to plan further operations. His replacement was Admiral Halsey, a proven carrier veteran who had been aboard the *Enterprise* when the Japanese had attacked Pearl Harbor. In fact, when one thinks of Halsey, one automatically thinks of the *Enterprise*.

With Halsey in command, the fleet became the Third Fleet. This helped to make clear to the Americans which man was in command, while at the same time confusing the Japanese about the number of American fleets in the Pacific. Also relieved of command for a while was Admiral Mitscher. His replacement was Admiral John S. McCain. He would be in command of Task Force Thirty-eight. Mitscher was also planning future operations.

Much had happened in the Pacific while the *Yorktown* was being refitted in Bremerton. The Battle of Leyte Gulf had been fought in late October. In that battle the Japanese lost four carriers and twenty other warships. The Americans had lost the carriers *Princeton, Gambier Bay*, and *St. Lo*, along with two destroyers; in addition the Japanese damaged six CVE's. The Japanese Navy had become a mere symbol. The two battles of the Philippine Sea had all but destroyed it. With the loss of most of their ships, the Japanese turned to a new and deadly weapon—the Kamikaze.

The Kamikaze Corps was a special air corps whose tactics were to crash into an enemy ship, set it on fire by the spread of gasoline and explode it with bombs. The Kamikaze pilot was killed in the crash. Against such fanatics as these the *Yorktown* would have her greatest test. It had become a battle between the pilots who wanted to die, and the gunners who wanted to live. It would be hard to shoot down a plane whose pilot was bent on killing himself while trying to kill you.

The Kamikazes had hit the *Franklin* while the *Yorktown* was away. She was badly hit and had heavy casualities. She burned from frame ninety aft, but was soon back in action against the enemy. Also hit on October 30 was the *Belleau Wood*. She was just aft of the *Franklin*, and caught one of the suicides trying to hit the *Franklin*.

Three days after the *Yorktown* arrived with Air Group Three aboard, the *Lexington* was hit by a kamikaze. She too headed for Ulithi for repairs. It had become apparent that the Kamikaze was the greatest threat to the Third Fleet since the early days of the war.

The kamikazes, a term meaning "Divine Wind" in Japanese, had been formed in October, 1944. The first Japanese flier to die hitting an American ship was Lieutenant Seki. He dived his bomb-laden plane into the *St. Lo*. His attack, and the planes following him, sunk the carrier. When the reports of the sinking arrived, the Japanese went wild with excitement. They had found an efficient weapon with which to sink American carriers. For the next eight months this would be their chief weapon in the war. Hundreds of young Japanese fliers volunteered for the one-way missions. To them, it meant honor; to the men of the *Yorktown*, it meant a struggle to protect oneself against fanatics who gave no thought to self preservation. Only skill was in the *Yorktowners'* favor. That skill would be found in gunnery, her damage-control workers, her pilots, and every other member of the crew.

On November 10, Admiral Halsey signaled McCain that a force of Japanese battleships and cruisers had been spotted heading toward Leyte Gulf. Immediately McCain signaled the *Yorktown* and the others to search out and destroy the remaining ships.

Turning toward the Philippines, the *Yorktown* plowed through the heavy seas at a speed of twenty-six knots. By dawn she was in launch position.

Throughout the night Jim Bryan's men had got the planes ready for takeoff. By 6:00 A.M. a few scouts had been sent up to look for the enemy warships. No ships were spotted, but the scouts did spot a troop convoy heading toward Ormoc Bay, which was located on the western coast of Leyte. Immediately "Pappy" Harshman, the air officer, bellowed over the squawk box, "Pilots, man your planes!" Quickly the pilots of Air Group Three headed for their planes. As the Hellcats flew into the air, the *Yorktown* had once again become a fighting ship. This was her first strike since July 28. Would she be able to maintain her reputation for being the ship which could launch and retrieve planes quicker than any other carrier in the fleet? Soon they learned the answer: it was yes. The crew still had its touch.

Soon the pilots of Air Group Three were attacking the troop ships and their destroyer escorts. The battle was furious as the pilots dived at the ships, into the hail of antiaircraft fire. When it was over the pilots of Air Group Three and the other air groups had sunk all of the transports, and four of the destroyers. Also, sixteen enemy planes were shot down. In preventing any enemy troops from land-ing, the *Yorktown's* planes had helped MacArthur fulfill his promise to return to the Philippines.

For the next four days the *Yorktown* hammered away at the shipping in the Philippines, doing great damage to the Japanese Merchant Marine Fleet. By keeping supplies out of the Philippines, the Americans hoped to defeat the Japanese. The

Japanese had taught the Americans this tactic in the early months of 1942. Now American forces controlled the seas and the air around the Philippines.

Despite this, the Japanese still managed to send up a few planes to harass the *Yorktown* and the other ships of Task Force Thirty-eight. The Americans decided to stop this harassment by destroying the airfields in the Philippines. On November 19 the *Yorktown* struck the airfields in the Central Philippines. After this raid she returned to "the barn," as the harbor at Ulithi was called.

Here the carriers lined up in what became known as "Marauder's Row." From a distance all the carriers looked the same, and only by noticing the few differences could one tell the *Yorktown* from her sisters. Only the *Enterprise* and *Saratoga* were different in their profiles.

In Ulithi, the fleet was relatively safe from attack. On the morning of November 20, a midget sub managed to penetrate the anchorage and blow up an oiler. Still, life in Ulithi was better than that in combat.

One of the favorite spots of the enlisted men at Ulithi was the island of Mog Mog. Here an enlisted man could buy beer, play softball, or just lie in the warm sun. For men like Kenneth "Parky" Parkinson and Ruben Kitchen, November had always meant cold weather and snow. But in the Pacific, the weather was still hot during these months. In fact, many of the men were swimming while their folks back home were bundling up against the bitter cold.

Getting beer on Mog Mog meant standing in long

lines. Each man was able to buy just a few beers with the paper tokens that he was issued. Some men did not drink beer, but their tokens did not go waste. Friends would be given the tokens. In that way a drinker with a few non-drinking friends could get all the beer he wanted. To a war-weary crew, Mog Mog was paradise.

On one occasion a small party from the *Yorktown*, which included Ruben Kitchen, missed the liberty boat back to the ship. They had lost track of time, and had been on the other side of the island when the call came over the PA for them to return to the ship. When they arrived back where the ships were anchored, they noticed that their friends were gone. Asking around, they discovered they had missed their boat. Not wanting to be late, they took the next boat going out. They found themselves on another carrier. Kitchen explained what had happened, and the officer of the day made arrangements for them to get back to the *Yorktown*. When they arrived at the *Yorktown*, they went aboard looking nonchalant. Nothing happened. The officer of the day just shook his head and let them pass.

Aboard the ship, Ruben Kitchen had met an old friend from back in Pike County, Kentucky. His name was Ralph Kendrick. He was an Airdale. They met by chance. About every day Kendrick and a friend of his would come down to the shipfitter's shop for a cup of coffee and a visit. The shipfitter's shop had the largest coffeepot aboard. The smell of coffee greeted a visitor as soon as he entered the shop, especially when the ship was operating in colder climates.

Kitchen had been on the *Yorktown* since May, and word had gotten around that he was a fair craftsman, who took pride in his work. As demand for his services grew, his skills became greater and more varied. At first he made a few watch bands and sold them to others in the crew. Then he made some knives. Next he was making ensign bars for the ensigns to wear, then Lieutenant bars. One day he found himself in the admiral's quarters making a telephone extension so that the Admiral could answer the phone without getting up. And once he was asked to make a stainless-steel lunch box for the admiral. This was used by the admiral's cabin boy, a Philippino, to bring the admiral his dinner while he was on the bridge. Kitchen's skill in making small items kept him quite busy on noncombatant days. He enjoyed the work.

On December 8, Kenneth "Parky" Parkinson went swimming in Ulithi Bay. In his next letter home he told his wife, Lula, about his swimming in December. In Illinois, Lula was wearing heavy clothes for protection against the chilly weather.

Soon the rest period was up in Ulithi. There was a war going on, and now the *Yorktown* must get back to it. On the morning of December 14, the *Yorktown*, with the rest of the carriers, began supporting the invasion of Mindoro in the Philippines. For three days American planes flew over the island, giving support cover for the landings. Because of victories in the past, none of the carriers was attacked during these three days.

After the strikes on Mindoro, Halsey planned to refuel the fleet at sea. After this, he planned to strike Luzon on December 19. On December 17, the oilers approached to refuel the carriers, while some of the carriers prepared to refuel their destroyer escorts. But nature was about to step in and change these plans.

Aboard the *Yorktown*, Ted Rohrbough and the others of the Fourth Division made preparations to refuel a destroyer that had pulled alongside. During normal refueling operations, the crew would line the railing on the destroyer and yell as with one voice, "Where is the ice cream?" But on this day the sky was gray and the sea rough; being topside aboard a destroyer was dangerous.

As the wind picked up, the sea grew turbulent, and the destroyer became a bobbing cork beside the *Yorktown*. The destroyer eased alongside the number one crane on the carrier. By this time, there were monstrous swells. The destroyer would raise up on a swell to the flight deck level of the carrier. Then it would fall into the trough and only the mast would be visible from the carrier deck. This process was repeated several times, but after expert line-handling by the Fourth Division and the men on the destroyer, fuel lines were connected between the two ships.

As the empty destroyer gulped the much needed fuel oil, the seas tossed it about like a toy. With near empty fuel tanks the destroyers rode high in the water. Because of their added antiaircraft guns, they were top-heavy. They needed the fuel not only to hold course, but also for ballast. The situation for the destroyers was becoming quite grave.

Topside on the destroyer, two men worked

furiously to keep the fuel lines from separating. These men were exposed to the wind and seas, but because of the need for fuel, they braved the elements while their ship gulped the fuel. Suddenly a swell came between the destroyer and the carrier. Tons of seawater hit the superstructure of the destroyer. When the swell passed, the fuel lines had parted, and the two sailors were gone. The water crushed them, and then torn them from their station. Refueling operations were cancelled. With her tanks only half full, the little destroyer rejoined formation.

Aboard the *Yorktown* the condition was "modified affirmed." Men were at their general quarters stations; the guns were manned and radar units searched for the enemy. The crew secured the hatches as the giant *Yorktown* started to get tossed around.

Throughout the night the storm raged; the barometer dropped, and the wind rose. The storm was approaching gale force. By dawn it was realized that the Third Fleet was lying directly in the path of the granddaddy of all typhoons. While the *Yorktown* was having some troubles, the destroyers were starting to fight for their lives. Fuel almost exhausted, they rode high in the water. The small destroyers would climb each swell with all their might, then drop down the other side until half the ship sliced into the next wave. Then the bow would pierce the air, and the process would start again. As long as they could head into the swells, they had a chance, but the high winds buffeted the superstructures, trying to turn them around and lay them down on their sides.

Aboard the *Yorktown* planes were lashed to the decks to keep them from sliding around and causing damage. Other cargo was secured, checked and double-checked to make sure it would not slide. Jim Bryan made sure that his men had secured all the bombs and torpedoes. A 500-pound bomb rolling across a pitching, tossing deck is deadly. The men went about their tasks quickly.

Aboard the destroyer *Dewey*, the bridge lost steering control at 8:20 A.M. Quickly, steering was transferred aft, for without steering, the ship would die. The barometer was still dropping; it read a little over twenty-eight degrees. Many had never seen the barometer read this, yet it was still falling.

On the *Cowpens*, an F6F which was triple-lashed to the flight deck broke loose and started on a forty-five degree roll. The plane smashed into the catwalk and started a fire. The men in damage control moved quickly to fight the fire, but, because of the rolling deck, they could not get near the burning plane. As the plane burned, the sea ripped away one of the 20-mm gun sponsons, then tore into the steel curtains on the hangar deck.

On the hangar deck, a bomb-handling truck broke loose and smashed into the belly tank of an F6F. Meanwhile, on the flight deck, the sea extinguished the flames of the burning F6F, and then knocked the smoldering plane into the white, foaming water below. The immediate danger was over as quickly as it started on the *Cowpens*.

Aboard the *Yorktown*, deep down on the eighth deck in central damage control, the seven men stationed there fought to keep the ship on an even keel. This was where the gyros were located, but even they were of little use in seas such as this.

As the wind increased, ship after ship dropped out of formation. It had become a battle just to survive. The swells were now seventy-feet high from their crests to the bottom of the troughs. No one had ever seen the sea this rough. In the CIC aboard the *Yorktown* men scanned the radar. What once was an orderly pip of lights on the screen had become a mass of confusion. Small pips of light were everywhere on the screen. Only the larger ships were able to hold formation.

On the carrier *Monterey*, fire broke out on the hangar deck. After a few minutes, the smoke forced men to abandon the number one and number two firerooms. Mere skeleton crews manned the boiler rooms which gave the steam to turn the props. While the men fought the fire, a gasoline-vapor explosion killed one seaman, another was burned to death after being trapped by the flames; a third died of asphyxiation.

A few men found breathable air topside. Although the *Monterey* was rolling and pitching, the men took the risk topside; at least the air was fresh. Suddenly the ship rolled, and five men lost their footing on the slick, steeply angled flight deck. A few of the men had close calls. One was sliding far across the deck. He saw the ocean coming closer, yet there was nothing he could do. His heels were trying to dig into the slick flight deck, but without success. As he was about to slide off the flight deck, his heel found the small steel rim surrounding the deck. As his slide was slowed, he rolled over onto his stomach and dropped into the catwalk that surrounded the flight deck, That man was Gerald R. Ford.

On the *Yorktown*, food was brought to the crew in vacuum bottles, with the caps sealed. Soup was the only hot meal which could be served. Sitting on the decks with their backs to the bulkheads, the crew drank their soup from the bottles. The mess tables were not even put up, because they could not stay in place on the pitching decks. Everywhere men had on lifejackets. The *Yorktown* was luckier than most of the other ships. Little gear had broken loose in the storm.

On the *Dewey* the barometer read 27.30, a record low. The small destroyers had the roughest time, with the light carriers and escort carriers next. The *San Jacinto, Monterey, Altomaha*, and others had planes break loose. Men jumped out of the way to avoid being crushed by sliding equipment. On the small carriers all hell broke loose.

The little *Monaghan*, a combat veteran with twelve battlestars to her credit, rolled in the angry seas. The wind pushed on the superstructure of the destroyer. Slowly she rolled over toward starboard. Men on the ship watched the boiling green water climb nearer as the ship rolled. She reached fifty degrees, but then slowly started to recover. As the small *Monaghan* recovered, the wind pushed against her superstructure. Slowly she started to roll over toward starboard again. The captain radioed that he was dead in the water. Only hope was left, for without power the ship was at the mercy of the sea and wind.

The wind in her furious wrath, then took the

Mohaghan. Driving at 110 knots, the wind pushed the destroyer toward starboard again. As the ship approached seventy degrees, it was evident that she would not recover. Water poured into the wheelhouse. The *Monaghan* slowly came to rest on her side. What the Japanese could not do in three years, the sea had done in just a few hours. The *Monaghan* went down with 256 of her crew.

Aboard the *Yorktown* the sea lashed at the forward gun mounts under the flight deck, yet no damage was done. The ship remained at modified affirm. Men checked the planes and other gear continually to see that they were secured. Some of the men drank their soup; others, because of slight seasickness, felt it was better not to try to eat. There had been only a few minor injuries. Captain Combs had inherited a well-trained crew, and a very stout ship.

Throughout the fleet strange things happened. On one ship a man was washed overboard by a giant wave, but was carried back onto the ship by the next wave. Ships rolled beyond their rated-degree-of-returning, yet they recovered.

The *Spence*, also a destroyer, went next. The sea spray caused her electrical board to short out. This killed all the electrical power aboard the ship. Compartments became dark, pumps quiet; the ship's heart had stopped. The body lived but not for long.

Without power, the wind pushed the *Spence* over to the port side. With the antiaircraft guns topside, and her fuel tanks empty, the *Spence* rolled over onto her side. One man, Lieutenant Alphonso Stephen Krauchunas, crawled along the bulkheads trying to find his way topside in the darkness. As he reached topside, the ocean entered the passageways, forcing him back; but he refused to die. Fighting, he managed to break clear. After *Spence* sank, he was the only officer to survive; he and seventy enlisted men were all who were left of the crew.

On the *Dewey* the crew fought for their lives. They were battered and racked. As the 110-knot winds pushed on the *Dewey*, she rolled to starboard. The captain had been wise enough to transfer the fuel oil to the port tanks on the morning watch. This added weight to the starboard side that would otherwise not have been there.

Slowly the *Dewey* settled toward the starboard side. As the degree indicator read sixty, sixty-five, seventy, seventy-five, then eighty, it became certain the destroyer would capsize. Suddenly the number one stack was carried away by the green sea. This lightened the topside weight. Because of this and the fact that all the fuel was in the port tanks, the *Dewey* had the chance she needed to live. As the water touched the starboard wing of the bridge, the ship started to recover from her roll. Slowly she righted herself. The *Dewey* had rolled eighty degrees and survived, the only ship on record to do so.

Shortly after the *Dewey* cheated death, death reached out for the *Hull*. With her fuel tanks seventy-percent full, the *Hull* was better off than her sisters; yet she could not handle the sea. Water began coming in through seams. The wind mercilessly pushed her on her side, holding her there long enough for tons of green sea water to enter the little ship. Slowly she died.

The crew of the *Yorktown* managed to hold course and fight the sea. Her size was a great help. As the wind settled down, the danger lessened. By late evening the seas were rough, but manageable. The *Yorktown* had survived nature's worst storm without mishap.

Later that evening, she, along with the other remaining ships, looked for survivors from the three capsized destroyers. The storm had done as much damage as a major engagement with the enemy would have done. Nature had scattered the Third Fleet over miles of ocean, and had taken the lives of nearly 800 men. Damage to ships and equipment was in the millions of dollars.

Halsey planned to go ahead with the Luzon strikes, but the storm had settled over that area, keeping planes from both sides out of the air. It was then decided to return to Ulithi to get the fleet back together, and to repair the damage sustained by the ships.

While the *Yorktown* anchored in Ulithi, the men had a chance to think about the approaching Christmas season. The scuttlebutt turned to Christmas. Ruben Kitchen remembered that December 20 was his birthday. He was nineteen years old that day, and was glad he had been assigned to the *Yorktown* in May, at Pearl Harbor. He had seen a lot of action, but he was still safe.

On the hangar deck, a Christmas tree was set up for the ceremonies to be held on Christmas Day. In the mailroom, Mailman Third Class Joseph Huber was sorting mail to be delivered on Christmas Day. This included letters and packages from home. Some of these packages had been sent in early October to insure their arrival by Christmas Day. These had been held back until December 25.

Don Seaman, in the pay office, got the pay ready for the crew. Money could be spent at Mog Mog. The pay office had taken pride in never being late for a payday.

Harland Bickford, Kenneth Parkinson, Lester Fisher, and others in the R-1 Division, were doing some small repair work on damage caused by the typhoon. A ship the size of the *Yorktown* was constantly in need of repair work somewhere: a broken water line, a loose board on the flight deck, even a curtain hanger which had come off the bulkhead in the captain's quarters. These men were the maintenance men of the ship on noncombatant days. Everyone hoped they would prove to be miracle workers if she ever was hit. Their main duties were controlling damage, fixing holes in the ship, and stopping fires.

Edward Johnson continued to practice his boxing for the smokers held on off-combat days while the carrier was refueling or taking on supplies.

Christmas Day found the crew of the *Yorktown* relaxing in Ulithi. On the hangar deck, Chaplains Moody and Wright held church services just yards away from a giant Christmas tree piled high with packages. The packages which Joe Huber and the others of the mailroom had sorted were waiting to be opened by the crew. Letters were read over and over again. Each man tried to make this Christmas like those spent at home. For some it was their first Christmas away from home; for others it was longer.

Christmas dinner included turkey with all the trimmings. Standing in line was Captain Combs telling each sailor, to "dish it up, eat all you want," and, "You can't live out here on love, sailor!"

Later that day the ship's band, under the direction of Chief Musician Reilly, played Christmas carols on the hangar deck. After a few hours of carols, the band broke out with "Beautiful, Beautiful Mog Mog" and other lively swing sounds. The band even played requests. One time a "Shavetail" requested that the band stop playing loud pop music. They just played louder.

On into New Year's Day the *Yorktown* stayed away from combat, but a strike had been scheduled for January 3, 1945, against Luzon and Formosa. For the next eight months the *Yorktown* would battle against a steady stream of Kamikaze pilots. With each day that passed her chances of surviving without being hit got slimmer. Would she be alive at the end of 1945? The crew believed so.

Chapter VII

The Japanese now began to realize that they would lose the war. Little hope was left for a Japanese victory, but they wanted to keep the Americans from attacking their beloved homeland of Japan. Their navy no longer had the air power to attack the United States Fleet, so the Japanese turned to land-based planes on Formosa to deliver the blows which were to convince the Americans to stop the war and let the islands of Japan remain unharmed. More and more young pilots volunteered for the one-way missions that would accomplish this. On Formosa, there were slightly over 100 planes of various types for use against the mighty carriers of the Third Fleet.

On the morning of January 3, 1945, the crew of the *Yorktown* made preparations to strike at planes located on the airfields in Formosa and Luzon before the Japanese had a chance to evacuate them.

In the ready rooms on the gallery deck directly below the flight deck, the pilots of Air Group Three went over the flight plan of the day briefly. Among these rugged pilots were Robert Thienes, Joe Mayer, William McLeroy, and Robert E. Lee. As Copper Bright, the air operations officer, went over the targets of the day, the men listening to him little realized what they were going up against. These men were used to fighting to live; they could not understand fighting to die.

With a good breakfast of steak and eggs under their belts, they were ready when "Pappy" Harshman, the assistant air operations officer, gave the word over the squawk box for the pilots to man their planes. Walking briskly up the ladder, the men emerged onto the flight deck.

It was still dark when they boarded their planes. The other members of the crew were already waiting in the TBM's and SB2C's. These men had got on earlier to check the radios and guns. The pilots in the F6F's, of course, flew alone. Suddenly the flight deck came alive with spitting, belching planes as each was started and warmed up. By looking closely one could see the flicker of blue flame from the exhaust of several of the planes. After a few minutes of warming up, the planes were moved into position for launching. At this point it became extremely dangerous for the Airdales aboard. A slip or a stumble could mean serious injury or even death.

Just before dawn, the first F6F rolled down the flight deck, followed by the rest of the planes. As the last plane left the ship, preparations were made for the next strike. All day long planes were sent out to bomb the airfields on Formosa. While the American planes were gone, the men in CIC scanned the radar for bogeys. On the guns, men watched for any plane that might have sneaked below the radar. Throughout the day no enemy was sighted, and the pilots of Air Group Three and the other air groups destroyed most of the 100 planes on Formosa. They also managed to sink sixteen small ships. The Japanese never managed to get near the fleet.

The next day was the same. American pilots carried out raids, while the Japanese remained unable to strike back against the carriers of Task Force Thirty-eight.

On the morning of January 5, some of the ships took on fuel as they proceeded toward Luzon. On the next morning, planes were launched. Because the skies were overcast, little was accomplished. The next day, the weather was clear over the target, but it was overcast in the launch area. Halsey decided to strike Formosa again. Maybe the weather would be better there.

Throughout the night, the *Yorktown*, along with the rest of Task Force Thirty-eight, steamed toward Formosa. Reaching the launch area in the early morning, the pilots of Air Group Three once again climbed into their planes in the predawn hours. By 6:00 A.M. the planes began leaving the flight deck.

On Formosa, unknown to the pilots of Air Group Three, the Japanese had constructed several mock planes. These planes were constructed of cardboard and plywood. From the air, in a fast plane, these mock-ups looked real. It was especially hard for a pilot dodging antiaircraft fire to tell the real from the mock planes. The Japanese had even camou-flaged these planes to make them look real. They also placed small cans of gasoline in the mock hulls so the planes would explode when hit, thus com-pleting the illusion. The real planes were hidden well off the airfields, in the jungle.

Air Group Three approached one of the airfields and the pilots bore their planes down upon the targets below. Fiercely the Japanese threw back their colorful antiaircraft fire. As each pilot brought his plane through the deadly hail of fire to drop his bomb and then strafe the field, none realized that they were only destroying a few dollars' worth of cardboard, wood, and gasoline. The Japanese, who honored bravery, wondered how each man would feel if he knew he was risking his life for these useless targets. The Japanese had fooled the pilots. It would be months before they learned what their targets had really been that day.

By nightfall all the planes were back aboard. Quickly Halsey turned his ship toward the Bashi Channel. It would be through this seventy-five mile wide stretch of water that the carriers of Task Force Thirty-eight would enter the South China Sea. This stretch of water was closely watched. With land nearby, it would be quite easy for the Japanese to send numerous kamikazes at the *Yorktown* and the other carriers. This was a bold step for Halsey. He was looking for the carrier-battleships *Hyuga* and *Ise*. The first carrier to enter the channel entered under the watchful eye of Captain Combs, for it was the *Yorktown* that spearheaded the rest through the channel.

Remarkably, the Japanese did not try to stop the ships. Once clear of the channel, the *Yorktown* turned toward Camranh Bay, looking for the *Hyuga* and the *Ise*. Here was the Third Fleet, complete with tankers, in enemy held waters and steaming unmolested. Quickly planes were sent up to find the remaining ships of the Japanese Navy. If they could be destroyed, the war could be shortened by months.

As pilots from the *Yorktown* searched for the Japanese fleet, the Third Fleet was spotted by planes from another task force. Task Force Thirty-eight had been keeping radio silence. This other task force, located outside of the South China Sea, had not maintained silence. One of the pilots radioed the other, "Hey, Joe, look at all them ships down there—hope they're friends."

The other pilot replied, "Yeah, gee, look at 'em. Must be the Third Fleet."

Radio silence was broken with this message. The Japanese surely knew the Third Fleet was in the area. The warships were not found, but the *Yorktown* did strike at the surrounding airfields and at some merchant ships.

While in the South China Sea, the pilots of Air Group Three flew strikes against Saigon. There were Japanese airfields nearby, and they had to be destroyed. Early on the morning of January 12, Lieutenants Robert Thienes, William McLeroy, Joe Mayer, and the others climbed aboard their F6F Hellcats parked on the flight deck. It would be their job to fly cover for the SB2C's and the TBM Avengers.

At a little after 7:00 A.M., word was given to launch the planes, fighters first. Quickly the F6F's took to the air, followed by the other planes. The flight to Saigon would be long. The distance was over 200 miles, some of it over enemy-held water.

As the planes from the *Yorktown* flew over the waters of the South China Sea, the men left behind began preparations for their return. In the CIC a constant watch was kept on the radar screens for any sign of enemy planes.

As Air Group Three attacked the airfields in the Saigon area, a few of the pilots had close calls. Lieutenant Bill McLeroy noticed that his wingman's plane swerved out of formation. Quickly, Bill called over the radio to his wingman, Bob Thienes. After a few minutes, Thienes answered. Bill asked Bob what was wrong. With some difficulty Bob managed to explain that he had been hit in the head. Blood was streaming down his face, and dripping onto his lap. He was also partially blind. He could hardly make out the instrument panel in front of him.

Next, there was silence from Bob's radio. Again Bill shouted to Bob. After a few minutes he was able to rouse him again. Bill knew now that Bob was passing out intermittently. It looked bad for Thienes, and McLeroy knew it. Thienes was wounded, partially blind, and passing out; and the *Yorktown* was over 200 miles away. Bill McLeroy knew that only with his help could Bob Thienes make it back alive to the carrier. With quiet determination, he decided he would not let his friend die here.

As the minutes passed, Bill could tell that Bob

was having trouble flying his F6F back toward the *Yorktown*. The injured pilot's plane would climb, and Bill would have to coach Bob to level off and fly straight. Then Bob would pass out again and fall forward. The F6F would then start a descent. Again Bill would coach him to level off. It went on like this for miles. Bob managed to fly only because of the constant coaching and encouragement that Bill gave him.

Finally McLeroy spotted the *Yorktown* on the horizon. Now would come the final test. Should he try to help Theines land aboard the carrier, or should he allow him to parachute out and be picked up by one of the destroyers? Either way, it would be risky. Thienes might pass out before he could pull his rip cord. It was decided between the two that Thienes would try to land on the Lucky Y.

As Thienes's F6F approached the stern of the *Yorktown*, Dick Tripp was on the landing-signal officer's platform ready to help with his signal paddles. Slowly Thienes approached the stern, guided by his own instinct and radio from McLeroy. McLeroy watched Dick's paddles and told Thienes how to correct his approach. Closer and closer Thienes approached under the watchful eye of Tripp and McLeroy. As he was over the stern, Dick gave the signal to cut power, and McLeroy yelled into the radio, "Cut power!"

Thienes cut his power, and his F6F settled onto the deck. Men raced to his plane; Thienes was back home safe. As Thienes was pulled from his plane, McLeroy made his own approach. Within a few minutes he, too, was safe aboard.

Immediately, Thienes was taken to sick bay, where it was discovered he had taken a Japanese AA shell in his skull. The shell had penetrated and stayed there. It was this that had caused the partial blindness. Thienes was alive only because McLeroy had stayed with him, and had helped him get back home safely.

Imagine flying over 200 miles blind, groggy, and unconscious most of the time, to a spot on the sea that was 800-feet long and 100-feet wide, with only the coaching of your wingman. Thienes was indeed lucky that day!

By now the *Yorktown's* presence was known to Tokyo Rose. She even singled out the *Yorktown*. "*Yorktown*." she would say, "you are a doomed carrier. You will never leave the South China Sea, because we will be waiting for you at the Balintang Channel. Remember, *Yorktown*, you are a doomed carrier." Every day she would mention the *Yorktown*, and every day her radio broadcast would be piped throughout the ship. Whether the crew of the *Yorktown* wanted it or not, they had gained fame among the Japanese.

Of all the *Essex* class carriers, the *Yorktown* was the one which had caused the most damage to the enemy, and still she remained unscratched. To hit the *Yorktown* would be no small victory to the Japanese; and they intended to hit and sink her. The *Yorktown* had become to the Japanese what the *Bismark* had been to the English. But the Japanese did not have the navy that the English had in the days of the *Bismark*.

The next day, January 13, the *Yorktown*, along

with the rest of Task Force Thirty-eight, steamed north to avoid a typhoon and to refuel. Because of the weather conditions, little flying was done on January 14.

Early on the morning of January 15, Fritz Wolfe, the skipper of the "Fighting Three's," sent his F6F's on a mission over Formosa and the China Coast. Flying from the deck of the *Yorktown*, the men of Air Group Three did little damage to the Japanese because of the lack of targets. Again, on January 16, there were no targets, and on that day the weather was bad for flying as well.

For the next two days the weather got worse, and finally on January 20, Halsey decided to leave the South China Sea and return to Ulithi. Just before the ships began their trip through the Balintang Channel, Tokyo Rose came on the air. Again she taunted the *Yorktown*. All ears listened as she told the men of the *Yorktown* that they were doomed men, and they would never leave the South China Sea: it would be their grave. All listened, but few took her seriously. They had gone through a lot in the past seventeen months, and they were still undamaged.

The mood aboard the *Yorktown* was nervous, even though the crew did not take Tokyo Rose's threat seriously, it did play on their nerves a little. As Task Force Thirty-eight began making preparations to go through the Balintang Channel, the Japanese were preparing to try and stop them. Japanese subs had mined and blocked the channel. Someone had to go first. That someone happened to be Captain Combs of the *Yorktown*.

Cautiously, Captain Combs guided the Lucky Y into the narrow channel. Air Group Three was already aloft searching out enemy bogeys, and attempting to knock them out of the air before they reached the ship. Even against these great pilots, some bogeys managed to break through.

Soon word came over the loudspeaker not to be surprised at anything. The Japanese were all around—in the air, under the waves, and on the islands nearby. Halsey had been bold in going through this channel a week before in the darkness, but now he was attempting to transverse it in daylight. Surprisingly, the task force managed to get through the channel without mishap; but there were a few tense moments.

By nightfall the Japanese were still flying missions, and one plane was shot down by the *Yorktown's* gun well after dark. These guns were fired by radar.

Upon leaving the South China Sea on January 20, the *Yorktown* changed course and made a run toward Formosa. Task Force Thirty-eight would hit this area before it retired to Ulithi.

As the men of Air Group Three flew toward Formosa to deliver their messages of death, the Japanese were flying toward the *Yorktown*. This time it was kamikazes on their one-way mission of glory and death. Tokyo Rose's warning was coming true. Four of these suicides, escorted by three other planes, made dives on the carriers. One plane made its dive on the CVL *Langley* and dropped two bombs. One bomb missed, but the other hit the flight deck, ripping it up and killing three men. As fires broke out, the damage control men raced to fight them.

At the same time that the damage-control men were fighting the roaring fire on the *Langley*, a kamikaze plunged into the *Ticonderoga*. The plane, its pilot, and its bomb penetrated the flight deck of the "Ti" before the 550 pound bomb itself exploded. With the explosion occurring on the hangar deck, death and destruction were spread everywhere. As the flames spread to the parked planes, they, exploded, adding to the destruction. Another suicide hit the Ti forty minutes later. Now the Ti was engulfed in flames, but she never lost speed. Thanks to her damage-control men, she was able to resume her way on her own. After the fires were out, a death toll was made: 143 men had been burned to death or died of suffocation. The ship that had been featured in the final shots of the movie *The Fighting Lady*, was now a hurt ship with death in her hull.

Meanwhile aboard the *Langley*, the crews had managed to put out the fires and resume operations in three hours. She had lost three men.

After the raid on Formosa, the men of Air Group Three returned to the Lucky Y. Again, she had not been hit. Her fame as a lucky ship was now spread throughout the fleet. Younger carriers had been hit; some had been hit hard. The only three carriers older than the *Yorktown*: the *Enterprise*, the *Saratoga,* and the *Essex*, had all been hit at one time or another. Fate had spared the *Yorktown*. Captain Combs had under his command a carrier that any man would want.

After the South China Sea venture was over, Task

Force Thirty-eight returned to Ulithi. Now the crew of the *Yorktown* could do some needed repair work, relax, and be the center of attention for the entire fleet. A surprise was planned for the *Yorktown* and her crew while in Ulithi Bay.

It was now time for some rest and recreation, and Ulithi Bay could give both. Here was the temporary home of Task Force Thirty-eight/Fifty-eight. Only a few months before, this bay had been in the hands of the Japanese. Now the large American carriers felt safe at anchor here, although every now and then a Japanese plane managed to break through.

Ulithi had three principal islands: Astor, Mog Mog, and Falalap, as well as a harbor large enough to anchor 1,000 ships. It was the islands that the crew liked most. Astor was used for staff parties for the officers, while Mog Mog was the enlisted man's paradise. Here he could have a cold beer, play softball, horseshoes, or other sports, and buy trinkets from the islanders. It did not take the natives long to find out that sailors will buy almost anything. If this war had helped the economy of anyone, it had helped theirs. Before the war, these people went for months without seeing a stranger. Now the island was full of sailors ready to spend money.

Nearby the *Yorktown* was anchored the badly damaged *Ticonderoga*. Rain had dripped through the holes in the flight deck making black streaks down the bulkheads from the soot caused by the fires. She even smelled of smoke and death. She was a sick ship, but would soon be in action again.

As the *Yorktown* anchored, Captain Combs thought of the surprise in store for the crew. He had them make the *Yorktown* shipshape for it.

The captain's speedboat needed some work done on it so he had the Fourth Division look after it. Coxswain Leonard Wasson was assigned to do the repair work. While he was busily working on the speedboat located on the starboard boat boom, he became seriously ill. Pain racked his right side, folding him over double. At once he was taken to sick bay where his trouble was found to be appendicitis. Without delay, the surgeon operated on him, and removed a badly ruptured appendix. Bed-rest for the next few days helped him to recover and return to duty in a few weeks.

The men of the Fourth Division were also put to work painting while in Ulithi. Crew members Rohrbough and Muller were told to paint the division peacoat locker. As the two men were painting the inside of the locker with white paint, they became ill. Both had gotten arsenic poisoning because they had not ventilated the area well enough. Taken to sick bay, the two men were given three IV units each. Within a few hours they were returned to duty.

Everywhere men were busy cleaning, painting, and making the ship look like new. The navy always had a reputation for being neat, but this was unusual. The *Yorktown* was a warship, not a luxury liner. The scuttlebutt was out, but the crew at large did not know what was happening. Captain Combs did, and he knew that the men would soon be proud that they were a part of the *Yorktown*.

Even with all the cleaning, the ship was still taking on supplies. The hangar deck was piled high with bombs, tools, crates, and other supplies. As soon as they were brought aboard, the men of the other divisions came and took the supplies to their respective areas on the ship.

Up on the flight deck the painters were busy painting false elevators. This was to give the kamikazes a false target to aim for, instead of the real elevators.

While the painters were painting on the flight deck, an electrician was working in a bos'n's chair over on the side of the ship. Suddenly, a bluish arc flew from where he was working, knocking him into the water. Men raced to the edge of the ship to offer assistance, but his body did not surface. He was either dead or unconscious when he hit the water. In any case, he was certainly dead now. Within a few minutes, the crowd dispersed and the men resumed their duties.

Two days later, the body of the electrician bobbed to the surface in the exact spot where it had disappeared. This was strange because the current was quite swift there.

While the ship was docked some of the officers had a party on Astor. This was a special party, because the guest of honor was Ernie Pyle, a well known war correspondent and a favorite among the fighting men. Ernie was a small man who seldom smiled or spoke. However, when an accordion player played "Lili Marlene" Ernie sang the song loudly, and then asked that it be played again. Again he sang, and again he asked for the song to be replayed. Finally, night fell and the officers returned to the *Yorktown*. With Ernie as the guest of honor aboard the Yorktown, something was going to happen.

Ernie Pyle was there for a reason. Although another ship, the *Ticonderoga,* had laid claim to it, the *Yorktown* was being given the title of Fighting Lady officially. The *Yorktown* was now going to have a nickname, a nickname that she had earned, and a nickname that was the most famous in the fleet. She would be the Fighting Lady.

The hangar deck was polished to look like a movie theater and over a large screen, signal flags spelled out the words "Fighting Lady." As evening approached, the ship was jammed with officers from throughout the Fifth Fleet. As Ernie Pyle came aboard, members of the crew followed him to Admiral Radford's cabin. In 1943, Admiral Radford had told Lieutenant Commander Dwight Long to film a movie about carrier warfare. The *Yorktown* was the carrier chosen for this film then. It was decided now to let the world know that the *Yorktown*, not the *Ticonderoga* (as the press had told the people back home) was the real Fighting Lady.

The movie had been filmed by both Navy and Hollywood cameramen under the direction of the renowned producer Edward Steichen. He had shot the film in color. This helped the Yorktown lay claim to the title. In late 1943, she was the only carrier that carried color film aboard ship and in her planes. Also, she was the only carrier to have a red stripe painted down the center of her flight deck. This red stripe showed up quite often in the film.

As evening fell, all the brass came aboard. A cake

in the shape of the *Yorktown* had been made for the occasion. Before the movie started, Captain Combs accepted a copy of the film from Lieutenant Commander Dwight Long. The *Yorktown* was now officially the Fighting Lady.

The lights were dimmed and the movie started. The opening scene showed a lone carrier emerging from below a cloud cover. The hum of a plane's engine could be heard above the narrator's voice. The voice began, "This is the story of an aircraft carrier; she is the Fighting Lady." The narrator went on to tell more about this carrier.

As he talked, many familiar faces appeared on the screen. The hangar deck became quiet as old friends appeared in the film. In the radar plot was Smokey. Plank owners remembered how he had begged Jocko to let him fly. He was now reported as missing in action. Also, the face of Lieutenant Commander Charles Crommelin appeared on the silver screen. He, too, was missing in action.

The film went on. There were many scenes filmed from the cameras on the planes of Air Group Five showing the deadly antiaircraft fire put up by the Japanese. Suddenly, a Japanese Zero flashed across the screen, only to be hit by deadly fire from a *Yorktown* plane.

The film continued, and the audience grew restless. The men were reliving the past. For the first time, they were observers of the action, not the actors.

Four planes approached the *Yorktown* low over the water. They were making their runs to hit her. Black puffs of smoke were visible all around the planes. As each was hit by the fire, it fell into the sea aflame. Only one plane continued on through the deadly hail of fire. Closer and closer it came. Tension mounted as it came closer. Finally, just yards away from the ship, the plane exploded and crashed into the sea. In the audience, as well as on the screen, a shout of cheer went up. As the cheering died down, one sailor was heard to say, "I thought that son-of-a-bitch was never going to stop."

The crew was captivated by the film's honesty and depth. It told their story as it really had happened. Truth was more exciting than fiction. After watching this fine film, the crew realized that they were indeed lucky to have gone through so much and survived, much less never to have been hit.

After the film was over, groups of men retired to different parts of the ship to discuss it. They congratulated one another in a joking manner for the part each had played in the film. They also reflected upon the impact this film would have back home. They could not have known then that this film would later be a classic among war documentaries and would be shown to thousands of naval personnel in the future. Nearly every film about World War II made in the future would have clips from *The Fighting Lady* in its action scenes.

The next morning the Fighting Lady resumed her normal duties. She now had a reputation to uphold. She was the proudest ship in the world.

The next day was very hot. Fresh clothes soon became sweat-soaked. Fresh water was used for drinking and cooking. Only saltwater was used for showers, and the salt soon chafed the skin in the heat. Only the cooks were allowed fresh-water showers and this was for sanitation reasons. But, by doing a little trading with one or two men in the R-1 Division, a sailor could get enough fresh water for a shower. Throughout the ship the policy of "you scratch my back and I'll scratch your back," was applied. A favor here and a favor there enabled the men to get various items and services. One special treat was the CO_2 used in making Cokes. In this heat a Coke and ice cream helped.

But now it was time to resume the war. Tokyo Rose again taunted the *Yorktown* with her predictions of doom. That night Lieutenant Commander J. Bryan III read the Plan of the Day. The last line said it all, It stated, "0830 Underway For Indian Country." Ever since Jocko had been aboard, the enemy waters had been called Indian Country.

The next morning Captain Combs was furious. The small destroyers were hovering around in front of the *Yorktown*. These destroyers were to lead the task force through the torpedo nets, but they were not acting quickly enough for Captain Combs. He expressed his disapproval to Admiral Radford who was himself fuming over the delay caused by the "tin cans."

From up on the signal bridge, Signalman Joe Leathers could see nearly 200 ships. Many more were beyond the horizon. This was the largest fleet to ever sail the seas.

Then the *Yorktown* began to move slowly. Captain Combs complained because they were moving at only nine knots. The destroyers were hindering the

Yorktown's speed. Admiral Radford told Combs to "go ahead; the destroyers will get out of the way". The ship went to "ahead standard," but the little destroyers still lingered under the bow of the carrier. Finally, at 9:00 A.M., the *Yorktown* cleared the torpedo nets. General quarters was sounded and the ship picked up speed. The other carriers fell in behind the *Yorktown*, with the two battleships behind them. Cruisers took up the flank. Over the bow was open water: over the stern was the rest of Task Group 58.4. The rest of Task Force Fifty-eight was in Ulithi Bay. Again, the *Yorktown* was spearheading the action.

Just below the flag bridge was a battery of 20-mm guns. That was where Don Seaman manned his gun along with five other gunners. As the *Yorktown* plowed ahead into Indian Country, one of these gunners was singing, "We're off to see the Wizard, the wonderful Wizard of Oz!" Over the bow, ahead of the newly painted "10" was a rainbow caused by the spray's being blown into the bright sun's rays. The song "Somewhere Over the Rainbow" might have been a better song. For somewhere over that rainbow was the enemy.

As the ships steamed toward Tokyo, the heat below decks became almost unbearable. Ventilating fans blew air below, but they did little to help. The cool waters off the coast of Tokyo would be welcome after the heat.

As the *Yorktown* proceeded toward Tokyo, she took on fuel. The tanker *Cacapon* came alongside, and once again Ted Rohrbough and the others of the Fourth Division wrestled the heavy fuel lines so that the Fighting Lady could get a drink of the precious liquid. As the *Yorktown* was refueling on the port side, the battleship *Washington* made connections on the *Cacapon's* starboard side. The three ships danced together in the blue-and-white waters of the Pacific. After refueling, the *Yorktown* and *Washington* broke away from the *Cacapon* and proceeded on their way.

The Fighting Lady neared Japanese waters. This would be the first time since the Doolittle Raid that Tokyo was bombed, and the first time it was ever bombed by carrier planes.

As the *Yorktown* neared Toyko, orders were given for all hands to keep shirts buttoned and sleeves rolled down. This was to protect the men from flames in case the ship was hit.

As the task force got closer, more patrol planes were sent out to search for any sign of the enemy. Surprise was necessary to avoid the deadly kamikazes. Early on February 15, five days after leaving Ulithi, contact was made with the Japanese. Two Hellcats sighted and sank a small fishing boat, and the destroyer *Hailey* was sent to pick up survivors. The others on the boat had all been killed. Only a seventeen-year-old boy was found. One of his legs had been broken by a bullet from an F6F.

He was transferred to the *Yorktown* shortly after being picked up so that he could be given medical aid. After his leg had been set. Bill Kluss was sent to question him. Bill learned a lot. His name was Sadao Watanabe, and he lived at Choshi on the island of Honshu. He was a fisherman and his boat had broken down twenty-nine days before. He and the others lived on rain water and fish from the sea since that time. As Bill was asking questions, a corpsman brought in a tray of food.

When the corpsman placed the tray on his knees, two peas rolled off the tray. Little Sadao searched for those two peas before he took his first bite. He was so hungry that he wanted to get all the food he could. Bill let Sadao eat before he questioned him further.

After Sadao was finished, Bill questioned him some more. There had been ten other men on the boat when it was sunk, and they had all been killed. Sadao thought that the planes were from China. When Bill explained that his boat had been sunk by the Americans, Sadao was not alarmed. He knew he had been treated well, and was among friends. In fact, he told Bill that he was going to enlist in the United States Navy after his leg healed, so that he could stay with his new-found friends. Bill then left Sadao, and wondered to himself how or why Sadao could feel that way. He liked his enemy better than his own. Strange indeed!

The Japanese still had not detected the *Yorktown*, and the plans remained to attack Tokyo on February 16.

That night most of the crew were restless. They knew that once they were discovered, the Japanese would throw everything they had into the air at them. They would be fighting a last ditch stand, and they would stop at nothing to destroy the Americans.

While the ship steamed closer to Tokyo, the condition was modified affirmed. In the shipfitter's bunkroom, Kenneth Parkinson wrote in his little diary. Ruben Kitchen and some others played cards. For the men in damage control, war was a waiting game. Their duties came only after the ship was hit. Until then, they could just wait and hope their services would never be needed.

February 16 began early for the men aboard the *Yorktown*. Fritz Wolfe had his Fighting Three pilots up at 5:00 A.M. After eating a hearty breakfast of steak and eggs, the pilots assembled in Ready Two. Despite the fact that these men were getting ready to make a raid on Tokyo, they were quite calm. No nervous tension or jitters; at least they did not show any.

The weather upon the flight deck had become foul. There was only a 300-foot ceiling. Everything was still wet from the rain that had fallen during the night. The large "10" on the flight deck glistened from the wetness caused by the rain and spray.

All around the flight deck and up on the superstructure men were manning the guns, waiting for Japanese planes to approach. In the last few days, the temperature had dropped considerably. It changed from hot, damp days at Ulithi to cold, damp days off the coast of Japan. Gunners now dressed in heavy clothing. The spray and wind from the 30-knot speed made their general-quarter stations miserable although still bearable.

Captain Combs and Admiral Radford discussed last-minute tactics on the bridge, while the pilots waited in the ready rooms for the signal to go. The ticker tape carried a message from Captain Combs. He encouraged the men with his words, and told them The Fighting Lady would be ready for their return. Then the ticker gave the order, "Pilots, man your planes."

When the pilots walked out onto the wind-swept flight deck, the Airdales had their planes ready. As each pilot boarded his plane, he made a check of everything to see if all was in order. Then, each plane was revved-up to check the instruments, oil pressure, and other items.

Soon all the planes were ready, and the first plane taxied into position. The roar became louder as the pilot reached for maximum rpm's. Then the signal was given, and he released his brakes. Quickly he picked up speed as he rolled down the flight deck toward the large "10." Almost near the edge, the little F6F rose into the air. As this plane cleared the deck, another rolled down on the opposite side. For the next few minutes the planes alternated in this pattern until all the planes were airborne and heading for Tokyo. On the flight deck an eerie silence ensued. Just seconds before, the deck had been deafeningly loud with the roar of engines; now all that could be heard were small sounds, and a few men talking.

In CIC Cooper Bright, Jimmy Smith, Commander Myron T. Evans, and others listened to the pilots' conversations on the radio. Occasionally a pilot would mention the weather or the rough job that had to be done that day. The men in the CIC were forced to play a waiting game. The men of Air Group Three were now on their own. They had been well prepared, but now all that the crew of The Fighting Lady could do was to get ready for the pilots' return and to wait.

By 9:00 A.M. Bill McLeroy, Robert E. Lee, Joe Mayers, and the others neared the city of Tokyo. Intercepters were sent up by the Japanese to knock the attackers out of the sky. Mayers and the others had expected this, but they did not expect what they saw next. The Japanese had run so low on planes that they were now flying pre-World War II biplanes into action. For a few seconds the men of Air Group Three were startled, but as the biplanes attacked, the pilots flew into action. Quickly, the F6F's chewed up the older planes, and sent them spinning out of control to the ground.

Elsewhere, other Japanese planes took to the air. As the flight neared Tokyo, an "Oscar" intercepted one of the planes of Air Group Three. Seeing that he was no match for the F6F, the Japanese pilot turned to escape the deadly guns of the highly manueverable fighter. As the F6F pilot closed the range, his guns spitting lead, the Japanese pilot jumped from the plane. At once the *Yorktown* pilot stopped shooting and watched. The Japanese pilot was not wearing a parachute. The F6F pilot watched as the unfortunate Japanese pilot neared his death. Then it was over; he had hit the ground with a deadly thud and then bounced once into the air. Why the pilot jumped was a mystery. His plane had not been hit and he had no parachute, yet he jumped to his death.

Because this pilot was watching the Japanese pilot fall, he failed to notice that the Oscar had made a shallow turn and was about to collide with his F6F. Although startled by the plane on its collision path with his, the pilot fired a short burst. The Oscar exploded in flames, then crashed into pieces when it hit the ground.

Over the radios, pilots could be heard talking as they made contact with the enemy. Although some Japanese planes got into the air to intercept the flyers from the *Yorktown*, most were caught on the ground at Konoike. These planes were soon left burning. Their mission over, Mayers, Lee, and the others returned to the carrier.

On the *Yorktown*, Cooper Bright, Jimmy Smith, J. Bryan III, and others in CIC were still in the dark as to what was happening over Tokyo. The time was now 11:00 A.M., and the waiting was beginning to get to them. The waiting was becoming difficult, but then the *Yorktown's* planes neared the ship. Soon Dick Tripp was bringing each plane in carefully, as he had so many times before. As each plane landed, the arresting-gear officer, Angie Pecciant, would have his crew get the cable off the hook and get ready for the next plane.

Plane after plane landed without incident. Then the bull horn warned of a damaged plane's approaching, and the men watched the stern of the ship anxiously. Dick gently brought the pilot down the groove, and then waved for him to cut his power. The plane, an F6F, settled softly down onto the deck. The arresting gear caught the hook, and the plane came to a stop. As the pilot taxied the plane forward, J. Bryan III noticed that the plane had twelve feet of its port wing shot away including the whole aileron.

Throughout the day, strikes were made against

Tokyo. While the strikes were organizing in the air over the ship, two *Yorktown* planes collided in mid-air. There were a few anxious moments, but the pilots managed to keep control of the planes. Preparations were made for the crippled planes to attempt a landing. Within minutes, the two pilots had their planes safely back aboard ship.

The last plane landed on the deck as the wet darkness settled upon the ship. The day's tally was fifty Japanese planes shot down out of the air and seventy-three planes destroyed on the ground. The men of Air Group Three earned their pay on February 16.

As darkness settled, general quarters was sounded. The Japanese liked to attack American ships as night fell. Eager eyes searched the darkness for any bogey that might manage to sneak through under the radar.

Elsewhere on the ship men listened to a broadcast of Tokyo Rose which was piped throughout the ship. Tokyo Rose talked in a warning manner. "*Yorktown*, we know that you raided Tokyo, and by tomorrow you, The Fighting Lady, will be on the bottom of the Pacific Ocean. Remember, *Yorktown*, you are a doomed carrier." But the *Yorktown* was avenging her predecessor.

The next day the *Yorktown* was again getting ready to launch strikes against Tokyo. As on every strike day, the pilots were up early and had a hearty breakfast. While the pilots were getting ready for the mission, the Airdales on the flight deck were getting the planes ready.

In the darkness, men were called to general

quarters. Ted Rohrbough, Edward Johnson, Don Seaman, Ed Wallace, and the others assigned to the guns rushed to their stations. In this northern climate in the wind caused by the forward motion of the ship, the men were soon wide awake. Cold, brisk air made the men wish they were now in Ulithi basking in the ninety-degree heat.

Soon it was evident that the coldness had made the engines of the planes so stiff that the starting cartridges would not turn the engines over quick enough to start. Men were soon put to the laborious task of pulling the prop to limber-up the cold engines. In this way compression was built up in plane after plane until each roared to life.

After all the planes were warmed up, Pappy Harshman gave the order, "All pilots man your planes!" Leaving the ready rooms, each pilot walked briskly to his plane, not so much out of an eagerness to fly, but simply to get out of the cold. Soon the first plane roared down the flight deck followed by another and another until the deck was left empty. Again, all the other men of the *Yorktown* could do now was to wait, and be ready for the planes' return.

Again the planes met with resistance over Tokyo. One pilot closed in on a Zero and shot a burst into the plane. As smoke poured from the Zero, its pilot climbed from the cockpit. The Japanese pilot lost his hold, and the force of the wind threw him into the rear tail section of his own plane, killing him instantly. As he fell, his chute opened and the dead man floated gently to earth.

As the planes returned to The Fighting Lady, the

bull horn blasted out a warning. An F6F was coming in for his landing. The plane, number two, had lost its tail hook. Standing on his small platform near the stern of the flight deck, Dick waved the paddles, showing the pilot how to get in the groove. Lieutenant Reitel was making his approach well and Dick gave him the signal to land. Upon hitting the slick flight deck, the F6F started skidding toward the wire barrier at seventy-knots. Within seconds the F6F hit the wire barrier. This slammed the feisty little fighter down onto the deck, nose first. Its spinning prop gouged chunks of wood from the flight deck. Reitel fell forward in the straps that held him in the plane. His arms fell out of the cockpit. Then the plane fell back onto the deck with a jolt. As men raced to the plane, Reitel climbed out of the F6F. He was shaken, but unhurt.

As night fell, the men welcomed a friend, Lieutenant Frank Onion. He had been shot down on February 16 in his F6F while raiding Tokyo. He came aboard and the men of Air Group Three were glad to see him. Looking at his hand, they noticed a bandage. Frank had lost one of his fingers when his plane was hit by enemy fire. Now that he was back aboard the *Yorktown*, he would be able to rest with friends. He had been lucky.

Again Tokyo Rose singled out the *Yorktown*. It seemed that the title of The Fighting Lady was getting to be known by the Japanese as well as by the Americans.

As the *Yorktown* left the Tokyo area, the marines were getting ready to invade Iwo Jima. This island had been hit by the *Yorktown* on June 15, 1944, just a few days before the Marianas Turkey Shoot. This time the Americans were coming to stay. Once again the *Yorktown* would pound the island with bombs. This island was near the Japanese homeland, so a fight was expected from the enemy.

As the *Yorktown* was steaming south to attack the island, a submarine was picked up on sonar by a screening destroyer. Quickly the destroyer went into action, dropping depth charges in a pattern, trying to kill the sub. Soon the sea was covered with exploding funnels of water. For several minutes the destroyer dropped the ash cans, but no contact was ever made. After a while contact was lost. The sub never attempted to make a hit.

For the next two days the pilots of Air Group Three pounded Iwo Jima, trying to help their land counterparts take the island. While the *Yorktown* was hitting the island, the old *Saratoga* was undergoing an ordeal that almost finished her.

The Sara had been operating with the Big E as a night carrier in Task Group 58.5. On February 21 she was assigned to the amphibious fleet just off the coast of Iwo Jima. She was almost at her destination when six kamikazes came out of the sky. The Sara was the largest carrier the Americans had. Sinking her would be a real victory for the Japanese.

At 4:59 P.M. the six planes made their death-dives toward the ship. Gunners put up a hail of deadly fire, covering the sky with black puffs of smoke. The first two planes were hit, and they crashed into the ocean with a bounce. But their bombs then bounced against the Sara and exploded near the waterline.

Plane number three sighted into the forward area of the flight deck. Flying through the deadly anti-aircraft fire, he managed to crash his plane into the flight deck.

The fourth plane was knocked out of the air, but the fifth also managed to break through. He, too, crashed into the forward area of the flight deck.

As gunners fired at plane number six, its pilot sighted toward the deck where the others had hit. Gunners were firing at the plane while he was sighting them in. He was going to try to take them out with him. He came closer, each side exchanged gunfire. The gunners stayed and fired at the plane. Then it hit. Parts of the plane smashed into the gun gallery, killing the men at the guns, the rest of the plane went over the side. The Sara was hurt and hurt badly.

Within three minutes she had sustained five bomb hits. The flight deck was damaged and fires raged everywhere. Men covered the flight deck with foam. Elsewhere corpsmen aided the wounded, while the chaplains comforted the dying. Down in the engine rooms, the engineers managed to keep the ship going at twenty-five-knots.

Aboard the Sara were two brothers from Flatwoods, Kentucky. They were Jesse and Eddy Clark. Each was at his general-quarters station and neither knew whether the other had survived. Each did his duty, trying not to think about the other. After two hours, order returned to the Sara. The two brothers each decided to go to the other's station to find out if he was safe.

Each brother walked toward the other's station,

and, to each other's surprise, they met in a passageway. While they asked about one another, general quarters sounded. The ship was secured, so they had to stay where they were.

Five more kamikazes came toward the ship. The first four were knocked from the air before they had a chance to hit. The fifth flew through the antiaircraft fire, and crashed near some guns on the flight deck. Flames from the exploding plane licked the air. Fire fighters fought the flames, and soon had them under control. By 8:15 P.M. the Sara was again recovering her own planes.

After the attack, the men were able to go about the ship again. Jesse and Eddy returned to their stations as soon as possible. Jesse went back to his compartment below decks, while Eddy returned to his gun mount. At least he returned to the area. The mount had been destroyed and most of its men killed. Fate had allowed Eddy to be away from his gun on that day, at that instant. Shaking, he looked at the blackened wreckage.

The Sara had lost 123 men; 192 others were wounded. She continued on toward the amphibious fleet, to wait until the *Enterprise* could take her place. In the small fleet was the escort carrier the *Bismark Sea*. Throughout the night, the Japanese attacked the small escort carriers.

At 6:45 P.M. the *Lunga Point* came under attack. The *Bismark Sea* opened fire and destroyed the attacking Betty. A few seconds later another Betty came toward the *Bismark Sea*. As the plane approached the ship, the gunners opened fire, and continued firing until the plane came so close that the

179

gunners could not get their guns down low enough to hit the plane. The kamikaze exploded into the side of the ship at 6:47 P.M.

The explosion sent the elevator down onto the hangar deck. With the cables parted, the elevator was now useless. The main water-line was broken, so there was no water to fight the fires on the hangar deck. Bombs rolled into the fires, and the open elevator shaft served as a beacon for another kamikaze. One pilot made a vertical dive right into the flaming inferno, adding to the destruction. Soon the ship was flaming from stem to stern. With no water to fight the fires, the captain gave the order to abandon ship at 7:00 P.M.

As the men raced over the side, the flames grew hotter. When the last boat had pulled a safe distance away, a torpedo exploded aboard the *Bismark Sea*. She burned and exploded for the next two hours, and at 9:15 P.M. she rolled over and sank. With the *Bismark Sea* went the lives of 218 men.

Jesse Clark, aboard the damaged *Saratoga,* watched as the ship sank. Aboard the *Bismark Sea* was a friend of his. Only after the war did he learn that his friend had survived that terrible night.

Back aboard the *Yorktown*, the prisoner of war, "Little Tojo," was regaining his strength. His leg was now in a cast, and several of the men signed their names on it. Lieutenant Commander J. Bryan III visited Sadao almost daily. Sadao still wanted to join the United States Navy and become a crew member of The Fighting Lady.

Later that night, a bogey appeared off the port side of the ship. The five-inch guns opened up with their loud "bam, bam," followed by the 40-mm guns. The 40's flicked red streaks into the dark sky, searching, climbing for the bogey. On the flight deck was an F6F-N, getting ready to go on night patrol. The pilot was sitting in the plane as the number one, five-inch mount cut loose with a few rounds of fire. The plane was directly under the muzzle of the gun as the crew swung the gun across the flight deck. When the first round went off, it shattered the canopy of the F6F and left the pilot dazed. Within seconds the gun stopped firing, but the damage was already done. Later, upon investigation of the F6F-N, it was noted the skin had caved in, the ribs were bent out of shape, and the rivets were cut from the skin.

Aft of the superstructure was a TBM. The aft gun had destroyed it also when the crew fired across the flight deck. The concussion had left the skin hanging loosely on the frame. Both planes were destroyed beyond repair. They were cannibalized, then tossed overboard.

After the airstrikes against Iwo Jima, the *Yorktown* turned north to strike at Tokyo once more before retiring to Ulithi. Aboard the carrier was a pilot from the carrier *San Jacinto*, and with him were the two crew members of his TBM. They had gone down at sea on February 21, and had been picked up by the destroyer *Hazlewood*. She then transferred them to the *Yorktown*. Today the destroyer *Craven* was going to pick them up, and send them back to the *San Jacinto*.

Quickly the men in the Fourth Division made plans to rig a bos'n's chair between the *Craven* and the *Yorktown*. Ted Rohrbough and the others had done this dozens of times before, and were proud of the fact they had never lost a person or a piece of cargo. As the sea foamed between the two ships, the TBM crew looked down at the white froth. The pilot was especially nervous, and jokingly requested a last breakfast.

Soon the chair was secured, and ready for the first passenger. Slowly the pilot positioned himself in the chair, took one last look around, and was sent on his way. The chair swung gently back and forth, with the white foam about thirty feet below the pilot's feet. Swinging and bouncing, the chair made its way across the water to the *Craven*. The pilot climbed out, then shook his head. Following close behind were his two crewmen.

Once the operation was over, Commander John W. Brady aboard the *Yorktown* told the *Craven* "Thank you!" and the *Craven* pulled away with her cargo.

Next, the tanker *Marias* pulled alongside, and once again, the men in the Fourth Division made connections with the ship. This time they connected fuel hoses, and the *Yorktown* gulped down precious tons of fuel oil.

While the *Yorktown* was taking fuel from the *Marias*, the cruiser *Biloxi* pulled alongside the tanker for fuel also. As she pulled near, the signalman started sending a message to the *Yorktown*. Signalman Joe Leathers read the message. The *Biloxi* was requesting some new movies.

As J. Bryan III entered the wardroom, he noticed a cartoon on the bulletin board. It showed George

Earnshaw, a former baseball pitcher and the current gunnery boss aboard the *Yorktown*, sticking his head out of a five-inch gun mount, looking at the wreckage of an F6F-N and a TBM. Below was a caption which read, "Three more and I'll be an ace!"

As *Yorktown* neared Tokyo, the sea began to kick up. The screening destroyers were bouncing over the ocean, and even the carrier was pitching a little. This made it difficult to land a plane. A pilot can fly down the groove without trouble, only to have the stern of the ship rise or fall as he cuts power for a landing. Navy pilots had to be the best in the world, yet even they could make mistakes.

As The Fighting Lady pitched from a height of twenty feet, a lone plane from the *Randolph* made its approach to land. Dick had him lined up properly, but just as the pilot let his wheels touch the flight deck, a large swell lifted the stern. The F6F slammed hard onto the deck. The shock jolted the six guns on the F6F and they fired a short burst; then the belly tank broke loose and slammed into the spinning propeller. The cleaver cut a chunk out of the tank, and gasoline poured onto the flight deck. Instantly, a spark ignited the gasoline. The F6F was engulfed in orange flames, yet the pilot managed to get out of it with only slight burns.

When the guns from the F6F went off, the bullets struck eleven men, wounding them slightly. Later it was also noticed that five planes spotted forward were damaged by the bullets. The landing of the *Randolph* plane would be remembered for a long time to come by the men who witnessed it.

The next morning, the *Yorktown* made ready for another raid against Tokyo. As the pilots took to the air, the flight deck crews watched and were glad the planes had taken off without mishap. On cold, damp mornings like that it was dangerous to be on the flight deck. With the spinning propellers kicking up high gusts of wind, it was easy to lose your balance on the wet, wooden flight deck.

One morning, one of the plane's captains waved a plane off. As the plane took off, the wind blew toward him. The deck was wet and slippery, and when the officer realized that he was being blown backwards, he attempted to drop to the deck. If there had been a few seconds more, he might have made it, but instead he fell into the whirling propeller of the plane behind him. He was killed instantly. A live flight deck was indeed extremely dangerous, especially on wet days.

As the men of Air Group Three winged over Tokyo, they met with resistance. The antiaircraft fire slowly climbed up to them. Joe Mayer was flying his F6F over the city when he felt the plane lunge to starboard. Looking quickly, he noticed his starboard wing had been hit. A 20-mm shell had found its way to his plane. Although only slightly damaged, Joe was still worried. Joe was highly superstitious and his plane was number thirteen. Only when he was safely back aboard the ship was he relaxed.

Joe had been keeping a list of happenings involving the number "13." The first man killed in Fighting Three was flying number thirteen. Aboard the *Ommaney Bay*, four out of five crack-ups involved planes with the number thirteen. The *Langley* once had a fire on the hangar deck. Of the five planes destroyed, three were Number thirteens. Joe feared the number "13."

That night Tokyo Rose called on the *Yorktown* again. She began, "Hello Fighting Lady, we know that you are still around Tokyo. All you sailors aboard the Fighting Lady, you have only a short time to live. The *Yorktown* will be sunk at all costs. I have forty suicide planes waiting especially for you. Remember, *Yorktown*, you are a doomed carrier."

The Japanese kept the crew of the *Yorktown* busy all day, and it was after 9:00 P.M. before most of the crew ate dinner.

After the raid against Tokyo, the *Yorktown* went back to Ulithi Bay. She steamed into the bay on March 1, 1945. As The Fighting Lady slowly made way to her berth, Admiral Radford came out onto the flag bridge and leaned on the railing. He looked all around at the other ships in the bay, up at the warm sun, and commented, "Nice trip."

Now that the *Yorktown* was in Ulithi, the men could go about their duties in more leisurely fashion. Shirts could now be unbuttoned and sleeves rolled up again. After the cold of the waters off Tokyo, the warm weather near the equator felt good. Cold-weather gear was put away for another day.

As spring rolled around, the crew started thinking about man's favorite subject, woman. One of the men, PhM3c Sam S. Pearl, decided that the ship should have a beauty contest; but where in the Pacific could he find eligible females? Then the idea hit him to write to *Life* magazine asking for entries from the millions of females in the United States.

Sam approached several of the crew and told them of his idea. Immediately, the men got together and wrote a letter to *Life*. They asked the editors to print their letter. The crew members hoped to get several contestants eager to earn the title "Miss Fighting Lady"; only time would tell.

When Little Tojo was told he would be taken to a hospital on the islands, he just sat in his bed with his head lowered. Soon after anchoring, he was sent off to the hospital. Sadao told Bill Klaus he would write him, and that he still wanted to join the United States Navy.

Smokers were planned for the crew to help them unwind, to relieve tension, and just to provide entertainment. Edward Johnson still held the lightweight boxing title and he could put on some pretty fair matches. Ed was in the Third Division as a 40-mm gunner. The Fourth Division had a champ also. He was Seaman Spickowski and he was the heavyweight champion aboard the *Yorktown*. Spickowski had one fight in which he knocked out his opponent just a few seconds into the first round.

The men who did not take an interest in boxing did other things to entertain themselves. One popular form of sport was the three-legged race. The spectators would line the edge of the flight deck while different divisions competed for the title. Down the flight deck they would race; every now and then one team would fall down, to the delight of the spectators. Pie-eating contests were also held. The winner of these would get a trophy—a pie.

But the form of entertainment that all the crew enjoyed was watching movies. When the *Yorktown* would finish her stock of films, she would contact another ship and work up an exchange. In this manner, new movies were taken aboard whenever the crew had a chance. Now that the war was nearing its end, the Japanese were fighting more fiercely. The only time movies could be seen was when the ship was in Ulithi.

Radio broadcasts were still coming from Tokyo, and Tokyo Rose was still singling out the *Yorktown* as a doomed carrier.

The weekend had rolled around, and Saturday night was movie night. This night the movie was entitled *Hollywood Canteen*. It was a musical with Spanish dancers doing traditional Spanish dances. With this movie, Captain Combs hoped to soothe the men's nerves. He read from the Plan of the Day, asking the men to guard against sour dispositions, and not to give the Japanese the satisfaction of causing quarrels among shipmates aboard the *Yorktown*. Tokyo Rose liked to tell the sailors about wives and girl friends back home who went out with men left behind. This played on the nerves of some men, even though their wives and girl friends stayed at home every night. Evil thoughts planted by Tokyo Rose could, in time, come to torment a man unendurably, until he finally took his anger out on his shipmates.

Fighting Three went over to Mog Mog for a little party one afternoon. Things were going along quite well until one of the pilots decided to pick on a marine there. One of the men, Gashouse, had drunk just enough to want to start some trouble. He walked over to a marine lieutenant, grabbed his paper cup filled with bourbon and Coke, and squeezed the cup until the contents spilled out over the marine's uniform. The marine grabbed Gashouse by the shirt collar, and was getting ready to strike him in the face when Bill McLeroy stepped between the two. He managed to get Gashouse away before any fighting started.

Aboard the *Yorktown* during those warm days in Ulithi, Ruben Kitchen made a stainless-steel jewelry case. Some of the other men in the R-1 Division were making large cases, but he had decided to make a smaller one. He did this in order to save time, but the smaller case actually took him longer to make. Everything had to be scaled down, which took time. The other men used items found in the ship's stores; Ruben had to custom-make all his parts.

On March 8, The Fighting Lady welcomed aboard another air group. Air Group Three left the ship with quite an impressive record. These men had shot down 91 enemy planes, destroyed another 166 planes on the ground, sunk 28 ships, and damaged 75 other ships. Their "probables" were 19 planes shot down, 260 planes destroyed on the ground, 18 ships sunk. Joe Mayer, Robert E. Lee, Bill McLeroy, Bob Thienes, Carl Carlson, Fritz Wolfe, Peter Grace, and the others of Air Group Three had left the *Yorktown*, but they would always be a part of The Fighting Lady.

Air Group Nine came aboard. Among these men were Jack Kitchen, Bill Ogdon, Val Valiquet,

Eugene A. Valencia, Harris E. Mitchell, Clinton L. Smith, and James B. French. It would be these men and their comrades who would fly from the decks of The Fighting Lady in the next few months, months that would be the worst in the *Yorktown's* history.

The day after Air Group Nine came aboard, Captain Combs put the *Yorktown* to sea to exercise the new pilots and to see how well they could handle themselves. Also, George Earnshaw and Pat Patterson wanted to give their gunnery boys a workout.

After the *Yorktown* got out of range of Ulithi, the tow planes flew nearby pulling target sleeves. When the planes came into range, the five-inch guns would open up. In one of the gun mounts was Edward N. Wallace. He was a mount captain, and it was his responsibility to see that his mount could fire visually and manually in case fire control was knocked out. On this day, however, fire control was working extremely well, as the following illustrates.

As the first plane came into range, the five-inch guns opened fire. Black bursts of fire filled the sky, until the bursts collided with the sleeve. As the sleeve fell, the men topside cheered, for it would be these gunners as well as the men on the 40's and 20's who would fight off any kamikazes that happened to get through to the *Yorktown*.

Four more planes approached pulling sleeves. Again the five-inch guns opened fire. This time the fire-control people had the range, and three of the four sleeves were knocked from the sky with the opening bursts of fire. George Earnshaw and Pat Patterson had trained the men well.

Next, Air Group Nine decided to show how well

trained they were. One moment not a plane was in sight; and the next instant, the sky was full of F6F's, TBM's and SB2C's. The huge TBM's were flown as if they were agile fighters, while the F6F's flashed by the flight deck. These men were quite impressive; in fact, they were plain good.

After this show of skill, the pilots brought their planes down for landings. They were sloppy in the holding patterns, and Dick Tripp had some trouble in getting the planes down safely. In fact, one of the planes had a barrier-crash, but it was not very serious. As one man said, "Carrier landings are nothing but controlled crashes." Dick was one of the best at landing these controlled crashes.

Even though Captain Combs kept the men busy to occupy their minds, he could not make them forget the heat. Sheets placed on beds were soaked within minutes after a sailor retired for the night. Uniforms and work clothes were the same. Heat rash also managed to get the best of some of the men, even with the fresh-water showers. When the *Yorktown* went to sea, all the men would be able to get would be salt-water showers.

On March 11, Tokyo Rose made her predictions about the *Yorktown* again. After some music, she called out, "*Yorktown*, I have a message for you. Think you're nice and safe at Ulithi, don't you, *Yorktown*? Well, we're fixing up a little surprise for you." She then played more music. All about the *Yorktown* were other carriers, but she picked her out as the next carrier to be hit. The Fighting Lady had earned the respect and hatred of the Japanese. The old "Yorkie" lying at the bottom of the sea near Midway would have been proud to know that her namesake had avenged her death so well that she was constantly being singled out by Radio Tokyo.

That evening the hangar deck was made ready for another movie. This would be the last chance to screen a movie for weeks to come, and there would probably be a big crowd for the night.

As the time for the movie got closer, men from the different divisions started to fill the huge hangar deck. Soon everyone who was free from duty was seated. Voices could be heard throughout, and then the lights were lowered and a hush fell on the crowd. The movie started.

The men were enjoying the movie when suddenly a loud explosion nearby attracted the attention of everyone. Instinctively, almost everyone hit the deck—everyone except Stew Lindsay. When everyone else hit the deck, he stood up for a better look in the direction from which the noise had come. This was a mistake. As he stood up, the man behind him hit the deck, taking Stew down with him. The result was a pair of skinned knees acquired when Stew was forced to the deck.

In Ted Rohrbough's section of the hangar deck there was a mad scramble in the darkness to get to general quarters. In Ruben Kitchen's section the men quickly, but calmly, walked to their stations. Men in different sections reacted differently in this crisis.

When the general quarters alarm went off, the men below decks had lights to help them get to their stations. But for the men who had battle stations on the decks, it was hell. No lights were allowed, and the men had to feel their way to the guns. Men raced up the superstructure and along the catwalk at the edge of the flight deck. Within minutes The Fighting Lady was at battle readiness. Off to her side, flames could be seen climbing in the dark sky toward the stars above. Some of the men began to remember Tokyo Rose's threat of a few hours before.

A kamikaze had crashed into the fantail of the *Randolph*, which was berthed next to the *Yorktown*. The resulting explosion had killed 27 men and wounded 130 more. Two Bettys had flown from Minami Iwo, over 800 miles away, to crash into the ship at Ulithi. Another plane crashed into the island after mistaking it for a carrier.

Fearing more attacks, the ship got underway. Men in the Fourth Division were told to man their boats in case they were needed. Quickly, Ted Rohrbough went to the number two whale boat. The boat was hoisted up on the port side by an electric winch fastened under the flight deck. As the boats were hoisted, the lines had to be kept straight. In the darkness the only way to do this was to feel each cable as the boat was hoisted up. This was done by leaning over the side of the ship, a dangerous job even in the daytime. Ted kept the lines straight with his hands. Finally the boat was ready.

When no planes appeared in the next few hours, the men were released from general quarters. The fleet would stay in Ulithi. The *Randolph* was badly damaged and it would be several weeks before she could engage the Japanese again. The *Yorktown* had missed being a victim by a couple of hundred yards.

The next day the fleet was still a little jumpy from the incident aboard the *Randolph* the night before. At 1:00 P.M. general quarters was sounded, but it was a false alarm. The men were relieved of their stations.

For the next few hours routine aboard the ship was normal. Ruben Kitchen did some work upon the island structure in the captain's quarters. Kenneth Parkinson, Harland Bickford, and the others in the R-1 Division got things ready for the action the *Yorktown* would soon see. The next day The Fighting Lady would leave for Japan.

Dick Tripp, J. Bryan III, and a few other men were in Dick's room putting ice on some beer they had acquired. Suddenly general quarters went off again. Quickly the men raced to their stations, but again the alarm was false. Finally, at 10:30 P.M., most of the crew was able to retire for the night. The beer in Dick's room was just right. Those men had one last beer before leaving Ulithi.

The next day Task Force Fifty-eight was reshuffled again. This time Task Group 58.4 got the *Intrepid*. Several men aboard were glad not to get her, because of the record the *Intrepid* had. She had been hit so many times and had spent so much time in dry dock that she was called "Dry I" by the men of the other ships in the fleet. If anyone got hit, it would be the *Intrepid*.

Chapter VIII

Early on the morning of March 14, Captain Combs eased the mighty *Yorktown* through the nets to open sea. The carrier was the flagship of Task Group 58.4, and was under the command of Rear Admiral Arthur W. Radford. Following closely behind the *Yorktown* were the carriers *Intrepid, Enterprise, Independence,* and *Langley.* Behind the carriers were two battleships. The group was flanked by one light cruiser, two antiaircraft cruisers, and fourteen destroyers. By noon Task Group 58.4 was well at sea. Task Force Fifty-eight followed in formation.

After lunch, replacement planes approached the *Yorktown.* As these planes neared, Captain Combs turned The Fighting Lady into the wind. Dick Tripp took his position on the small platform near the stern, off to the starboard side. With the skill acquired from thousands of landings, Dick brought the planes in without a mishap—all but the last three.

The first of these was an F6F Hellcat. Dick managed to get the plane down safely, but, as the fighter hit the deck, both of its tires blew out. After skidding, the plane came to rest short of the barrier. The pilot was uninjured.

Next an SB2C approached for a landing. The Beast made good its approach, and Dick gave the cut signal. The heavy plane hit the deck, then bounced thirty feet into the air. As the bomber came down upon the deck, its own weight caused its landing gear to collapse. Its prop then cut into the teakwood flight deck. The spinning propeller cut huge gashes into the wood. The prop went all the way into the ACI office below the flight deck. Again, no one was injured.

The last replacement plane to land was an F6F. This plane had to make ten passes before Dick would allow the pilot to land the fighter. Finally all the planes were safely aboard, and the *Yorktown* turned back toward Japan. On the 20-mm gallery below the bridge, one of the men played a harmonica. Flying fish leapt about the carrier.

As darkness fell, the ships of Task Force 58.4 seemed to disappear; only their silhouettes showed up. Only Joe Leathers and the other signalmen could distinguish the battleship *Missouri* from the battleship *Wisconsin*, or the antiaircraft cruiser, *Alaska* from her counterpart, *Guam*. But, after all, that was part of their job. Nearly everyone could tell the difference between the *Intrepid* and the *Enterprise*. As for cruisers, there was only the *St. Louis*.

The fourteen destroyers were more of a challenge.

J. Bryan III read the Plan of the Day, noting again that everyone was to keep his sleeves rolled down and his shirt buttoned. The Fighting Lady was getting ready for combat again.

As the *Yorktown* drew closer to Japan, she took on the fuel needed to fight the enemy, as well as some last minute mail. Two of these letters were from Little Tojo. Sadao had written one letter to Oliver, the pharmacist's mate who had taken care of him. The other was to the entire crew. In it he thanked everyone for the help he had received while aboard the *Yorktown*, and hoped that some day he could become a member of The Fighting Lady.

Flash-proof ointment was issued to all hands. This was a thick, gray cream that dried and caked on the skin. It was supposed to lessen the severity of burns in case of flash fire. Ruben Kitchen, in the shipfitter's shop, decided to test it before he put it on his face. He put a small amount in a pan, and then put a flame to it. It immediately ignited and burned. He got his division officer, Lieutenant Fred Weatherford, and repeated the experiment for him. Fred watched, and decided that each of his men could decide for himself whether to wear it or not. What caused the flash-proof ointment to burn was the alcohol put in it to keep it a cream until it was put on. After a few minutes the alcohol would evaporate, leaving a protective coating. The only question left was, "What if we get hit before the alcohol evaporates?"

On the evening of March 17, Father Moody's voice came over the loudspeaker telling the men what to expect the next day. The men now knew they were headed for Japan.

After Father Moody gave his short talk, Captain Combs told the men to be on guard for anything that might happen, and to be ready at a moment's notice. The kamikazes were beginning to hurt the American Navy in the Pacific, and many could be expected the next day. It was up to the men to keep The Fighting Lady in the war until the end.

As Captain Combs finished his speech, the sound of guns was heard on the flight deck. While an F6F was being respotted, its guns got off a short burst. The wings were folded at the time and the bullets hit six men on the hangar deck who had been working on an SB2C. A lone bullet then went through the flight deck, the hangar deck, the second deck, and two hatches, finally hitting a man who had been in sick bay, on the third deck. Luckily, no one was seriously injured.

That night Ralph Kendrick went down to the shipfitter's shop to visit Ruben Kitchen. Ever since these two had gone to school together, they had kept in contact with each other. As the two sat drinking coffee, they talked about old school days; they were trying to get their minds off the action coming up. Finally, after about thirty minutes, Ralph returned to his area. Each man would need his rest on the next day.

Early the next morning the pilots of Air Group Nine ate their breakfast of steak and eggs. After a hearty breakfast, the men retired to the ready rooms to learn about their targets. They were going to hit airfields on the island of Kyushu. As they went over

197

the tactics of the strike, a civilian was upon the flag bridge. He was Ralph Delahaye Paine, publisher of *Fortune* magazine. Admiral Radford had given him permission to watch from there. He would have a ringside seat for the action that was to come about.

General quarters had been sounded an hour before daylight. Men were ready for the Japanese, for the men who believed in dying for the emperor.

At 5:00 A.M. the pilots walked to their planes. Seventeen minutes later the first F6F left the deck, passing over the newly painted "10" on the bow of the flight deck. Soon Eugene Valencia, Harris Mitchell, Clinton Smith, James French, Johnny Orth, Jack Kitchen, and the others were in the sky heading toward Kyushu, Japan. Their targets were the airfields.

While these men were flying toward Japan, others were flying toward the *Yorktown*. Kamikaze pilots were flying toward the carrier hoping through their deaths to bring death to the *Yorktown*. These men had trained for weeks under Captain Motoharu Okamura. On this day fifty of them would fly to their deaths and to glory. That is the way the Japanese saw it.

At 7:37 A.M. the first enemy plane was sighted. A bogey had broken through and dropped a bomb onto the deck of the *Enterprise*. The bomb failed to explode, but it started a small fire, killed one man, and wounded two more. The *Enterprise* quickly put out the fire and continued operations within thirty minutes.

At 8:00 A.M. it was the *Yorktown's* turn. Off to the port was a "Frances." The pilot had the twin engine bomber on a direct path toward The Fighting Lady. As the pilot sighted his plane toward the ship, guns opened up, firing at the dealer-of-death. As he came closer, the five-inch guns increased fire. The bomber was directly over the destroyer *Melvin* when both engines exploded in flames. The pilot tried to hold his course, but crashed into the sea 1,500 yards off the starboard bow. The five-inch guns hit the plane almost as soon as they opened fire. George Earnshaw's men had been well trained. Two men aboard the *Melvin* were wounded by fragments when the plane exploded.

Five minutes later another Frances dived on the *Intrepid*. The plane came toward the *Intrepid* and the guns fired away at the plane. As it got closer, it seemed that the pilot would succeed in his mission. Finally the plane was shot down, but she had been knocked out of the sky so close to the ship that water from her crash sprayed over the bridge of the carrier. Fragments of the plane killed one man and wounded thirteen more. Of the three carriers in Task Group 58.4, all had been attacked, but only the *Yorktown* remained unhit. The Lucky Y still had her luck with her.

Later in the day, guns from the other ships opened fire on a lone plane. The *Yorktown's* guns remained silent. The reason for this was that the lone plane was an F6F. The pilot tried to convince the gunners that he was friendly, but was knocked from the sky before he could get his message across. The gunners on the other ships felt bad about shooting down one of our own, but the jitters had got the best of them.

At 12:00 noon, lunch was served to the crew. The ship was at modified affirmed, so the men ate sandwiches and soup at their battle stations. The gunners ate while scanning the sky for enemy planes. Below decks the men ate and listened for sounds from above to get an idea of what was going on outside. To the men below decks, war was a waiting game; this was especially true for the men in damage control. Only when the ship received a hit did these men go into action.

Ralph Paine was getting some stories for his magazine. This was turning out to be the busiest day in the *Yorktown's* career. Today he would really have a story to write.

As the day dragged on the men were tense with the excitement and the cold. This was winter in the sea off Japan. The gunners and their loaders stood near their guns in the thirty knot winds. The air was cold, but the forward motion of the ship made it seem about twenty degrees colder to anyone exposed to it. Hot, black coffee helped to ward the chill off.

Just forward of the number two elevator was a battery of 20-mm guns. The marine division aboard The Fighting Lady fired these guns, but some sailors acted as loaders. One of these men was Joseph Huber. During general quarters, he acted as a loader, but at other times he was a mailman third class in the K-Y Division. He was helping scan the sky, when at 1:09 P.M., a "Judy" appeared off the bow of the ship.

The kamikaze began his dive toward The Fighting Lady. Every gun in the task group fired at the single engine bomber. As the plane neared, the guns aboard the ship opened fire at it. The starboard five-inch guns opened fire, throwing their ejected brass onto the flight deck. All the forward guns fired. Joe Huber loaded his 20-mm gun as quickly as the marine gunner fired. Joe could see that the plane was coming directly toward them. That made his gun crew fire even more efficiently. The kamikaze approached. Black puffs of smoke exploded all around the plane. Joe and his gunner stayed, firing their 20-mm gun. If the plane hit, they would probably be killed, but they were trained to stay and slug it out with the plane.

Just as it began to seem that these would be their last moments on earth, the plane faltered and crashed into the sea. Just before the plane crashed, the pilot dropped his bomb. The projectile fell toward the ship, and hit the water near the number two elevator and Joe Huber's gun. Brown water fountained into the air higher than the stack of the ship, only seventy-five feet away. As Joe and the others looked up the ship seemed to jump high out of the water. They would live another day to fight again. Several of the men noticed that they were not cold anymore. The tension had caused their blood to race through their bodies, warming them to the point of sweating.

Down in repair three, Ruben Kitchen, Ken Parkinson, and the others felt the ship jump out of the water. They were sitting on the deck at the time, and each man bounced a few inches into the air from the concussion of the near miss. Lieutenant Fred Weatherford was sitting nearby waiting for orders over the phone, but after a few minutes realized that the Lucky Y had escaped damage again.

As the men in repair three sat out the fighting, they were bounced again less than eight minutes later. These men were three decks below, and they could only guess at what was happening topside. All they could do was wait for orders to go to some damaged area. Again they did not receive a call, and again the Lucky Y had escaped a hit.

When the second Judy came in for the kill, she was flying only 500 feet above sea level. Quickly the gunners zeroed in on the plane. The pilot dropped his bomb which crashed into the water only 100 feet off the starboard side. He then proceeded to fly by the deadly fire of the gunners. As the pilot flew along the starboard side, the gunners flamed him and he crashed into the sea just astern of the ship.

Down on the seventh deck in central damage control, the men felt the jar from the bomb more than some men in other parts of the ship. The shock waves knocked the two gyros out of commission. Without these the *Yorktown* would pitch more than usual. Quickly the eight men here put the gyros back into commission. The ship never stopped because the sea was fairly calm. Still the Lucky Y had never been hit by enemy action; near misses that do not kill or wound anyone are not considered hits.

It was now 2:30 P.M. The crew had been at general quarters since before dawn. The gunners were getting tired; they had put in a hard day so far; in fact, everyone had put in a hard day.

Ralph Paine was taking notes on the day's activities for his article in *Fortune* magazine. The movie The Fighting Lady had caused quite a stir back home. People were wanting to read more about the carrier that was helping to defeat the Japanese. Millions had seen the film, and it was only now that the public was learning the identity of the ship. Stories of the *Yorktown* were good selling material.

As the day dragged on, Don Seaman and his turning operator, Elmer Jekel, were scanning the sky for planes while they drank hot coffee to help keep warm. It had been over an hour since they had come under attack, and the ship was at modified affirmed. Next to Elmer was the gunner of the other 20-mm gun, Powell Barnette. He was a quiet man with little to say.

Upon the superstructure in quad seven was Edward Johnson. He was a loader on gun number three, which was located just aft of the funnel. From here Ed had seen lots of action, especially when all the planes landed on the deck. He had one of the best seats in the house for observing landings.

Down in repair three on the third deck, Lieutenant Weatherford decided to go up to check on the other stations under his command. Since the ship was at modified affirmed, this was perfectly legal. He left telling the men in the repair three locker that he would be back soon.

Edward Wallace checked the batteries of three quad mounts located on the starboard side of the ship along the hangar deck. He was in charge of these mounts which had been put on in Bremerton, Washington, during the last fitting-out stateside.

The afternoon was still chilly. At 2:45 P.M. one of

the flights began returning from the raid. The boys of Air Group Nine had done considerable damage on Kyushu, and this flight was getting ready to land for the day.

As the planes approached for a landing, the assistant landing officer, Lee Spaulding, went up to relieve the weary Dick Tripp. Dick was glad to be relieved, because the cold cut right through him out on the platform.

Lee brought the first plane down safely; but as the second plane landed, two live rockets were jarred loose from its wings. All along the flight deck men ducked to avoid the skidding rockets. After the rockets stopped, several of the flight-deck men raced out to get rid of the rockets before they had a chance to explode. One man walked over to one of the live rockets, picked it up, patted it on its warhead, and then tossed it over the side of the flight deck.

The fifth plane to land could not get his tail-hook down. The F6F, number fifty-seven, made three approaches without success. Each time Lee would wave him off. It was decided to let him make a fourth pass. As he came down the groove, the five-inch guns on the flight deck began turning toward the starboard. A Judy had dropped out of the clouds unexpectedly and was dead ahead.

Seconds after the plane was sighted, its pilot dropped his bomb. This travelled almost horizontally toward the ship.

The gunners managed to knock the Judy out of the sky as its pilot attempted to pull his plane out of the run. The pilot was picked up, but the other man in the plane was killed. As the gunners were shooting the Judy out of the sky, the *Yorktown* was hit by the enemy.

The bomb hit the starboard side of the signal bridge and sheared smooth a brass rim on the porthole of Admiral Radford's sea cabin. The bomb then ripped a squawkbox off the bulkhead, slashed two small pipes, and tore out a two-foot section of the incinerator vent. The bomb cut through steel like a knife through butter.

Next, it cut a five-foot hole out of the deck of the signal bridge, just in front of the hatch coming out of the superstructure. J. Bryan III was on the port side of the bridge at the time, watching number fifty-seven try to land. Chief Mueck, the flag's chief signalman, was on the starboard side of the bridge. What he would see in the next few seconds would startle him.

Only a second had passed since the bomb had hit the ship. The next few seconds would change the lives of twenty-three men. Without warning, the bomb hit the 20-mm gun gallery below the signal bridge. Don Seaman was firing his gun when he saw his turning operator, Elmer Jekel, fall. The bomb's fins had cut his legs off as the bomb passed by him.

Over on gun mount five, next to mount seven, (Don's mount) the gunner, Paul Barnette, was hanging in his harness. The fins had also cut his legs off, and he hung there with his life's blood dripping from his stumps into the hole on the deck left by the path of the bomb. The two men were fatally wounded, but still alive. Before Don could help his turning operator, the bomb exploded below the gun gallery.

But before the bomb exploded, it had travelled to the level of the hangar deck and exploded in one of the new 40-mm gun mounts put on at Bremerton, Washington. The explosion wiped out this mount, killing one man and fatally wounding another. Other men were wounded, but not fatally.

As the explosion forced its way upward and inward, it wounded many more men and killed one more. Ed Johnson, on the superstructure in the aft 40-mm gun mount, was thrown about fifteen feet into the air. The blast threw Ed backward, which probably saved his life. If he had gone forward, he would have been tossed overboard into the water seventy-feet below; and, if he were wounded, this would have meant certain death. Instead, he came back down upon his gun.

Lieutenant Fred Weatherford had left repair three just a few minutes before, while the ship was at modified affirmed. When the ship went to general quarters because the planes were returning from their strike, he was not able to return to repair three. Seeing that he would have to stay up on the hangar deck, he went to the shipfitter's bunk room to rest. He entered the bunkroom and decided to lie down on James Mack's bunk. There he rested, waiting for modified affirmed so he could return to repair three on the third deck.

Lieutenant Weatherford probably never knew what hit him. When the bomb exploded, it riddled the bulkhead next to the bunk he was lying in. The bunkroom was turned into junk in an instant. The life of Fred Weatherford was wiped out. Lieutenant Weatherford was the only officer killed by the bomb.

Down in repair three, Ruben Kitchen, Ken Parkinson, and others were playing cards to pass the time. Unknown to them, the bomb was making its way down the side of the ship. Suddenly, they were all lifted about a foot off the deck, then slammed back down upon it. They knew the ship had been hit, but where? and how bad? They did not know that their leader and friend, Fred Weatherford, had been killed.

Quickly, Ruben picked up the headphones and listened for orders. They were not called. Crews on the other decks would handle the damage. Again it was a waiting game for them.

The bomb had done its damage. Holes were ripped into the side of the ship. Some men were killed, others were wounded. Small fires had started. Mount seven was burning, while mount five was silent. One 40-mm quad was wiped out, and a five-inch battery was out of commission.

As the smoke began to clear, men rushed to the aid of the wounded and dying. Edward Wallace rushed to the 40-mm quad that was under his command. When he got there, he saw the destruction. Men were lying about everywhere, bleeding and moaning. Ed could clearly see that mount thirteen was the point of explosion for the bomb. This mount was ruined. The men remaining there were lucky not to be dead.

Within seconds after the bomb had exploded, Father Moody was rushed out onto the flight deck to give aid where it was needed. As Father Moody rounded the corner of the island, he saw a marine rubbing his eyes and screaming in pain. His eyes

207

were bleeding from fragments that had hit him in the face. Lying beside this marine was another marine. He had a large gash in his leg, and he was clasping the wound trying to stop the flow of blood. Quickly, Father Moody got three corpsmen to help him and rush the two wounded men to battle dressing one, located at the forward end of the superstructure.

Up higher on the superstructure the men of the 20-mm gun gallery were lying in a clipping room. They had been moved there by sailors to protect them from the elements. There were six wounded men lying on the deck when Father Moody arrived there. Two of the six had their legs cut off, two were stretcher cases; and the other two were able to walk by themselves.

Father Moody leaned down beside Elmer Jekel. Father Moody could tell that Elmer was in shock from the loss of his legs. Carefully, Father Moody lifted Elmer onto a stretcher and helped carry him down the ladder to battle dressing one. As Father Moody and the corpsman carried Elmer into the small compartment, Dr. Bond was bandaging a burnt arm. Father Moody called out to Dr. Bond, telling him he had a bad case. Dr. Bond glanced at Elmer and made the statement that all feared, "He's gone, put him aside." Father Moody gently lowered the stretcher, but there was no time for mourning. There were other wounded men who needed help.

Father Moody started back up the ladder, but was met by two corpsmen carrying Paul Barnette. He, too, was legless and going into shock. Father Moody sent him ahead to the dressing station, then climbed up to the other four men.

Father Moody helped get the men ready; then he helped take two of the stretcher cases down to the dressing station. The other two men were able to walk.

By now, dressing one was overcrowded with wounded. Dr. Bond asked Father Moody and Chaplain Wright to find a way to get the wounded to sick bay. The ship was at general quarters, and getting to sick bay meant going down to the third deck. All the hatches were dogged, and could only be opened by special permission.

Father Moody went to get permission, while Chaplain Wright looked for stretcher bearers. Pappy Harshman gave Father Moody permission to use number three elevator. Soon Chaplain Wright returned with two stretcher bearers. Most of the men who could have helped were busy fighting a fire at the after turrets. Dr. Bond released two of his corpsmen. This made a total of six to carry the stretchers down to sick bay. There were twelve stretchers in battle dressing one. It would take four trips to get all the men into sick bay.

When two of the stretcher bearers started to pick up the stretcher with Paul Barnette on it, he told them to take someone else first, because he was all right. They went to another stretcher. The six men started down to sick bay with their human cargo. As they stepped onto number three elevator, it began its descent to the hangar deck.

As the elevator stopped on the hangar deck, the men noticed the automatic sprinkler system had kicked on. The sprinklers were turning the hangar deck into a rain forest. The water was cascading down, drenching everything on the deck. The six men stepped off the elevator into the downfall of water, sheltering each wounded man the best they could.

The hangar deck was packed with planes. The only way to get over to the open hatch that led to sick bay was to crawl between the wheels and the wings of the parked planes. It took five minutes to reach the open hatch, with each stretcher being pulled by one man and pushed by the other. By the time they reached the hatch they were drenched.

After reaching the hatch, they had to go through ten more hatches and down two more decks. After they went through each hatch, they had to dog it behind them. This part of the trip took ten more minutes. The total time for each trip down was fifteen minutes. It took five minutes to make the trip back up to the dressing station for more wounded.

On the second trip, two of the men picked up Paul Barnette again. He was being given plasma to help with the blood he had lost from having his legs cut off by the bomb fins. With only six men to carry the stretchers, there was no one left to hold the plasma bottle. Seeing this, Paul told them he would hold the bottle. As the men made the fifteen minute trip down to sick bay, Paul firmly held the bottle.

Finally, after the fourth trip, all the men from the dressing station were in sick bay. Those who had been wounded on the hangar deck were already in sick bay. Fred Weatherford, Elmer Jekel, and Robert Lueck were already dead. Everyone hoped that the bomb would not claim any more lives.

The F6F, number fifty-seven, that was trying to land when the bomb hit was told to land in the water. After the plane landed, a destroyer picked up the pilot.

Throughout the evening Father Moody and Chaplain Wright stayed with the men in sick bay. They passed out cigarettes, gave drinks of water, covered the men with blankets, and helped the doctors.

The *Yorktown* stayed at general quarters until 9:18 P.M. The tired men ate supper. In the wardroom, Pat Patterson was down in the dumps. His roomate had been Fred Weatherford. The men in repair three also felt the loss of Fred; Ruben Kitchen said that Fred had been like a dad to him since he had come aboard the *Yorktown*.

Down in sick bay, the lonely night passed. The men stood the pain the best they could. Father Moody sat down beside Edward Sherman. He had been badly wounded when the bomb exploded in mount thirteen. Both his arms were broken and his body was riddled with bomb fragments. His face was smeared with blood and smoke. Everywhere blood oozed from bomb-fragment wounds. Father Moody softly asked Ed if he wanted a beauty treatment. Looking up with his blood-caked face, Ed grinned and said, "Sure."

As Father Moody gently wiped the blood and smoke from Ed's face, they talked. Shortly after midnight Ed called to Father Moody. He spoke a few words and then died.

By early morning, shock and the loss of blood had taken its toll on Paul Barnette. He died less than fourteen hours after he had been wounded. The Fighting Lady had lost a total of five men. They were the only men to ever die aboard her as a result of direct enemy hit by a bomb or torpedo. Never again did she receive a hit from the enemy. To many on the other carriers she still deserved the name of the Lucky Y. The other carriers had lost hundreds as a result of enemy action. The *Yorktown* had gotten off lightly during World War II, and only the *Enterprise* and *Saratoga* had seen action before her.

The next day Air Group Nine struck again at Kyushu, Japan. Again the Japanese sent kamikazes at Task Force Fifty-eight. That day their target was Task Group 58.2. This group included the carriers *Hancock* and *Franklin*. Aboard the *Franklin* was the *Yorktown's* original air group, Air Group Five. One of the pilots, Joe Kristufek, had asked for permission to be assigned to the East Coast after leaving the *Yorktown*. He was granted permission to stay. This act of fate quite possibly saved his life.

Also aboard the *Franklin* was Captain Arnold J. Isbell, the man who was to replace Captain Combs as skipper of the *Yorktown*. As Captain Isbell was getting ready to take over his new command, he did not know that all hell was getting ready to break out aboard the *Franklin*. At 7:09 A.M., a Judy managed to break through the *Franklin's* defenses. Within minutes the *Franklin* was a blazing inferno. Orange flames and black smoke filled the sky. The *Franklin* was hurt badly.

Aboard the *Yorktown*, men upon the bridge could see the black smoke rise into the sky. Soon they learned the damaged ship was the *Franklin*. Hearing this news, many men felt a kinship with the CV-13. Air Group Five was aboard the *Franklin*; this meant that some of their old friends would probably die before the day was over. Quietly, one man after another would glance in the direction of the smoke, then look back into the sky for enemy planes.

Heroics were the order of the day aboard the *Franklin*. Men led others through the smoke and flames to safety. As the day wore on, the *Franklin* started to win her war against the sea, but at a cost of many dead and wounded. Some of these dead were members of Air Group Five. Two of these dead were Joe Kristufek's former crew members. If he had not gotten the transfer, he too would have probably been killed. When one compartment was opened, the body of Captain Isbell was found with fourteen others who had been trapped by dogged hatches and had suffocated. Captain Isbell had died before reaching his new command, the *Yorktown*.

As the *Franklin's* crew fought to save her, the crew of the *Yorktown* was ready at its guns; waiting, searching, and hoping the enemy would not show. After picking her way through drifting mines, the *Missouri* fired at a mine and missed. She dropped a smoke marker to show its location. The carrier behind, the *Independence*, pulled wide and left it for the *Wisconsin*. The *Wisconsin* dropped another marker. Finally a destroyer fired at the mine, but the *Yorktown* changed course before Captain Combs could see whether the destroyer had been able to explode the mine. Up on the signal bridge, J. Bryan III remembered a poem he had made up the previous night:

"Wisconsin, Missouri, Alaska, and Guam,
Sleep tight! The *Yorktown* will keep you from
harm."

The crew had spent the entire day at battle
readiness, eating soup and sandwiches at general
quarters. Finally darkness fell over the Pacific. The
crew could get some rest at last.

The next day the crew of the *Yorktown* had a sad
task to perform. On the fantail were the five bodies
of men who had been killed on March 18. At 2:00
P.M. the five bodies, each now covered with an
American flag, were brought up on the flight deck.
All the men who were not on duty assembled on the
flight deck facing the port side. Chaplain Wright
and Father Moody read the services as the wind
blew across the flight deck, ruffling the flags draped
over the bodies. After the two Chaplains finished,
the band played "Onward Christian Soldiers." The
marines fired three volleys, then the number two
elevator was lowered to the hangar deck. The five
bodies were tilted into the sea. All the ships around
the *Yorktown* had their flags at half mast. After the
last body was lowered into the sea, word was passed
to carry on and flags were brought back to full
mast.

These five men, Lieutenant Fred G. Weatherford,
Seaman First Class Elmer Jekel, Seaman First Class
Powell M. Barnette, ART2c Edward Sherman, and
ART2c Robert Lee Lueck, would always be a part
of the *Yorktown*. These were the only men to ever
die as a result of a direct enemy hit.

During the day, the *Yorktown* had gone to

general quarters three times. During the third general quarters, the destroyer *Heerman* was transferring three POW's. When the carrier's guns opened fire, instead of casting-off and letting the third prisoner drown between the two ships, the destroyer stayed until the man was safely aboard. Then she dashed for open sea where she could use her guns. This small act quite impressed the editor of *Fortune* magazine, Del Paine. The captain of the *Heerman* had risked a hit on his ship to save the life of the enemy.

After going to general quarters four times, the *Yorktown* finally settled down at 9:00 P.M. The men were tired and looked ragged, but still they managed to keep the enemy from making further hits on The Fighting Lady. Captain Combs had stated before going into this battle, "The enemy will only attack an easy target, so make the *Yorktown* a hard target."

For the next several days the crew of the *Yorktown* became weary from the constant calls to general quarters, and the refueling operations which occurred every fourth day. Only when the ship withdrew to refuel could the men relax. Even then, daily duties had to be performed.

It had been over a week since the bomb hit the side of the ship. Most of the men were back at their duties; but the survivors of gun mount seven and the 20-mm gun mount, where the two men had their legs cut off, were transferred to different sections of the ship. These men had gone through hell, and the trauma caused by the bomb had left scars on them. Don Seaman, one of the gunners, was transferred to central damage control, deep in the bowels of the ship. Here he helped keep the ship on an even keel by watching the gyroscopes. Don's turning operator and the gunner next to him had been killed by the fins of the bomb as it passed through the gallery.

Elsewhere in the Pacific, the *Franklin* was getting ready to take the long voyage back to the United States. More of the missing in action were being added to the killed-in-action list daily as more compartments were opened. The *Franklin* had almost sunk from her wounds of March 19, and hundreds of her crew were killed in the attack. Yet, like her *Essex* class sisters, she had been able to take punishment. This factor made the *Essex* class carriers among the best warships ever built.

On Thursday, March 29, a flight of bogeys was spotted off the starboard side of the ship. At the same time, several pilots from the *Langley* also spotted the Japanese. Thinking the planes had not been picked up on radar, one of the pilots dove his F6F toward the plane closest to the *Yorktown*. He opened fire, as did the guns of the *Yorktown*. All at once the enemy and the F6F were surrounded by antiaircraft fire. The *Langley* pilot quickly saw his error in chasing the Japanese, but he was too slow in his escape. His plane, along with the enemy plane, was hit. Both crashed off the port quarter.

Aboard the *Yorktown* at this time, the gunners thought they saw two planes attacking their ship. A friend does not attack toward his own lines, as it appeared the F6F was doing. The Japanese had the Lucky Y's bore sighted. It was pilot against gunners. Shells were passing each other in the air between the plane and the ship. Still the two planes, one behind the other, flew toward the ship. The back plane began to veer off, but was hit before it could make good its escape. The lead plane continued on. In quad ten the gunners and loaders were sweating, even in the cold climate. The kamikaze was coming directly at them. Closer he approached until he filled the sky in front of the guns. The plane burst into flames, and passed over the heads of the men in quad ten by ten feet. So close did it pass that the flames from the burning plane singed the hair on the heads of the men in quad ten. The plane crashed into the water and exploded.

The second plane then passed overhead and also crashed into the sea. It was then that the gunners saw that the plane was an F6F. The plane and pilot both sank into the Pacific. The gun crews felt badly about the incident for days, yet the pilot of the F6F had erred in chasing the Japanese plane down to the *Yorktown*.

When the enemy plane hit the water, it exploded, throwing a column of water into the air just fifty feet from the port side of the ship. Dick Tripp had been landing planes at the time the Japanese attacked, and as the burning plane came toward him, he jumped into the safety net around the landing platform. The plane passed just a few yards from where Dick was lying in the net. When the plane exploded upon impact with the water, a piece of its cylinder hit in the safety net right next to Dick. Had it hit him, it would have killed him.

Because the *Yorktown* was landing planes at the time, the flight deck was crowded with them. If the

Japanese pilot had been successful in his kamikaze attempt, the *Yorktown* would have gone up in flames and smoke as the *Franklin* had, ten days earlier. The Lucky Y had pulled it off again.

For weeks the *Yorktown* and other carriers had been sending their planes against Okinawa, softening the enemy's defenses. That day, Easter Sunday, American amphibious forces were going to land on the island. A bitter fight was expected since this was the last island before the Japanese homelands.

Shortly after midnight on the first, a bogey appeared on radar. Admiral Radford was entering flag plot at the time. Yawning, he walked over to the radar screen. As he was being filled-in on the talk between ships, the Betty was shot down. Admiral Radford raced to the bridge, and watched as the flaming plane splashed into the cold Pacific. The Admiral turned to J. Bryan III and stated with a yawn, "That'll teach him!"

At sunrise the troops landed on Okinawa. At first, little opposition was met, but later in the day the Japanese began their defense of the island. For the first time in weeks, the *Yorktown* had an easy day. The Japanese were too busy fighting on the island to concentrate on the carriers.

Chaplains Moody and Wright sent Easter blessings in the Plan of the Day. Elsewhere, men were getting airborne strikes ready to help with the invasion. The troops would need these valuable planes in the weeks to come if they were going to take the island and hold it. For one man, Peter D. Joers, Easter Sunday meant a promotion. He was now the communications officer, promoted from assistant communications officer.

That night The Fighting Lady sent her night fighters aloft. The enemy was strong on Okinawa, and more troops were expected there. As the night fighters roamed the area around Okinawa, they spotted a group of transports heading for the island. Quickly, Johnny Orth and the others strafed and sent rockets into the transports. The escorting cruiser and several destroyers sent up a barrage of antiaircraft fire, but not before the Japanese had beached the transports and abandoned the mission. At least these few hundred enemy soldiers would not kill any of our troops on Okinawa.

A few days later another storm hit the task force. This storm was not like the one in December, but it did cause the small CVL's to roll and pitch heavily, as well as the destroyer *Franks*. Aboard the *Franks* were an injured captain and a comunications officer. The *Franks* had collided with the *New Jersey* the night before. The battleship received little damage, but the *Franks* was badly damaged and her crew received several severe injuries. With the destroyer bouncing like a cork in the heavy seas, the injured were taking a severe beating. Their wounds and broken bones brought on terrible pain as each man was jolted in his bunk.

To complicate matters even more for the *Yorktown's* task group, the *Missouri* lost a man overboard. Thanks to some fine seamanship, though, he was picked up twenty-two minutes later by a screening destroyer.

This man had been lucky. He was sighted and picked up. Others were not so fortunate. During one landing operation, Ralph Kendrick was on the flight deck waiting for his plane to come back from a strike. It was nighttime, and the blackness filled the air. Suddenly a plane landed with a crash. The sliding plane headed directly toward Ralph. Instinctively he dived for the small catwalk surrounding the flight deck. In his haste to escape the runaway plane, he jumped too hard. He missed the catwalk, and splashed into the dark ocean below. In he darkness he could not be spotted. He drowned and was never seen again.

A few days after that incident, Ruben Kitchen asked where Ralph was. He had not been coming down to the shipfitter's shop for coffee, which had been his habit. He was told what had happened. Ralph had been a school mate of Ruben's back in Pike County, Kentucky. Ruben wished that his friend had been as lucky as the man from the *Missouri*.

While the storm raged, the *Yorktown* had to take on fuel and ammunition. Again the men in the Fourth Division had their work cut out for them. Ted Rohrbough and the others sent lines over to the tanker, only to have them snapped by the violent rolls the two ships took. Finally, with expert ship handling, line handling, and a little luck, the *Yorktown* gulped down her fuel and took on the much-needed ammunition.

In sick bay was Danny Carveth. He had been blinded by the explosion caused by the bomb on March 18. J. Bryan III visited him every few days to read to him. Although J. Bryan III was not an actual crew member, but rather a visiting staff member, he had become a member of the *Yorktown*, caring and feeling about the others on the ship. The Fighting Lady somehow or other made everyone a part of her family. As J. Bryan III was getting ready to read to Danny Carveth one evening, he was told that Danny had to have another operation. The reading would have to be postponed for a few days until Danny could recover from the operation.

While the troops fought on Okinawa, the Japanese sent kamikazes at Task Force Fifty-eight. On April 7, the Japanese sent the largest kamikaze in the world toward the fleet. With no carriers left, the Japanese knew their fleet was destroyed. In one last-ditch effort to stop the ships of Task Force Fifty-eight, they turned the giant *Yamato* into a suicide ship, with only one mission: sink as many ships as possible before being sunk herself.

The giant *Yamato* had been laid down in 1937 and slid down the ways four years later in 1941. She was the giant of all battleships, displacing 72,809 tons and carrying nine eighteen-inch guns which fired shells weighing 3,000 pounds a distance of over twenty miles. Compared with the largest American ship, the *Missouri*, she was indeed a giant.

The *Missouri*, which was in the *Yorktown's* task group, displaced 59,300 tons. She carried nine sixteen-inch guns; these threw shells weighing one ton a distance of twenty miles.

The giant *Yamato* had never been very successful for the Japanese. She had been built in an aircraft-carrier age. Her giant guns never did get to engage enemy forces as they had been intended to do. Carrier planes had kept her in protected waters throughout the war; now she was going to slug it out with the Fifth Fleet until the end.

Aboard the *Yorktown*, word was received that the Japanese task force was preparing to launch an attack on Task Force Fifty-eight. Among the attacking ships was the *Yamato*, the legend of the Japanese Navy. As the men ate lunch, there was talk of this floating legend. One man stated that he had heard she was as large as the Empire State Building. Another replied, "Hell, if she is that big, maybe one of our BB's could hit her." (Carrier men called themselves the fighting navy, while they referred to the battleship navy as the spit and polish navy.)

As lunch was being served aboard the Lucky Y, general quarters sounded. Quickly the men raced to their stations. Off to the port, smoke was rising into the sky. The *Hancock* had been hit, but the fire was soon under control and the Japanese attacker shot down.

As the *Yorktown* sped through the water, the crew scanned the sky for more enemy planes. Most of the planes of Air Group Nine were out after the *Yamato*, which left some of the defense up to the gunners themselves.

Meanwhile, in the sky between the *Yorktown* and the *Yamato*, the pilots and their crews made last-minute checks on their equipment. In one of the planes, an SB2C, Harry Worley chatted with his rear-seat man, Earl Ward. The men chatted to calm their nerves. Every man in Air Group Nine knew that the *Yamato* was the prize of the Japanese fleet, and she would be well protected.

Aboard the *Yorktown* the men in CIC listened to the radio for some word of contact, and watched the screen for bogeys. The waiting was nerve-racking. Would they find the *Yamato*? Would they stop her if they did? Many questions were going through the crew's minds. What if the *Yamato* succeeded in escaping the planes? Could the *Missouri* and the other battleships stop the giant? If they could not, she could make mincemeat out of the *Yorktown* and the other carriers. Of course, many of these worries were unfounded, but the possibility of danger did exist.

As the giant *Yamato* steamed toward Task Force Fifty-eight, Captain Gihachi Takayanagi readied his ship for the worst. He had been sent on a one-way mission with only enough fuel to reach the Americans. Here he would slug it out until his ship went under. The crew had been told not to sacrifice themselves needlessly, but to leave the ship once she started down. Word had already been sent from the island of Amami-Oshima that American planes had passed overhead. The *Yamato* would come under attack shortly. The men aboard the *Yamato* raced about making last minute preparations for the upcoming air battle. They hoped that the 16.5-inch armor plating would stop the airborne torpedoes, and that the heavy armor on the deck would allow the bombs to explode harmlessly. Soon word was sent that the American planes had been sighted. Hatches were bolted shut as the Japanese prepared for the fight.

The first planes the crew of the *Yamato* sighted were from other air groups. Air Group Nine had been sent up for the second wave, and was still on the way. When the carrier pilots sighted the Japanese task force at 12:32 P.M., they circled overhead. Bursts of antiaircraft fire exploded around them. Then, after what seemed an eternity, they dove toward the ships below.

These planes from other carriers strafed the giant ship from fore to aft. The bullets tore up the wood-deck planking, sending splinters flying through the air. Several of the Japanese were hit as a result of the strafing, but still no bombs or torpedoes had been dropped. On the next pass, bombs were dropped at the speeding giant, but without success.

In the wheelhouse, the officers tried to keep in contact with the rest of the ship. Suddenly, bullets ripped into the area, wounding several officers there. Still the *Yamato* was undamaged. But it was evident the destroyers could not keep the planes away. Soon more planes were spotted.

This time the American pilots managed to make a few hits on the battleship. In the air, just a few miles from the fighting, Air Group Nine was getting ready to make its runs. Harry Worely and Earl Ward had been listening to the action over the radio. They were determined to make a hit on the giant.

Finally, Torpedo Squadron Nine, led by Lieutenant Thomas H. Stetson, was over the *Yamato*. The *Yamato* steamed below them. The few previous hits had hardly slowed her. She was smoking from them, but all the men in Air Group Nine knew was that she was still deadly.

On the *Yamato*, the Japanese could not believe their eyes. Here were more planes. They had taken a few hits, but the odds were going against them with each passing minute. Looking up, they could see the planes dive toward them.

Harry Worely watched the others make their passes on the ship while he waited his turn. He was determined to make a hit. He watched the deadly antiaircraft burst around the others in his air group. He watched as the others made hits on the ship. Then it was his turn.

Harry flew his SB2C toward the ship, antiaircraft shells bursting all around him. In the rear seat, Earl Ward was watching for any Japanese planes that might try to stop them. Harry flew nearer. Then, suddenly, a shell burst into the cockpit. Harry was hit. He had received a head wound. He realized he would never make it to the *Yamato*, or back to the *Yorktown*. In the rear seat, Earl was unaware of what was happening. Suddenly, Earl felt the plane make an unexpected dive. He knew that his pilot had been hit, and that his fate was sealed along with Harry's.

Harry tried to dive into a nearby destroyer. He would make a hit at all cost. As the SB2C neared the target, Harry died from his wounds. The plane, now out of control, crashed into the sea directly in front of the destroyer. The destroyer steamed past the stricken plane. Both men were dead.

Aboard the *Yamato*, all hell was breaking loose. Air Group Nine had been more successful than the other air groups. Within minutes they had put five torpedoes into the giant, five out of the eight she received during the attacks. These five fish dealt the *Yamato* her death blow. She could have survived the first three hits, but the following five were too much for her.

Below decks men were sealed in compartments that were now taking on water. The hatches were not broken, and the men were left to their fate. In other compartments, steam lines burst, scalding men where they stood. Every compartment was becoming a tomb for the men inside it. The compartments that were not damaged would carry their occupants down as the ship sank, until water pressure crushed the bulkheads.

Topside, men began scrambling over the side as the *Yamato* listed. Mangled bodies slid across the decks as the list increased. The *Yamato* had become her own worst enemy. Deep inside her, muffled explosions could be heard. These ripped her belly apart, letting in more of the ocean. Suddenly the ship started her plunge toward the bottom. Men up on the decks were thrown from the ship as she sank. Within a few minutes, all that was left of the *Yamato* was some flotsam and 269 survivors. There had once been a crew of over 2,760 men.

Aboard the *Yorktown*, Father Moody sent the word over the intercom that the *Yamato* had been sunk along with the *Agano*, a heavy cruiser. No one cheered, possibly because they knew the fate those Japanese sailors had received. War had become a dirty, cruel, tiresome job. Kill or be killed. That day the Americans had killed.

Throughout the day, the *Yorktown* had gone to general quarters three times, but had not fired a shot. The waiting was almost as bad as the fighting itself. As Captain Combs appeared on the bridge, the planes from Air Group Nine appeared on the horizon. These tired, weary men were home at last. Dick Tripp brought them down for safe landings. As the pilots emerged from their planes, they went to their ready rooms to talk about the sinking of the *Yamato*.

In one ready room, a pilot was sitting, shaking his head. As he sat there, he mumbled to himself. He had been flying a Hellcat, and had watched as the torpedo planes made their attacks, flying through the deadly antiaircraft fire. It was then that he realized he had been drinking the alcohol in the guidance system of the fish. Without the alcohol, the fish would go only a couple of hundred yards. Never again would he sneak some of the alcohol, or "torpedo juice," from the torpedoes, for refreshment.

Later that night, the men of Air Group Nine made up a victory song, "Yamato Been a Beautiful BB, but BB, You Should See Yourself Now!" Air Group Nine had put into the *Yamato* the fish that had finally caused her to go to the bottom.

In later years, a model manufacturer would make two models: one of the *Yamato*, the other of the *Enterprise*. Material accompanying these models would explain how these two ships had engaged in the greatest battle between two ships that the world had ever seen. In reality, the *Yorktown* was the ship responsible for the sinking of the *Yamato*, not the *Enterprise*.

The battle for Okinawa had been going on for eleven days, and the crew was getting worn down. The Japanese knew Okinawa would be their last stand before the invasion of the homelands, and they were putting up a fierce fight with numerous sacrifices, as the sinking of the *Yamato* had shown. The kamikaze effort was now at its peak, with missions daily. That day, April 11, the Japanese once again sent a large-scale attack at the task force.

When it became obvious that a large-scale attack was coming, the fighter pilots of Air Group Nine took to the air. Jack Kitchen was the skipper of "Fighting Nine" and he knew he had proven veterans flying with him. Quickly, the pilots took to their nimble Hellcats and flew off the deck of The Fighting Lady to intercept these men who were willing to die for the emperor. Among these courageous fighter pilots leaving the deck of the *Yorktown* were four men who made teamwork pay off.

These four men were under the leadership of Lieutenant Eugene A. Valencia. He had trained this four-man division to the point of near perfection. The others in the group were Harris E. Mitchell, Clinton L. Smith, and James B. French. Together these four men would set a record with the events that were to take place within the next few days.

As the kamikazes flew toward the *Yorktown*, Valencia and his division flew toward an interception point. The kamikaze planes had to be stopped. Soon the few planes that had managed to break through the defense put up by pilots from the *Bennington* and *Bunker Hill*, appeared through the windshields of the four fliers. The four flew into the pack of enemy planes.

Immediately, orange flames began spitting from

the barrels of the wing guns on the F6F's. First one kamikaze, then another fell from the sky in flames. In just a few minutes, Valencia and his division had knocked several of the bomb-laden planes from the air. Seeing they had managed to stop this attack, they turned back toward the *Yorktown* to wait until they would be needed at a later time.

While Valencia and his division were engaged in their air attacks, enemy planes managed to break through at other places. Aboard the *Yorktown* the men were eating lunch when the call to general quarters sounded. Those eating left their unfinished lunch on the mess tables, while those still in line had to leave before they even got their food.

The wind was cold, and gun crews stood in that cold, guns ready. Soon the signal was given to return to normal duties. The enemy plane had been shot down by carrier pilots before it had gotten within range of the task group. The men then returned to the mess halls to finish their lunches.

Again, while some were eating, the sound to general quarters was heard. Again the crew raced to their stations. The Japanese were becoming a real annoyance. It had been going on like this for the last few days, and the crew was starting to get tired.

This time, after the gun crews manned their guns, they got to use them. A "Jill" approached the *Yorktown* from the starboard. Instantly the guns opened fire on the plane. The Japanese pilot flew his plane right on top of the water, below radar detection. Skillfully he flew about 200 yards astern of the ship, almost touching the wake. Every aft gun was firing at the plane as the pilot skipped out of sight behind a light cruiser and a destroyer. These two ships then opened fire on the fast-flying plane. With skill and luck, the pilot managed to evade all fire, and swerved back toward the *Yorktown*.

All guns on the ship opened fire once again at the kamikaze. The pilot must have realized that he would never make it through the deadly fire to hit the "Lady," so, surprisingly, he straightened up and flew toward the *Missouri*.

He crashed into the *Missouri* at water level. His bomb failed to explode, and he did little damage to the ship. Within minutes the small fire was out, and the dead pilot's body recovered. The time was 2:42 P.M.

Four minutes later the gun crews were hammering away at another bogey. This Jill also came from the starboard side of the ship at the water level. At a distance of 3,000 yards, the gunners zeroed in on the luckless pilot. Soon the murderous fire was converging in one spot, the Jill. Flames began to break out, and the plane started erratic flight. At 1,800 yards, the plane hit the water, leaving a small flaming spot where it crashed. Another enemy had died for the emperior, this time in vain.

For the next few hours all was quiet. Planes landed and took off, searching for more kamikazes. Dinner was served to the crew while at general quarters. That day was turning into quite a busy one. The gun crews, exposed to the cold, welcomed the hot coffee brought to them in thermos bottles. Ted Rohrbough, Ed Johnson, and the others stationed at the guns were starting to feel the cold to the bone. Soon, though, they would forget the cold.

By 6:51 P.M. darkness had already fallen on the Pacific, but out of that darkness came one more kamikaze. This time the plane was a twin-engine job, and it was already burning from an attack by a fighter. The pilot picked the *Yorktown* for his target. As the burning plane came into range, the gunners opened fire. Soon the expert gunnery that the ship was noted for knocked the plane from the sky. The small fire on the ocean lit up the area for several minutes until the plane finally sank into the dark, icy depths of the ocean.

Finally, at 11:43 P.M., the ship was secured for the night. The task group had come under fire nine times. The crew was dead tired, and getting almost to the point of becoming inefficient.

This had been the first combat Captain Walter F. Boone had been in since he arrived aboard the *Yorktown* on April 9. Captain Boone had come over from the *Enterprise* aboard a TBM. He was to be Captain Combs' replacement, Captain Arnold J. Isbell, Combs' first replacement, had been killed on the *Franklin* before he could reach the *Yorktown*.

Captain Combs had been promoted to the rank of admiral, as had his two predecessors, Captain Clark and Captain Jennings. He would be the last captain to make admiral aboard the *Yorktown* during the war.

On April 13, word was given out that President Roosevelt had died in Warm Springs, Georgia. The new Commander-in-Chief was Harry S. Truman.

President Truman was untried, yet all felt he could handle the job. Most figured that the Japanese would use the President's death as a form of propaganda. Throughout the task force, flags were flown at half-mast in respect for the late President.

As the *Yorktown* steamed through the waters of the Pacific, she took on three prisoners from the destroyer *Melvin*. These three men had been flying in a float plane that had been shot down by a night fighter. The *Melvin* was sent to pick them out of the water, but, because of pride, the men would not accept the aid. Sailors aboard the *Melvin* had to drag the three men from the water. They felt that they had been disgraced by being captured. Later they were taken aboard the *Yorktown* for interrogation. Medical aid was given to the men. One of them was seriously burned. His face was swollen, red, and raw. He was in bad shape.

On Sunday, services were held for President Roosevelt. Fighting Nine's skipper, Jack Kitchen, read a poem, which emphasized the length of time that Roosevelt had been president.

Since this was a refueling day for the ship, she was out of combat range. The crew took a few hours rest from the heavy combat they had been engaged in for the last several days.

After the services, the Fourth Division once again did their duty of sending fuel hoses over to the tanker. While the *Yorktown* gulped down her fuel, the Fourth Division rigged a stretcher and sent the three prisoners over to the tanker so they could be sent to a camp, and receive better medical aid. One man's face now looked frightful; the burns had become infected because of the hours he had been in the water.

Since Captain Combs had been made admiral, he wanted his stars. There were none anywhere on the ship, but one officer remembered that a sailor in the shipfitter's shop had been making ensign and lieutenant bars for many of the officers. He also remembered this sailor had been doing work in Admiral Radford's quarters on the superstructure. He felt the work was good, so he went looking for this man.

He entered the shipfitter's shop, and asked where Kitchen was. A sailor pointed him out. Walking over to this man, he asked, "Are you Ruben Kitchen?"

The sailor answered that he was. The conversation went on for a few minutes. Ruben agreed to make the stars, but said he would need a pattern. He was given a commodore's star to use as a pattern, and he was told to get anything he needed from the ship's stores. He got the materials he would need, and proceeded with the work. Admiral Combs was probably the only admiral in the navy with handmade stars.

Again the *Yorktown* set sail for the combat zone. Again she would be fighting it out with the deadly kamikazes. These men were quite unpopular with Task Force Fifty-eight, mainly because of the tactics they used. How do you kill a man who wants to kill himself? He does not fear death, therefore he cannot be stopped except in death.

The morning of April 16 was a little warmer than the previous mornings had been. Planes were launched for the work of the day. Okinawa was still in the hands of the Japanese, and American planes were needed to soften up the Japanese strongholds. The people on Okinawa were putting up a last-ditch stand, and the ground forces were fighting the hardest battles since the war began. The Japanese on the island, like the kamikazes, would rather die fighting than surrender. These suicidal tactics were costing American lives. Some of the enemy would pretend to be dead; when a group of soldiers came near, they would explode hand grenades, killing several ground troops as well as themselves.

The civilians were to be pitied. They had been told by the Japanese army that American marines killed babies and ate them. They had also been told that in order to be a marine a man must kill his own mother. Tales such as this caused widespread panic among the civilian population. Many threw their children off the high cliffs of the island to the rocks below, then jumped after them. They feared Americans more than they did death. War was indeed hell!

Aboard the *Yorktown*, off the coast of Okinawa, the men in CIC reported several bogeys on the screen. Further investigation showed that none of the planes were nearby, so the men on the bridge could begin to relax. The time was 1:19 P.M.

Suddenly, one minute later, five planes appeared from out of nowhere. They had avoided radar detection. Like mad hornets, these five planes swarmed the ships of Task Group 58.4. Quickly the *Yorktown's* gunners began firing, as did the gunners from the neighboring ships. This attack would have to be stopped by the guns from the ships; it was too late to get aid from the fighters.

The first plane dropped his bomb, which missed; then he was shot from the sky, just outside the rim of the formation.

The second plane made it into the circle of ships. Skillfully, he avoided the deadly rain of fire being thrown at him. Seconds after the first plane hit the water in flames, he hit near the stern of the *Missouri*, throwing up a column of brown water higher than the mast of the battleship. Two had been downed, but three remained.

The third plane zeroed in on the *Yorktown*, but because of the deadly fire thrown up, the plane hit alongside the destroyer *McDermott*, which was next to the *Yorktown*. At the same time that the plane crashed alongside the destroyer, a five-inch shell from the *Missouri* hit the *McDermott* at the waterline. Two men were killed, and seven injured.

The fourth and fifth planes picked out a fat, juicy target, an aircraft carrier. They did not choose the *Yorktown*, but rather her luckless sister, the *Intrepid*. These two pilots came in together on the luckless ship, forcing the gunners to divide their fire and giving their planes a better chance. The fourth plane hit the water close to the starboard bow on the *Intrepid*, but the fifth pilot ended his life in a raging fire as he crashed into the flight deck. Flames poured from the *Intrepid* as she pulled away from the formation. The *Yorktown* made an emergency turn to avoid any other planes that might be in the vicinity. Luckily, there were no other planes around.

As the five planes attacked, the flight deck of The Fighting Lady was full of men. The action came so fast there was no time for some of these men to get to their stations. Some elected to remain on the flight deck. The excitement caused many to rush from one side to the other for a better view of the action. Pappy Harshman shouted at them over the bullhorn, but the excitement made the men deaf to his words. Soon they understood the situation and dispersed.

Minutes after the fighting was over, the *Yorktown* landed her 23,000th plane, less than two years since the first Hellcat flew into battle during the Marcus raid.

The *Intrepid* was holding her own after taking the kamikaze. She had been laid out the same day as the *Yorktown* and in the same yard, but she had received all the bad luck, while the *Yorktown* had received most of the good luck. The *Intrepid*, too, had earned a nickname, Dry I, because of the time she had spent in drydock.

Aboard the *Intrepid* the fires were soon brought under control. Nine men were killed and forty injured. Forty planes were destroyed. Like the *Franklin* though, she was a hardy ship, and a worthwhile target for further raids.

At 3:15 P.M. three more kamikazes appeared in the area. Because the *Intrepid* was already wounded, these three chose her as their victim. Like jackals, the three pounced upon the wounded *Intrepid*. The first released his bomb, which was a near miss. He was shot down over the carrier. The second likewise dropped a near miss, then flew across the stern of the *Yorktown*. The *Yorktown's* gunners finished off the plane. The third was chased off by antiaircraft fire before he could make the drop. The *Intrepid* had been lucky this time. Even though she had been unlucky at times, she, like all the *Essex* class carriers, would survive the war.

After this attack, another milestone was passed aboard the *Yorktown*. The number two, five-inch gun had fired its 1,000th round. The bakeshop baked a cake for the occasion, and it was presented to the gun crew. Even in times of war, certain occasions must be celebrated.

Eugene Valencia's division had been making a name for itself during the Okinawa campaign, but it was on April 17 that this highly efficient division did their best.

Aboard the *Yorktown*, in the CIC, a large blip was picked up on the radar. Immediately the center hummed with activity. A large wave was coming toward The Fighting Lady. Word was sent for the pilots to man their planes. Quickly, the fighter pilots raced toward their waiting planes. The crews in the VIA Division had the fighters armed and ready; Jim Bryan saw to it that the planes were always ready.

Jack Kitchen climbed into his waiting F6F. The others, including Valencia and his division mates, strapped themselves into their Hellcats. The signal was given, and off the deck flew Jack, skipper of Fighting Nine, followed by the others. Once in the air, Eugene and his division started to get the feel of the upcoming action.

At about 9:00 A.M. on the morning of April 17, Eugene raced his division toward a bogey sixty miles away. A few minutes later they spotted ten planes; then there were twenty-five planes. The four pilots were all that there were between the enemy and the *Yorktown*. Eugene sent out the call to send help, and then the four Hellcat fliers attacked the twenty-five enemy planes.

Coming from out of the sun and using all the skills they had picked up in the last few months, the Valencia "Flying Circus" fired their first shots at the oncoming enemy. It wasn't until two of the bombers exploded that the Japanese realized that they were being attacked. The others immediately dropped their bombs and tried to make good their escape. The Flying Circus was everywhere, knocking planes from the air. The "Chrysanthemums" were falling from the sky.

Soon the Japanese managed to make good their escape, but not before the *Yorktown* "Mowing Machine" had managed to knock down or damage twenty-seven of the thirty-eight planes in the formation. Only eleven planes escaped the short, but savage, fight. As for the planes of the Mowing Machine, not one of the four had a bullet hole in it.

In this action Eugene Valencia himself downed six of the enemy, while James French knocked down four. The other two pilots, Harris Mitchell and Clinton Smith, downed three and one respectively. By the time the war was over each man was to become an ace, with Eugene becoming the third-ranking ace in the navy. Together these four men accounted for fifty enemy planes being shot down without a loss to any of them. This was a record that was never beaten.

Eugene wrote later that each man was given his chance to make the kill; usually the man with the lowest score was given first chance. He believed in letting each man have a chance to show his skills in flying and fighting. This was teamwork and it paid off.

As the four men landed aboard the *Yorktown*, each held up his hand to show how many he had shot down. Eugene grinned and held up both hands showing six fingers. Captains Combs and Boone were on the bridge. Captain Boone stated that not long ago pilots like Valencia received the Congressional Medal Honor for such actions. Now they were expected.

Later Captain Combs was looking over some photos of the *Missouri*, which had been hit on April 11. Looking at them, he noticed that the crew had given the Japanese pilot a burial with honors. He stated that he figured that was the decent thing to do, but that he liked the way the *Intrepid* handled the body of the kamikaze that had hit her the day before. They sent the *Yorktown* a dispatch saying, "Have thrown pilot's remains over the side."

The *Intrepid* was sent back for repairs, and her replacement was the *Randolph*. She was now patched up after the hit she had received in Ulithi Bay on March 11, and she was ready for action.

Since the campaign for Okinawa had begun, five of the large CV-type carriers had been hit and were withdrawn from the action. Only six of the original eleven were left. Some of these carriers had been hit hard, yet the fighting spirit of the navy had kept them afloat. The *Yorktown* was one of the luckier carriers.

It had now been a month since the *Yorktown* had

received the first and only hit of her entire career. The temporary patch on her starboard side was now rusty. The rust stain was running down her side, washed down with the water that had been sloshed up the side from the seas and the rain. Except for this small patch, the *Yorktown* looked as she always had.

April 18 was Father Joe Moody's birthday. He was now forty-one years old, but looked years younger. Things had calmed down a great deal after all the action of the past month. Father Moody had been extremely busy on March 18.

Pilots flew daily combat missions over Okinawa. One of the pilots of VB-9 had an unusual experience. Ed Wiezorek and his rear gunner were flying over Okinawa on a mission when he began his dive toward enemy positions. His plane was carrying bombs with instantaneous fuses. Ed dove to within 600 feet of his target, then released his bomb. As he pulled out, the bomb hit the target and exploded. The explosion damaged Ed's plane because he had dropped the bomb while flying close to the ground. He was unable to make it back to the ship. Still in control, Ed brought the plane down on a shallow reef. Minutes after he landed, an army ambulance drove out to pick him and his rear gunner, Carlton Walker, up. Neither were injured from the experience.

Once again the *Yorktown* had to pull to the rear area for fuel. As she was heading toward the rear, ceremonies were held on the flight deck, turning the *Yorktown* over to Captain Boone.

The crew was assembled on the flight deck for the

change of command. Admiral Radford was in charge of the ceremonies. He presented Captain Combs with the Legion of Merit, and then the executive officer gave the captain a new admiral flag. Admiral Combs stood proudly, and upon his shoulders he wore the custom-made stars, made aboard The Fighting Lady.

The next day the *Yorktown* took on fuel. The men in the Fourth Division sent three of their crew mates to the tanker. The first was Harwell Profitt, from Tennessee, who drawled when talking on the TBS. His voice was recognized throughout the task force. The second man was Admiral Combs. The third was a plank owner of the *Yorktown*. He had seen most of the action, including the Marianas Turkey Shoot. He had been the landing signal officer on duty on night of that battle. His name was Dick Tripp. Dick would miss the *Yorktown*, but would get back with her in later years. Soon all three were safely aboard the tanker. The Fourth Division bragged that they had never lost a person or any cargo. As the tanker pulled away, the carrier *Shangri-La* joined Task Group 58.4, along with the battleship *Iowa*.

It was during the Okinawa campaign that the *Yorktown* welcomed aboard three marine pilots. These three marines were flying with VMF-312, a part of Air Group Thirty-three, based at Katena airfield on Okinawa.

These three pilots were flying a patrol when they became lost over the ocean. Seeing that they were lost, they sent out an emergency call, which was soon picked up by the *Yorktown*. With radio and

241

radar, these three pilots were vectored to the *Yorktown*.

As the three pilots approached the ship, their fuel gauges showed that their planes were almost empty. This made the situation tense. To add to the troubles, none of the pilots had ever made a carrier landing before, and only one had made simulated carrier landings. The LSO would have his hands full with these three.

Standing on the small platform near the stern was Lieutenant (jg) J. E. Cozzens. He had been the third LSO to come aboard. Now that Dick was gone, these would be his babies. It was decided that since the three had never made carrier landings before, Lieutenant L. F. Spaulding would talk to the men over the radio during the landing. It was hoped that with the combination of radio and visual assistance the pilots would be able to land.

The first to attempt a landing was Lieutenant Ken Dodson. His plane was nearly out of gas; in fact, he did not even have enough to land in the traditional pattern, and so came in from the starboard instead of the port. "Hazy" Cozzens began bringing the marine in with the aid of Spaulding on the radio. It was this time or in the drink. Carefully and skillfully they brought Dodson to a fairly smooth landing on the flight deck. As his plane was being pulled away, it was noted that there were only five gallons of gasoline left in its tanks. If he had landed using full rpm's, instead of half of the required rpm's, he would probably have run out of gas before the landing had been completed.

The next two pilots were soon brought in for safe

landings. One of the marines wanted to know what Hazy was doing, waving those paddles back and forth. He was soon informed that he had been given a wave-off. Luck was with him; he made a perfect landing. The marines always said that they could do everything.

The battle in the Pacific was at its hottest, but in Europe the Allies had finally won. On May 7, 1945, the Germans surrendered unconditionally to the Allies. Victory celebrations were held in America, but in the Pacific men were still dying.

Normal practices were carried on aboard the *Yorktown*. One of these duties was checking the lifeboats. On this particular day, Ted Rohrbough was told to check the number two whale boat, since the seas had been kicking up for the last couple of days. Ted lifted the cover to see whether the rations were still intact. As he checked, he noticed two gallon jugs that were not supposed to be in the boat. Upon closer inspection he noticed these jugs were filled with a homemade wine. The jugs had been placed here to cool.

Ted took the two gallons of wine back to the division locker where he and several of his friends toasted the end of the fighting in Europe. There were probably some angry sailors on the ship when they discovered that the fruits of their labor had been taken away from them.

The *Yorktown* continued to give support to the invasion of Okinawa. It was now evident the Japanese would lose the war. Their air power was nearly gone, and almost all their carriers were now at the bottom of the ocean. What few carriers they had left were useless in port. The giant *Yamato* had almost been worshipped by the Japanese; for that reason, the Japanese public was not told of the loss of it. But the land-based kamikazes were still a threat to the Fifth Fleet.

On the carrier *Bunker Hill*, Admiral Mitscher was readying his fast carriers for more attacks against Okinawa. Shortly after 10:00 A.M. on May 11, a Zero dived toward the *Bunker Hill*. The kamikaze pilot released his bomb which hit the flight deck and passed out the side of the hull, exploding at the waterline. The pilot then crashed his plane onto the number three elevator. On the flight deck were several fighters being readied for takeoff. Amidst the flames and explosions many sailors were killed.

Seconds later another plane, a Judy, released its bomb, hitting the ship. This pilot then aimed his plane at the superstructure. He hit the structure at the base, causing more fires. This plane exploded less than 100 feet from where Mitscher was standing on the bridge. The explosion knocked him back, but he quickly regained his composure and walked onto the starboard bridge. At the same time another kamikaze crashed into the sea nearby; it had been shot down before it could make good its attack.

Most of the flight deck was smoking and burning. Amidst the molten remains of the parked planes were the bodies of the pilots and of the crews who had been readying the planes. These men never had a chance. As the fires were brought under control, the death toll stood at 402 men. Only the *Franklin* had been hit harder. Later that day Admiral Mitscher transferred to the *Enterprise*.

The *Yorktown* had been hitting the enemy since March 16. She now retired to Ulithi for rearming and replenishment. As he left the combat area, Captain Boone had the gun crews practice their anti-aircraft fire. When not in combat the gun crews practiced for two hours a day, thus keeping their marksmanship honed to a razor-edge sharpness.

As the ship entered Ulithi, the crew knew they would get to stand on solid ground again. As soon as possible, part of the crew was given leave to go ashore at Mog Mog. Being on this tropical paradise helped the crew to get rid of tensions built up during the Okinawa campaign. They had just come through the heaviest fighting of the war, and compared to most of the other carriers, they had been lucky. The *Franklin, Bunker Hill, Enterprise, Intrepid, Wasp,* and *Hancock* had all been hit, some seriously. Yes, the *Yorktown* had indeed been lucky!

On Mog Mog the war was forgotten for the time. Beer was available, and so were swimming and sports. Each man was given an opportunity to go ashore, while others remained to carry out normal duties.

Meanwhile, off Kyushu, Admiral Mitscher was aboard the *Enterprise*. Again his flagship came under attack. This time the task force came under attack by twenty-six kamikazes. Twenty-five were shot down, but the last one crashed into the *Enterprise*. The plane hit behind the forward elevator. The ship was seriously damaged, but only thirteen men were killed by the bomb. Once again Mitscher had to go to another ship. This time he transferred to the *Randolph*. As for the *Enterprise*, she was sent to Ulithi were she arrived on May 14. From there she sailed on to the United States. Her war career was over. The war would be over before she could return to action. The *Enterprise* had been hit by kamikazes on three different occasions. For her, the *Franklin*, and the *Bunker Hill*, the war was over.

The *Yorktown* was now ready for the combat zone again. When she reentered the zone, she became part of the Third Fleet. Halsey was in command of the operations. The *Yorktown* had been on the line for only six days when the weather started to kick up. Halsey was caught by another typhoon.

As the wind increased, the waves rose to fifty feet in height. Planes were lashed down to the flight deck. Admiral Radford watched as Captain Boone handled the ship with the same expertise his predecessors had. Again the *Yorktown* had a winning team. Other ships were not so fortunate.

Jocko Clark made the mistake of sending his task group into the center of the storm. As a result, the carriers *Bennington* and *Hornet* had the forward areas of their flight decks damaged by the giant waves. The cruiser *Pittsburg* had over 100 feet of her bow torn away by the violent seas. The *Yorktown* rode out the storm like the lady she was.

On June 6, 1945, the *Yorktown* topped off her fuel tanks with oil from one of the tankers. For the next seven days she would provide air cover for the troops on Okinawa. The island was almost in American hands; by June 13, air cover would be provided from the island itself. On June 6, another carrier joined Task Group 38.4. This carrier had at least one thing in common with the *Yorktown*. The name she carried was once intended for the Yorktown's. The carrier was the CV-31, the *Bon Homme Richard*. It had taken that name almost three years to reach the Pacific. The CV-10 had been renamed *Yorktown* in honor of the CV-5. The cycle was now almost complete. The former *Bon Homme Richard* was now sailing with the new *Bon Homme Richard*.

Now that the Okinawa campaign was over, the *Yorktown*, along with the rest of Task Force Thirty-eight, steamed into Leyte Gulf. At 11:55 A.M. on June 13, the *Yorktown* dropped anchor in San Pedro Bay. The most prolonged and furious carrier action of the war was now over. The crew was given shore liberty, and the islanders were ready and waiting for the sailors.

Yorktowners, and men from the other carriers, swarmed ashore at Leyte and Samar. Here the men played softball and saw what they could of the native customs. The military tried to keep the islanders and the sailors separated when possible, but the natives still managed to sell hats, grass skirts, and other locally produced items. Of course, there was a rise in the prices of the items. Knowing the sailors would be eager to buy gifts for wives and girl friends back home, the natives charged over ten times the normal price, and the sailors paid it.

It was here that Air Group Nine left the *Yorktown*. When they left, they left behind the most impressive scoreboard of the Fighting Lady's career. Now the ship would get a new air group, Air Group Eighty-eight, under the command of Commander Searcy. These were the pilots who would be flying from the Lucky Y when the war came to an end.

On July 1, 1945, the *Yorktown* sortied with the rest of the fleet. The action they planned would be against the home islands themselves. For the next month strikes were made against the Japanese islands. The Japanese were helpless to stop them. Except for the invasion of the islands themselves, the war was over.

As the *Yorktown* steamed north at twenty knots, the men on the bridge could look in all directions: all they could see was ships. With the *Yorktown* this was the largest fleet the world would ever sees. There were sixteen carriers, eight battleships, seventeen cruisers, and seventy destroyers. This fleet would carry the war to the enemy homelands.

The weather became colder as the *Yorktown* neared Japan. The crew got out their cold-weather gear; several days before, they had been roasting in the heat of the Philippines.

While the *Yorktown* steamed north, she conducted intensive training exercises. This intensive training had enabled her to be the luckiest ship in the navy, and Captain Boone was going to see that she stayed lucky. The gunnery crews practiced and sharpened their skills even more, while Air Group Eighty-eight trained daily. This got them used to the ship and the "we-are-first" attitude the ship maintained.

One of the pilots, Lieutenant Commander J. Clifford Huddleston, was the skipper of *VR-88*. He had brought his men from training to the war in the Pacific. As he flew his Avenger high in the air over the Pacific one morning while still at Leyte, he saw the sun come up over the horizon. Seeing how beautiful the sun was, he thought about the days of training at Martha's Vineyard and the men who were not with the air group now.

He remembered Lieutenant (jg) Willaman. Willaman had been a combat-experienced pilot who had joined Air Group Eighty-eight at Martha's Vineyard. Willaman was given the Distinguished Flying Cross one morning by Commodore Rowe. Willaman was proud of the medal. Thirty minutes later, he went aloft to calibrate a glide angle in his Avenger. As he dove toward the ground high over the field, his plane gave one loud popping sound followed by another popping sound. Both wings of his Avenger had torn loose from the plane. Spinning toward the ground, he was unable to get out of the plane. As his plane hit the field in a fiery explosion, Willaman died.

Next, Huddleston thought of two Avengers that had gone aloft one night during training exercises. In one plane were Lieutenant Bill Dorney and Lewis Jones. In the other were Ensign Wallace Brinkley and Dean Shaffer. In the dark of the night the two planes flew into eternity. Both planes and their crews vanished without a trace. Yes, several men had lost their lives in order for Air Group Eighty-eight to make it this far.

The humming of the engine brought Clifford back to the present. The sun had only been up a few minutes; he decided to land back on the field for a unique experience. As he touched down on the runway, he saw the sun come up again. That day he saw the sun rise twice. A few days later he was aboard the *Yorktown* heading for Indian Country.

On July 10, Air Group Eighty-eight hit Tokyo. The heavy bombers of the army had leveled much of the city, but only carrier planes could give the precise bombing that was required for the destruction of enemy planes and airfields. Little opposition was met, since the Japanese were saving their remaining planes for the invasion of the islands themselves.

Next the *Yorktown* moved swiftly north to Hokkaido. This city was an important center for the raw materials and foodstuffs that were shipped south to the larger cities. This move was quite unexpected by the enemy, and the attacks were a success. The Fighting Lady had carried the war to a part of Japan that had never been hit before. Railroads were destroyed along with other important targets.

When the planes landed back aboard the ship, one of them was missing. Lieutenant Commander Richard G. Crommelin was shot down in his fighter over Hokkaido by antiaircraft fire. The next day, Lieutenant (jg) Heman B. Chase was knocked from the air over Otaru Harbor. Air Group Eighty-eight was adding its men to the list of those who had paid the ultimate price while serving aboard the *Yorktown*.

Because the pilots of the carriers in the fleet were getting all the action, it was decided to let the other capital ships pound the coast of Japan. Under the watchful eye of the carrier pilots, the battleships and cruisers moved into range. Here they threw their eight, twelve, and sixteen-inch shells into the cities along the coast. After a few hours of this, they returned back to the open sea and to the protection it offered from the Japanese shore batteries.

The Japanese were almost beaten, but they held on. On July 18, it was decided to hit the remaining ships in Tokyo Bay. Here were the few remaining ships of the once-proud Imperial Navy. One of these ships was the battleship *Nagato*. Without airpower, she was helpless. With deadly accuracy the pilots of Air Group Eighty-eight slammed five direct hits into the *Nagato*. She soon became a useless piece of junk.

Next came Kure Naval Base, the strongest base in Japan. Here ships were burned into piles of charred debris and sunk. The Japanese were defeated, but pride would not allow them to surrender.

This pride caused President Truman to make one of the most important decisions in the history of warfare. The United States had a weapon like no other ever used before. This weapon could kill thousands with one blow. It was the atomic bomb. It became evident the Japanese were not going to give up, so President Truman gave the go-ahead for the dropping of the atomic bomb.

On August 6, the men of Air Group Eighty-eight were pounding the airfields on Honshu, getting the island ready for the upcoming invasion. At 7:30 P.M. word was given out that the world's first atomic bomb had been dropped on Hiroshima. The Atomic Age was born. Three days later the second bomb was dropped on Nagasaki. The Japanese had been the victims of the worst weapon in history, but would they ask for peace?

On the evening of August 9, a kamikaze sneaked

in with some returning Corsairs. The plane dived at the *Wasp*, which was next to the *Yorktown*. The gunners on the *Yorktown* flamed the plane, and it crashed harmlessly into the sea. These were the last shots fired in anger by the ship's guns during World War II.

The next day word came that the Japanese would consider accepting the terms of the Potsdam ultimatum, provided the emperor could retain certain prerogatives. This offer was refused by the Allies. The attacks were ordered to resume on Tokyo.

On August 15, The Fighting Lady sent a strike toward Tokyo. A first strike had already hit the city, and the second strike was on the way. At 9:45 A.M., Captain Boone announced over the intercom system that the Japanese had accepted the terms of the surrender. The crew was overjoyed—the war was over. Men were patting each other on the back; it was almost a party atmosphere.

In San Francisco, word was out that the war was over. People mobbed into the streets. V-J Day had been a long time in coming, and the people in America were ready to celebrate.

Meanwhile, in the air over Japan, word that the war was over was sent to the pilots flying the second strike. Many thought at first that it was a Japanese trick; but when they realized that it was true, the air crews went wild. On orders, they jettisoned their bombs into the ocean. Many of the pilots of Air Group Eighty-eight forgot they were flying in formation, and when they dropped their bombs into the ocean, several bombs almost hit planes flying below. Radio silence was broken; the war was over.

As twelve planes from Air Group Eighty-eight were flying back to the *Yorktown*, they passed over Atsugi Airfield. The time was almost 10:00 A.M. Suddenly the twelve fliers were surprised by a large group of Japanese planes. These planes began firing at the twelve unsuspecting planes. Before the *Yorktown* pilots could recover from the attack, four planes had been shot down. Within minutes, though, the remaining eight pilots downed twelve of the enemy and drove the rest away. The war was over; but below on Japanese soil, lay the bodies of four *Yorktown* pilots. Lieutenant Howard M. Harrison, Lieutenant (jg) Joseph G. Sahloff, Ensign Eugene E. Mandeberg, and Ensign Wright C. Hobbs, Jr., were the last men to die in World War II. The *Yorktown* would be the last ship to have her people fight in the war. She had carried the war to the bitter end.

By 10:20 A.M. all planes were recovered. Because of the treachery displayed by the Japanese, Admiral Halsey ordered that all Japanese planes be shot down "in a friendly manner." The Japanese could not be trusted.

For the next several days Air Group Eighty-eight flew combat air patrols. Relief flights were also flown to drop food into the POW camps.

Clifford Huddleston was flying one of these relief missions when he spotted a name on the roof of one of the buildings in one of the camps. In six foot high letters was the name "Pop Condit." Pop had been the first pilot lost aboard the *Yorktown* during the Marcus raid on August 31, 1943. It was thought that he was dead, but here was his name, along with "VT-5" and "Yorktown." Huddleston and Condit had trained together for carrier flying. Some of the men aboard the ship still remembered Pop and were glad to hear he was still alive.

Elsewhere signs were painted on rooftops giving praise to the *Yorktown*. For many of these prisoners, the *Yorktown* planes were the first contact with the outside since they had been captured. As one POW stated, "When we looked up and seen the planes from the *Yorktown*, we knew that the war was over, and that we had won."

MacArthur wanted to occupy the islands, but he was hundreds of miles away in the Philippines getting ready for the invasion. While he was on his way to occupy Japan with his army, a plan was devised for landing naval personnel if it became necessary. Many of the men aboard the *Yorktown* were given 45's and told to practice, using oil drums towed in the wake for targets. Luckily, though, MacArthur found out about this and ordered that only the army be allowed in Japan until it was safe for others.

This made several pilots angry. They had carried the war right to the Japanese, but, on orders from MacArthur, they would not be allowed to land until the army had control of the country. One *Yorktown* pilot decided to let it be known that he resented the fact that he could not land. He landed, against orders, on Atsugi Airfield where, only days before, four of his fellow crewmen had been ambushed after the war was declared over. Getting out of his plane, he made several Japanese paint a sign. After the sign had been painted and posted, he left.

Several days later the army landed at the airfield. As the soldiers climbed from their transports, they were greeted with the following sign: "Welcome to the U.S. Army from the Third Fleet." MacArthur was furious when he was told about the sign. Admiral Halsey tried to act angry, but instead he smiled slightly. The navy had been first again, with the *Yorktown* in the lead.

Finally, on September 2, 1945, the terms of the surrender were signed onboard the battleship *Missouri*. The war was finally over. But before the *Yorktown* was finished, she had one more important job to do. She and several other carriers were picked to transport the thousands of Army personnel back to the United States. Operation Magic Carpet would be the code name for this last operation the *Yorktown* would perform in the 1940's.

As arrangements were being made to transport some of the soldiers back to the States, The Fighting Lady dropped anchor in Tokyo Bay. As the sun set, Mount Fuji was silhouetted in the background. The victor had reached the end of the trail.

For the next several days the crew was given liberty to go ashore in Tokyo. The city was heavily damaged, but surprisingly, the Japanese had now accepted their defeat. On the streets the civilian population would bow humbly to the sailors whenever they happened to meet them. Some of the sailors accepted this form of greeting, but to most it was embarrassing. Few understood the Oriental customs, and most wished that the Japanese would not bow to them.

Street vendors sold what goods they had in the

streets. Ruben Kitchen, Ken Parkinson, and several others were walking down one of the streets when Ruben saw a vendor selling Japanese flags. He decided to buy one as a souvenir. He approached the elderly gentleman and asked how much he wanted for the flags. Luckily, the man could speak broken English, and replied that he would not sell an American one of the flags. Before Ruben had a chance to make a comment, the elderly vendor stated his reasons. He asked, "If you had lost the war, would you have sold me your flag?"

Ruben thought for a moment, and then replied, "No, I don't believe that I could."

The vendor then surprised all by stating, "You understand, therefore I will give you one of the flags." He then handed Ruben one of the small, silk rising sun flags. Ruben still has the flag.

While in Tokyo Bay several new men came aboard the ship. One of these was Charles E. McKellar. He had missed being aboard The Fighting Lady while the war was on, but he still became a part of the Lady's family.

On October, 3, 1945, the *Yorktown* left Tokyo Bay. At last she was homeward bound. Streamers and balloons flew from the ship. Men could now enjoy the warm rays of the sun. At night the hangar deck curtains could be opened as the crew watched movies. Fresh air felt good as it blew through the ship, as hatches were now left open.

From Tokyo Bay, The Fighting Lady steamed to Buckner Bay on Okinawa to pick up about 700 Army personnel for the return trip home. From there she steamed to Kwajalein Island to unload excess supplies.

While at Kwajalein, Captain Boone decided that all the beer rations should be unloaded along with the excess supplies. When word spread that the beer would be leaving, the beer began disappearing. The beer was being taken by members of the crew, and cooled with CO_2 from the fire extinguishers. So much beer was taken that Captain Boone ordered a boat watch at the stern where the beer was, until it could be taken from the ship the next day.

After the excess supplies and the beer were unloaded, several more passengers were taken aboard. Next the *Yorktown* sailed for Pearl Harbor.

At Pearl Harbor the yard crews installed salt-water showers on the port side of the hangar deck, and bunks down the center of the deck. Now the *Yorktown* was ready to sail to San Francisco. When she left Pearl Harbor, she had 1,600 passengers aboard; most were Army personnel, but a few were Navy people. The Navy people were assigned to the ship. This allowed them to eat with the crew and to sleep in compartments with the rest of the crew.

As the ship sailed for home, the executive officer, Commander John W. Brady, was at the helm. On October 23, The Fighting Lady sailed under the Golden Gate Bridge. It had been one year and ten days since she had left San Francisco the last time. As she entered the bay she was greeted by many boats, all of which were sounding their horns. The fire boats were sending streams of water high into the air in salute. Aboard the *Yorktown*, the edge of the flight deck was lined with sailors and soldiers alike. Here, at last, was home.

After unloading her passengers, the *Yorktown*

was turned into a floating attraction. On Navy Day, October 27, open house was declared, and hundreds of San Franciscans came aboard to view the ship. In this group were friends and relatives of the sailors. Proudly the sailors showed off their Lady. To them she was the best ship in the Navy. Many of the open house visitors were awed at the scoreboard on the superstructure showing what the *Yorktown* had accomplished during World War II. That night the visitors left. Many would remember the day they walked the decks of the gallant ship.

The next day The Fighting Lady would meet someone special to her. Back in the spring, several of the sailors had written to *Life* magazine asking for help in finding a girl to represent the ship. Upon returning to the States, the crew was given over 1,200 entries to the contest. For three days a committee went over the photos before they found the right one. Today, she would arrive in San Francisco.

When the plane landed at Mills Field, Sam Pearl and several others greeted her. Here she was: Betty Jo Copeland, from Fort Worth, Texas. From the more than 1,200 girls who entered, she was chosen as Miss Fighting Lady.

As she was brought aboard, she was given full honors. Then the lucky men who had been selected as guides showed her the ship she represented. The two Fighting Ladies met. For the next four days Miss Fighting Lady was taken to dinners and dances. Finally she boarded her plane for home, stating that she had had the most wonderful time of her life.

The Fighting Lady was then taken over to

Hunter's Point, where she was outfitted as a troop ship. Here she was fixed with bunks on the hangar deck and in all excess compartments. In some cases the bunks were stacked four high; they were made out of black iron pipe and had canvas bottoms. Also installed were more showers and galley facilities. After a few days she sailed for Guam. Operation Magic Carpet had just started.

When she left for Guam it was early November. Upon her arrival there, she picked up 4,312 passengers. On November 29, she again headed for California. Upon arriving at Alameda, she unloaded her cargo of men, then steamed toward the Far East. She arrived at Manila on December 23, and stayed until after Christmas. This time The Fighting Lady picked up 4,570 passengers and set sail for Alameda, California again. Here she unloaded her last group of passengers. For the *Yorktown*, Operation Magic Carpet was over. All that was left were her sea trials, before she sailed for Puget Sound.

After completing her sea trials, the *Yorktown* sailed toward Seattle, Washington. She stayed here, off the coast, for nearly a month. In late April word was given for her to sail into Bremerton Naval Yard for mothballing. The World War II career of the CV-10 was over. Sailing through Puget Sound with a new captain at the helm, Captain Maurice E. Browder, she caught up with the *Essex*. Throughout both ships' careers they had been competitors. Here was the chance for one more victory. Both ships turned on the steam, and it was a wild race through Puget Sound, *Yorktown* against *Essex*. One more victory was added to the *Yorktown's* log.

In May, tugs pulled The Fighting Lady to pier ninety-one; she was now part of the reserve fleet. Among those last to leave the ship were Charles E. McKellar and Don Seaman. Don was in the payroll department. It is quite possible that he was the last enlisted man to leave the ship. When he left, the records were transferred to the battleship *Colorada* with him. The *Colorada* was used to hold the records of the mothballed ships.

Now the *Yorktown* was sitting alone with the other heroines of World War II. The *Essex* and *Ticonderoga* were on one side of her, while the *Lexinton* and *Bunker Hill* were moored on the other side. She, like the others, was sitting, waiting for the day she would be needed again. Unlike the other carriers she would never be forgotten. She had had a glorious career in the last few years. Although no one knew it then, the future was still bright for the U.S.S. *Yorktown, CV-10*, better known as The Fighting Lady.

CVA-10
1952-1957

Chapter IX

Throughout the peaceful years from 1946 to 1950, the navy mothballed all the older *Essex* class carriers. It was the younger sisters and the new Midway class carriers that sailed the seas to protect the United States. Of the ships in this class, only the *Boxer* and *Antietam* had been completed during World War II; the others were completed after the war. Some of these new carriers carried the names of battles the *Yorktown* had been engaged in during the war; others were named after older battles and other ships.

These new ships would soon be needed in another

way; and so would their older sisters. In June, 1950, the North Koreans attacked South Korea, and the United States was at war again. This one was a land war; but carrier-based planes would be needed to bomb the North Koreans, and to stop their advance.

The first carrier to be recommissioned was the new *Princeton*, named after the CVL that had sunk during World War II. Next came the *Essex* and *Bon Homme Richard*, followed by newer *Essex* class carriers. These ships rejoined the fleet, now called the Seventh Fleet, to help fight the enemy.

Although the *Yorktown* would not be used in the Korean War until the end, one of her most famous skippers had an active part in the war. Jocko Clark was given command of Task Force Seventy-seven in the fall of 1951. He was given command of the Seventh Fleet in May, 1952.

One year before Admiral Clark took command of the Seventh Fleet, the *Yorktown* was taken out of mothballs and given the SCB-27A conversion. Jets were the plane of the future, and in order for the *Yorktown* to be able to handle these heavier and faster planes, she would have to be modernized. SCB-27A changed the look of The Fighting Lady. Her island structure was redesigned. The familiar five-inch guns fore and aft of the island were taken away. This gave her an uncluttered appearance. Also taken away were the 20- and 40-mm guns on the superstructure. No longer would the superstructure be crowded with gunners and their crews. The radar mast was made stronger, and the two bridges on the island structure were enclosed in glass. No longer would the captain or admiral have to stand out in the foul weather to watch strikes take off and land.

Many of the guns along the flight deck were removed, and new five-inch guns were placed on the starboard side alongside those already there. At the bow was placed another tub of 40-mm guns. The bow was widened to make the Yorktown look more like her younger sisters. The pilot ready rooms were no longer directly below the flight deck. This had been a bad place for them because it offered pilots waiting to go on a strike no protection. Many pilots during World War II had been killed in the ready rooms from bomb hits; but because of the state of technology then, the ready rooms had to be placed there.

Now the ready rooms were located below the hangar deck, where more protection was offered to the pilots. In order for them to get to the flight deck in a hurry, an escalator was installed on the starboard side. It took the pilots from the second deck to the island structure where they emerged onto the flight deck.

Elsewhere improvements were made on the *Yorktown*. Ten years had passed since her keel had been laid, and much had been learned in those years. On January 2, 1953, she was recommissioned into the United States Navy as CVA-10.

Before the *Yorktown* could be recommissioned, she had to have a crew. Men were brought from all parts of the navy to make up this crew. On December 15, 1952, the *Yorktown* was given her eighth captain, Captain William M. Nation. Captain Nation would get the ship ready for her duties later in 1953.

Also included in the new crew was Boyd Ingram. Boyd came from Moffet Field, California, to Puget Sound, Washington, where he was assigned to the V-7 Division. This was the aviation-gas-handlers group. These men saw to it that all fuels were handled safely, and that all thirty-three fueling stations were kept in working order. This was a time-consuming and important job.

Soon after Boyd had gotten the hang of that job, he and twelve others were sent to Philadelphia, Pennsylvania to learn how to operate the new H-8 catapults that were going to be installed aboard the *Yorktown* during SCB-27A. After completing the school, he was assigned to the V-2 Division. Here he was assigned to the retracting panel board as an operator by the catapult captain, E. P. Fripp.

Elsewhere in the United States something was happening that would later have an enormous effect upon the *Yorktown*. For the past five years, former members of the *Yorktown* had been holding reunions. These reunions started in 1948 in New York City, and many notable people in the navy were guests of honor; all had served aboard the *Yorktown*.

At the 1952 reunion, there was no guest of honor. This time the members of the U.S.S. *Yorktown* CV-10 Association honored a fallen comrade. Lieutenant E. T. Smokey Stover was the man they honored. After the war, it was discovered that Smokey had not survived. How he died is still a mystery; but it is believed that he was shot the day after he was brought down by the Japanese. He was executed in retaliation for the raid on Truk in 1944.

Smokey was remembered by his shipmates after eight years. More honors would come to him in later years.

Finally the *Yorktown* was finished with SCB-27A and with her sea trials. Off to the waters off Korea she headed. Before she could get to the war zone, a truce was signed; the Korean War was over. Upon arriving at the zone she was made flagship of the Seventh Fleet, while some of her younger sisters retired to a well-earned rest.

In command of the *Yorktown* now was Captain Arnold W. McKechnie. Captain McKechnie was a man who was proud of the ship that he commanded. To show this pride he made The Fighting Lady stick out in the crowd of younger carriers. While he was in command of the *Yorktown*, she earned a new title. The carrier became known as "A Fighter, a Feeder, and a Task Force Leader." Somehow, the spirit that had made The Fighting Lady a winner in the 1940's was still alive in the 1950's. Once again the *Yorktown* was taking the lead.

Captain Jackson, the executive officer, had made it his policy to attend at least one meal a day to see that the crew were being fed well. This sat well with the crew, as it showed them that the officers cared about them. Because of this, the crew would do anything for the captain and the executive officer. This attitude showed up in the effectiveness and cleanliness of the *Yorktown*.

Soon after the *Yorktown* was recommissioned in 1953, a practice of chow-line jumping began. The lines were long. To avoid waiting, one man would get in line and then when he got near the front, he would let several friends get in front of him. Each man in a given group would take his turn holding a place in line for the others. This got to be quite a problem on The Fighting Lady. The crew was getting unruly at meal times.

Captain Jackson got wind of this, and he began standing in line, observing the practice. The next day a statement appeared in the Plan of the Day. This said, "Anyone caught jumping the chow line, and the shipmate that lets him in front of him, will automatically get three days in the brig on bread and water. There will be no mast, no excuses. The MAA's will take the guilty parties from the chow line right to the brig."

The next day four sailors went to the brig, and on the day after that two more went. After that no one ever cut into line again. The men appreciated the firm stand the executive officer had taken. No sailor ever had to wait in line for more than twenty minutes after that. Paying attention to small matters like this had always paid off for the *Yorktown*. Jocko had done it, and so had all the captains who followed him.

As The Fighting Lady sailed into the China Sea, there began a cruise of seventy-seven days without liberty for the crew. In peaceful times, this was fairly hard for the crew to accept. Soon the *Yorktown* pulled into the port of Sasabo, Japan to unload two A-J aircraft that were aboard. The ship was going to be in port for only a few hours, but Captain McKechnie granted two sections liberty for five hours each. A few of the crew came back intoxicated; but because of loyalty to the captain and to

266

the *Yorktown*, all the men reported back as scheduled in spite of the fact they had been at sea for seventy-seven days.

The spirit of the *Yorktown* lingered on, and the new crew was just as proud of The Fighting Lady as had been the crew that had earned the title for her.

Elsewhere, in Washington, D.C. the Pentagon had a new Chairman of the Joint Chiefs of Staff. This man was Admiral Arthur W. Radford, the first navy man to be given the post. Admiral Radford was the man who had ordered the movie *The Fighting Lady* to be made during World War II. He carried his flag aboard the *Yorktown* during 1944 and 1945. His outstanding career aboard the *Yorktown* helped him in acquiring the new position.

The *Yorktown* led the task force on exercises in the Northern Sea of Japan. The exercise was code named "iron man." It was during this exercise that the *Yorktown* met with an accident.

Boyd Ingram was operating the pumps that built up pressure to retract the catapult to the battery position so that it could be fired again. On the first catapult shot the firing recorder broke. This recorder consisted quite simply of a string and a pencil attached to the crosshead to record the full run of the catapult. The firing recorder had broken before. Boyd repaired the string before the next shot. But Boyd left his normal position so that he could see what made the string break. As the catapult started to operate, the launching cable broke and slammed into the operating panel where Boyd would have been standing if he had not been trying to find the reason for the string's breaking.

The panel board was destroyed. If Boyd had been standing there, the cable would have torn his head off.

Boyd was nonetheless injured as the cable flew by him, knocking him seventeen feet from where he had been standing. Boyd ran outside the room as pieces of metal flew about his head. Once he was outside, the others could see that his elbow was crushed and his face cut badly. The glass that had been covering the gauges shattered and flew into his face. Once outside, he passed out. Quickly he was taken to the ship's hospital for surgery. Later he was transferred to the Naval Hospital in Yokosuka, Japan. After a few weeks, he was back aboard the ship.

Naval aviation began building larger and heavier jets. The *Essex* class carriers once again needed to be rebuilt to take the punishment. The *Yorktown* was scheduled for this modernization in 1955.

The Fighting Lady was still off the coast of Japan. Before she left, the crew decided to collect some money for the Shriners Crippled Children Fund of San Francisco. This would probably be the last chance for most of the crew to visit Japan. That gave some the idea for the following fund-raising plan: for a $10.00 contribution a sailor would be served breakfast in bed by any member of his division whom he chose, including his division officer, for a $20.00 contribution, a sailor would get a weekend in Tokyo, at his own expense, of course. Captain Gerald L. Huff agreed to this plan. By the time the fund-raising drive was over, the total amount of money raised came to over $30,000. The crew had the spirit now. The *Yorktown* was helping in peacetime as she had helped in wartime.

By mid-summer of 1955, The Fighting Lady once again entered Bremerton Naval Yard. This time she would change her appearance under SCB-125. She was given an angled flight deck and a hurricane bow. There she took on the appearance that she still has. She was finished on October 14, 1955, and rejoined the fleet with her complement of fighters and bombers.

By the following year she received the mirror-light landing system in San Francisco. No longer would men like Dick Tripp be needed to direct planes back in after a mission. The pilot would line the lights up in the mirror and land by them. The world was changing and so was the *Yorktown*. Soon she would be too small to be considered an attack carrier, or CVA, but still she would be needed in the fast-changing world of warfare.

As the year 1957 came to a close, the U.S.S. *Yorktown* CV-10 Association had its annual reunion. This time the reunion was held in San Francisco, and it was held aboard The Fighting Lady.

This time the reunion was special, not only because it was held aboard the ship, but also because of the man who was honored that day. In ceremonies held aboard the ship, the association presented the *Yorktown* with a sculptured plaque honoring E. T. Smokey Stover. Smokey was the symbol of all the men who had made The Fighting Lady one of the most famous ships in naval history. This plaque would remain on the ship for the rest of her career, showing the younger sailors in another age how a group of men in the early 1940's felt about one of their shipmates. As the ceremonies closed, the officer of the deck, Lieutenant (jg) W. L. Fadner, saluted the plaque honoring Smokey. Smokey was once again aboard his ship, although only in memory.

Chapter X

It began to seem that the years had caught up with the *Yorktown*. No longer were the *Essex* class carriers the largest in the fleet. The *Midway* and larger *Forrestal* class carriers were giants beside the *Essex* class carriers. Several younger *Essex's* had already been reclassified when, on September 1, 1957, the veteran *Yorktown* was reclassified as the CVS-10. She was now an ASW (anti-submarine warfare) support aircraft carrier. Upon her decks now flew helicopters and tracker planes. Removal from the attack roll did not dampen the spirit of the ship that Jocko Clark had commissioned in 1943. She would carry with pride the classification of CVS just as she had carried the CV and CVA classifications.

Among those men aboard her when she was reclassified were Donald Lampley and Jack Jones. Jack had been in the jet fuel division while the *Yorktown* was a CVA, but after her reclassification he was transferred to the oxygen shack where he made liquid oxygen. While the ship was still a CVA, Jack went to a tattoo parlor in port one night. When he came out he had "CVA-10" tattooed to his right arm. This is an example of the affection the crew had for the ship.

Donald Lampley had come aboard in 1956 while the ship was homeported in Alamada, California. He was assigned to the signal division. The superstructure was now much different than it had been when Joe Leathers was a signalman. Now the bridge was uncluttered. Joe probably would not recognize his old station on the superstructure.

When the *Yorktown* left to rejoin the fleet, she was on the lookout for a new threat, the submarine. The Russians were building a large submarine fleet, and it would be ships like the *Yorktown* that would search out and destroy these undersea vessels if the need came.

She rejoined the Seventh Fleet, and soon she took on another name; she became known as "Mother York." In fact, she played the role of a mother to the fleet. She was the center of the task group; and she was still a floating, seagoing air base, a mobile command center, and a logistic depot for destroyers. Whenever other ships called her, they referred to her as "Big Dipper."

For the next several years, the *Yorktown* had quite a peaceful role in the Pacific. The world was at peace, except for the French, who were waging a limited war in a small Asian country called Vietnam. Except for a few special assignments, the *Yorktown* led a normal, routine life.

In the summer of 1960, President Eisenhower made an official visit to the Far East, and the *Yorktown* carried the presidential press party. The press was impressed with the history of the ship. Captain Charles E. Gibson saw that members of the press were treated well. As for the crew, they were proud to show off their Lady.

This was not the first time the *Yorktown* had been the center of attention. She had, of course, been the star of the movie *The Fighting Lady*; but in 1954, she was also the star of the movie *Jet Carrier*. Also, in 1960, she made the news when she rescued the fifty-two man crew of the British freighter *Shn Lee*. The ship had hit Pratas Reef and was in need of assistance. Soon the *Yorktown* was at the scene, taking off the crew before any harm could come to them. This was a small action when compared to other deeds, but to the fifty-two men aboard the damaged ship, it was the greatest feat of the *Yorktown's* career.

It was 1961. Fifty years before, Eugene Ely had flown the first plane from the deck of the *Birmingham*. A couple of months later he landed on another ship, the *Pennsylvania*. Neither ship had been designed to both launch and land planes. The *Birmingham* flight ended on shore, while the *Pennsylvania* flight began on shore. To celebrate the fiftieth anniversary of the first carrier flight, the "Tennessee Ernie Ford Show" did a special program on naval aviation. This was taped live on the flight deck of the *Yorktown*. People all over America were getting to see some fine entertainment as well as World War II's famous Fighting Lady. The *Yorktown* was getting her share of publicity.

Throughout the early 1960's, she continued to operate in the Pacific either as an ASW task force, or with the Seventh Fleet. Task Force Seventy-seven was not very large compared to Task Force Thirty-eight/Fifty-eight. In fact, a single task group of Task Force Thirty-eight/Fifty-eight was larger than the entire Task Force Seventy-seven.

In 1965, the *Yorktown* again came to the public's attention. Again she was on a television show, and again it was a popular show of the time. Dick Clark, from "American Bandstand," decided to do a show about the rock and roll stars of the day. This show would be filmed at various locations across the country, and it would be entitled "Where the Action Is." What likelier place than a naval ship for one of the segments?

The show began with an aerial view of an aircraft carrier. On the flight deck was a large "10." As the camera zoomed down to the flight deck where the Where-the-Action-Is dancers were performing, Dick Clark stated, "Below you is the World War II aircraft carrier *Yorktown*, better known as The Fighting Lady. During World War II this ship sent over 100 Japanese ships to Davy Jones' locker." To many people this figure was astonishing.

By the mid 1960's, America was again engaged in

a war. This one was unpopular, and it was beginning to tear the country apart. Much had happened in the decade of the 60's. A popular president, President John F. Kennedy, had been shot and killed in Dallas, Texas. America had sent men into outer space, and was engaged in a race to the moon with Russia. By 1967, peace demonstrations were on the news every night along with films of the war in Vietnam. For the first time in history, people were watching a war from the comforts of their home. As for the *Yorktown*, she was getting old. She was now twenty-four years old, an old age for a warship.

The war in Vietnam was beginning to escalate, and even though it was mostly a land war, the navy played an important part in the action. Carrier planes were launched to attack communist troops in North Vietnam, and the Viet Cong located in the south. Among these carriers was the *Yorktown*. She launched her air groups with the same dedicated vigor that she had during World War II. Although neither she nor any other American ship came under attack, she earned two medals for her part in the war that no one seemed to want.

For her early activities in the war she was awarded the Armed Forces Expeditionary Medal for the months of February, March, and April, 1965.

From February to July of 1966, she was awarded the Vietnam Service medal. She also received four battlestars for her active role in the Vietnam War. Although this was a highly unpopular war, the crew aboard the *Yorktown* then, like all of her previous crews, did its duty and did it well.

Once again the *Yorktown* was in need of modernization. This time the work would be done at Long Beach, California. On March 31, 1967, the *Yorktown* entered the naval yard at Long Beach. Among the men aboard at the time was Melvin L. Bien, Jr. Melvin remembered that during the overhaul period he and the others in his division chipped paint and repainted the Lady inside and out.

The *Yorktown* was getting old, and several things happened during the overhaul period that would have never happened a few years before. The boilers gave trouble, the catapults were in need of repair; these and other things caused the Lucky Y to stay in the yard longer than expected. Years of the wear and tear of military life were taking their toll on the ship.

The yard workers worked hard to make the *Yorktown* one of the most modern ships in her class. White flood lights were added on to the flight deck. For the last few years night operations had been done under the glow of red lights. Now new flood lights were being added that would light up the flight deck like an all-night golf course. During World War II all night operations had been done in the dark, except for the one night that Marc Mitscher had the lights turned on, an event that became known as one of the most daring happenings in naval warfare.

New center-line strobe and drop-line lights were added to aid in night landings. These lights were arranged in such a way as to give the pilot the illusion that the flight deck was longer than it actually was.

Also added was a new nose-gear tow catapult. This catapult attaches to the nose gear of the plane instead of to the underside of it. This would help in producing faster and safer operations.

Hook-up lights were also added. These lights, placed in the flight deck, illuminate the under side of the planes, thus making hook-up of the catapult easier and faster.

And, finally, the flight deck was refinished. This job required that all worn out wood be replaced with new wood. The new wood was then sanded to be even with the old wood that was left. The grooves were then sealed, and a polyurethene coating was added to the wooden deck. On top of this a gray non-skid paint was applied.

The finishing touches came when the markings were painted onto the flight deck. Finally, after five months in the yard, the *Yorktown* was ready for the sea.

While The Fighting Lady was docked at Pier E, she greeted a new skipper. Captain William E. McCulley, Jr., had served as a skipper of the ship since May 7, 1966, and now he was going to turn the ship over to another man. On July 19, 1967, he and Captain William L. Bennett inspected the crew on the flight deck. Captain McCulley offered high praise for the crew after the inspection, and then he presented letters of commendation to RD3 Richard Delisa and RD3 James Townsen. These would be the last awards Captain McCulley would present to the crew of the carrier. The next day he would turn the ship over to Captain Bennett.

On July 20, about 125 guests were present to see the transfer of command. Among those present were Vice Admiral Shinn and other rear admirals.

Chaplain R. E. Foelber gave the invocation and Chaplain D. F. Steward recited the benediction. Afterwards a reception was held at the Allen Center Officers Club on the Long Beach Naval Base.

Many important persons attended this reception. One guest who may have welcomed the chance to be at the reception more than the others was Jocko Clark. Since he had put the *Yorktown* in commission, she was still his "girl," and he was proud of the record she had established during the last twenty-four years.

When Captain Bennett put the Lady to sea on October 16, he had only forty percent of the old crew aboard.

Sea trials were carried out off the West Coast, and soon the crew was having refresher training. The older men helped the new, raw recruits learn how to do their duties. The ship was in less-than-glamorous shape when the yard workers had turned the ship back over to the crew. Now the men were taking a new-found pride in their ship and themselves. They were becoming a part of the ship. A spirit was taking possession of them, a spirit of pride.

Next came ORE, ORI, NTPI, and carrier qualifications. Captain Bennett had the crew at general quarters at all hours of the day and night. This was done to help the men learn their duties well, and to help avoid tragedies like the ones that had occurred on some of the other carriers in the last several years, especially fire.

Fire has always been the enemy of carriers. Because of the aviation fuels, bombs, rockets, and the lightly armored decks, fire can start easily and burn a carrier to the water line. Japan lost many of her carriers during World War II not to the bombs and torpedoes, but to the fires that ran wild in the ships after they were hit. The Americans lost the old *Lexington* at the Battle of the Coral Sea to gasoline-fed fires. Captain Bennett was going to see to it that his ship would be safe from fire. It has been stated that, "The aircraft carrier is the most potentially dangerous ship afloat." Fire is the reason for that statement.

Soon the men were acting as one. The weeks of training were paying off, and once again The Fighting Lady had the best crew in the navy. Not only were they good, but, as always, they were also the happiest crew in the navy. Many men would state that of all the ships they had served on, the *Yorktown* was the best. This statement was made by many twenty-year men; they had served on many ships, including the largest carriers afloat today.

Finally the ship was ready. December 28, 1967 would be the date for deployment to the waters off Vietnam. But before that time came, there was to be a couple of weeks for the crew to get leaves. Just before Christmas, a Christmas party was held on the hangar deck for the crew and their dependents. But the day before that party, a special show was held for the crew and their families.

At 8:00 P.M. on December 15, the hangar deck was transformed into a large entertainment hall. The Hollywood Variety Show was here to give a replay of the previous year's show. Vince Barnett, an actor and a Beverly Hills Navy Leaguer, was the producer of the show, and he had many fine and talented people at his disposal. Included in his troop was Jo Stafford, John Forsythe, and many others. As the curtain rose at 8:00 P.M. the audience was in for a treat. Everyone remembered later how well the show had been produced and how well the entertainers had performed.

The next day the hangar deck was crowded with children. They were waiting for that jolly old man from the North. While they waited below, they could hear a plane landing on the flight deck above their heads. Santa Claus was making his first landing ever on the *Yorktown*; he came by plane.

After getting from the plane, Santa slid down a chimney to the hangar deck where 350 happy children were awaiting his jolly laugh and his gifts.

After Santa arrived, he presented each child with a toy and a sweater. The Westminster High School Choral Group sang Christmas songs which everyone enjoyed; and then refreshments were served to the children and the other guests. Santa was played by Robert Middletown, a well known character actor and a Navy Leaguer.

At last Christmas Day arrived, and the crew on board ship had a wonderful Christmas dinner, with turkey and all the trimmings. Three days later all the crew was back aboard the ship. The *Yorktown* had already steamed to North Island, near San Diego, to pick up her air group, Air Group Twenty-three. VS-23 was commanded by Commander Donald Richard Hubbs. He flew an S2E, a plane that was used to seek, track, and destroy enemy submarines in all types of weather.

After picking up the air group, the ship headed for Pearl Harbor. Here the crew welcomed in the New Year. In early January, 1968, she steamed toward Yokosuka, Japan. As the crew left Pearl Harbor, the weather was warm, and, on the beaches bathing beauties were out enjoying the sun. The crew enjoyed the sun as much as they could, because, like the men twenty-three years before them, they were heading into a cold climate. In Japan it was winter, with cold winds and temperatures below freezing. At least this time the crew did not have to worry about combat conditions as the crew of 1945 did. As the ship proceeded north, warm-weather clothes were put away, and cold-weather gear was broken out.

While the *Yorktown* was steaming toward Japan, another ship was operating in the waters off the coast of Korea. This ship was under the command of Commander Lloyd M. Bucher. Aboard the ship were eighty-two other men. The ship was the ill-fated *Pueblo*.

The *Pueblo* was operating near the coast of Korea when it was attacked by four North Korean gun-boats. Having little to fight with, Commander Bucher ordered all secret papers to be destroyed. Immediately several of the men began destroying the papers. Among these men was Duane Daniel Hodges. He was busy destroying secret papers before the boarding party could capture the important documents. Gun fire was all around, and suddenly Hodges fell to the deck. He had been hit by a bullet. A couple of the crew members went to his aid, but they could see that it was hopeless. As

Duane lay dying, he began singing a Christmas carol. After a few minutes Duane died, and the *Pueblo* was captured. For the first time in over 100 years a United States naval vessel had been boarded. Trouble was stirring off the coast of Korea, and immediately ships were sent to the area.

As fate would have it, the *Yorktown* was near that area. The large carrier *Enterprise* CVN-67, was already in the area, but the navy decided that more ships should be there to make a more impressive show. The *Yorktown* immediately steamed toward Korea, leading her task group. Once again the Lady was first in her class, and under the leadership of Captain Bennett, she was ready.

As The Fighting Lady steamed toward Korea, the wind blew snow so hard that at times the flight deck was invisible from the bridge. The wind buffeted anyone standing on the flight deck, and the seas rolled the ship. Still the Lady continued on her course. The North Koreans must be shown that America would be ready to fight if it was necessary.

For forty-six days The Fighting Lady prowled the coast of Korea. She was the first carrier to enter the Sea of Japan. As she patrolled the coast, she herself was watched by the Russian sub tender that the crew had nicknamed "Getalong." This little ship would cut across the bow of the larger *Yorktown*, trying to get Captain Bennett to change course. As the Getalong disappeared from sight near the bow, the men on the bridge would wait to feel the crunch of metal against metal. But the small ship would always manage to slip out of the way. For days it was a game of nerves, and for days the *Yorktown* was closer to the Korean coast than any other capital ship. Tempers finally cooled, diplomats began talking about a settlement, and the *Yorktown* was pulled out to go to her station in the South China Sea. She was supposed to have relieved the *Kearsarge* in late January, but the *Kearsarge* had to stay until the *Yorktown* arrived in early April.

The weather in the South China Sea was welcome after the weather the crew had been experiencing. Off Korea the temperature including the chill factor, was forty degrees below zero. At times the snow blew so hard that members of the crew had to use snow shovels to clean off the flight deck so the planes could take off and land.

Also off the coast of Korea, The Fighting Lady lost four of her crew. This made five lost since the first of the year. The first man killed was Lieutenant Commander Don Stebbins. Don had been flying an S2E plane near Barking Sands, Hawaii just a few days after the start of the new year. Like so many of the fliers before him, he had finally touched the face of God.

While flying missions near Korea, another plane was lost. This time the plane had four men aboard, with the commander of *VS-23* in the pilot's seat. For several days the *Yorktown* and the other ships in the task force looked for Commander Donald Richard Hubbs, and his crew, Lieutenant (jg) Lee David Benson, AX2 Randall John Nightingale, and ADRAN Thomas David Barber. Like many other navy fliers, they had disappeared into the sea without a trace.

For the next few months the *Yorktown* operated

off the coast of Vietnam, supporting the troops and bombing the enemy installations. The ship operated in the Tonkin Gulf, and the crew was allowed to go to Japan or the Philippines every thirty days for a four-to-seven day visit. The war off the coast of Vietnam was now becoming routine.

Since the routine was now well established, boxing teams were established to help entertain the men during smokers. The administration officer, CWOII Ramsdell, organized the boxing bouts, and "Win" also handled the ring announcing. The bouts were refereed by Lieutenant Al Penta and HM2 China Smith, while Dr. Bob Fellman kept a watchful eye over the boxers. Of course, no boxer would be any good without a good trainer. Aboard were two of the best, AO1 Frank Englebright and AO1 George Morgan. These men and the many good boxers aboard, made many a night more than just another dreary night at sea.

Luckily for the other ships in the *Yorktown's* task force, The Fighting Lady had her own television network. The Beverly Hills Naval League had installed the system on the ship during the recent overhaul at Long Beach. She was the first naval ship to ever have the facilities to make and transmit her own shows, and well as to transmit the family favorites that were being shown at home. Television had come to sea. When these bouts were fought, they were sent to the other ships in the task force for the entertainment of these men as well. The network was YKTV-TV, the first of its kind. The Fighting Lady as always was striving to be first.

The system had also been used to provide the crew

with some unusual pictures in March of 1968. The *Yorktown* had been covering the *Pueblo* incident when she bent one of her giant fifteen foot props. The prop was bent eight-inches backward, which was serious, but did not affect the operating capacity of the ship.

When the divers went over the side, they took with them a portable camera. As the divers worked to correct the damaged prop, the crew topside on the carrier were watching the progress on television. This was the first time in history that the crew of a naval ship watched the underwater repair of their own vessel.

On July 26, 1968, the *Yorktown* received yet another skipper, her twenty-fourth. Captain Bennett had done wonders for The Fighting Lady and now it was time for another man to skipper her. The new man for the job was Captain John G. Fifield, and while he was aboard the ship would be in the public's eye more than once.

The combat career for The Fighting Lady was now over. She had reached old age and a long rest was in her future. By mid-October of 1968 she was drawing the attention of one of the television networks. The successful television show "Get Smart," which was a comedy about a bumbling secret agent named Maxwell Smart, needed a ship for one of its episodes. The producer looked around, and picked the *Yorktown* as his prop.

On October 16, Captain Fifield welcomed the television crews aboard. The star, Don Adams, who played Maxwell Smart, came aboard; but the crew wanted to see his assistant, Agent Ninety-nine, who was played by lovely Barbara Feldon. The welcome mat was out for everyone, and the crew did their best to extend to the television people the warm hospitality the *Yorktown* had shown all over the Pacific.

While the actors and actresses played their scenes, the crew watched in silence; but after each scene was filmed they would shout their approval. During breaks the stars would sign autographs for members of the crew, and during lunch they would eat with the crew, thus affording some glimpses of their personal lives to several members of the crew. Finally, after two days of shooting, the stars and production staff left for the studio. They left behind a happy crew.

Next on the *Yorktown's* schedule was to have the flight deck painted, but the people doing the painting would not be members of the crew. Twentieth-Century Fox was sending over a crew of prop people to paint the deck. The *Yorktown* was to have a part in another movie, but this time she would play the Japanese carrier *Akagi*. Not many people realized as they watched the Japanese planes take off from the *Akagi*, that the carrier in the scenes was really the *Yorktown*. The movie was *Tora! Tora! Tora!* It was about the attack upon Pearl Harbor on December 7, 1941, and the carrier in that movie was, of course, the *Yorktown*.

The flight deck was painted to look like the deck of Admiral Yamamoto's flagship, the *Akagi*. From this flight deck thirty planes, made up to look Japanese, flew toward Pearl Harbor, in the movie. The actual filming was started on December 2, 1968 off the coast of San Diego, California. Since the movie crews knew nothing about carrier operations, *Yorktown* crew members did the actual launching and landing of the planes. Twentieth-Century Fox furnished Japanese flight-deck uniforms, and the superstructure was covered with anti-splinter matresses like those used on the *Akagi* on that fateful December morning twenty-seven years before.

It was ironic. Here was a ship that earned the nickname of The Fighting Lady by sinking 119 Japanese ships from 1943 to 1945, playing the part of a Japanese carrier. The flag that the crew of World War II had fought so hard to keep from flying over the heads of all free men, was now flying from the staff of the carrier that Tokyo Rose had said was doomed. Time does heal all wounds, and the *Yorktown* was now playing the part of her enemy of twenty-three years before, an enemy who was now her ally.

After the filming, Captain Fifield steamed for Pearl Harbor with his cargo of thirty Japanese planes. These planes would be needed for the rest of the filming that would take place in Hawaii. Although the last couple of weeks had been different, the crew enjoyed the opportunity to help show the story behind that "day of infamy."

Within days after the Japanese planes were unloaded, the *Yorktown* was getting ready for her part in man's greatest venture. President Kennedy had promised in the early 1960's that the Americans would land a man on the moon before the 1970's. At Cape Kennedy three men were getting ready to leave the earth for the moon. These men were Colonel Frank Borman, Captain James Lovell, Jr., and Major William Anders. These three men would be the first men to ever see the moon close up, and the *Yorktown* would be waiting for them when they made their splash-down in the Pacific.

As the three men were preparing for the lunar mission, the crew of the *Yorktown* was getting ready for their return. NASA had provided the crew with a dummy capsule, called "boilerplate." With this dummy, the Apollo VIII recovery crew would be able to practice so that they would know exactly what to do on the actual day of recovery.

Boilerplate would be lowered over the side, and the Underwater Demolition Team Twelve would go into the water and practice adding the flotation collar to keep the capsule from sinking into the Pacific. The UDT 12 practiced, and they successfuly picked up boilerplate up three times during daylight hours and three times during night. Not only did the UDT boys have to practice, but so did the men in the weapons department aboard the ship. These men would be responsible for picking up the capsule and for putting it onto elevator number three. After six successful attempts out of six tries, they were ready for the real thing on December 27.

On December 21, 1968, man began a journey that he had been longing to take for centuries. He was leaving the gravitational pull of the earth and heading for another heavenly body, the moon. Aboard the *Yorktown*, everyone was ready for his role in the most dramatic undertaking in America's history.

While the three astronauts were in the cold void of space, the crew of the *Yorktown* was enjoying the warm weather of the Pacific. In fact, swim calls were allowed for the crew while they waited for December 27. Two of the swim calls were cut short, however: one because of rough seas and the other because of the most dreaded creature of the seas, sharks.

The weather was good on the whole, and the *Yorktown's* own meteorologists, Lieutenant Commander Neil F. O'Connor and his staff of eleven men, were keeping NASA informed as to the weather conditions in the recovery area. O'Connor and his staff made upper-air and surface observations every three hours during the Apollo VIII mission. After the mission was over, O'Connor would have yet another job. He was also the public relations officer aboard the ship. This task would keep him very busy during the recovery operations.

The three astronauts arrived in lunar orbit on Christmas Eve, and as these three men scanned the moonscape below their capsule, they read from the Bible. Millions all over the world watched and listened as these three humble men read from the first book of the Bible. A more fitting Christmas present to the people of the earth would have been hard to find.

The next day, Christmas Day, the bake shop of the *Yorktown* was humming with excitement. CSCS Marlin Buirge had designed a cake to celebrate the mission of the three astronauts. His design called for the baking of sixty sheet cakes, arranged so that on top of the seven-foot by three-foot cake, there would be an open book. On the pages of this book would be the names of the three men in orbit around the moon as well as the name *Yorktown*.

With the design established, CS2 Samuel Clements was given the task of baking the thirty chocolate and thirty white cakes. When finished with his baking, CS2 Clements discovered that he had baked 450 pounds of cakes.

Next the icing was made. It contained twelve pounds of shortening, seventeen pounds of butter, fifty-seven pounds of powdered sugar, and nine teaspoons of vanilla. When the icing was finished, CS1 Steven Grasteit and CS1 C. T. Calhoun covered the cake with the ninety pounds of icing. Although they were not professional cake decorators, they did a professional job on this cake. The total weight of the cake was 540 pounds. Because of the weight of the cake and its size, it was assembled near a bomb elevator so it could be brought up to the hangar deck for the recovery ceremonies on December 27.

The crew was getting ready for the ceremonies that would take place when the astronauts splashed down, but this was not all they were doing. Every night either Chaplain Lucian R. Brasley or Chaplain Dean K. Veltman led the crew in prayer for the safe return of the three men so far from earth, and for their families, and for the men aboard who would be taking part in the actual recovery of the space craft when it hit the water.

On Christmas Day, a joint Catholic-Protestant prayer service for world peace was held on the flight deck. As the choir sang Christmas carols, these simple, yet meaningful songs carried out over the blue Pacific, and gave a peaceful atmosphere to a warship that had seen more than her share of fighting and death.

After the services, the crew gathered beneath makeshift Christmas trees to open presents from home as more carols were sung over the sound systems. The spirit of Christmas was in the air. Friendship and peace were felt everywhere. The news media was welcomed by the crew. Nowhere was there a stranger. The *Yorktown* was like a mother with her children safe at her side for this special day.

Christmas had always been special aboard the *Yorktown*, but every year after Christmas the crew had had a job to perform and this year was no different. December 27 was only two days away, and the world would be watching the performance of the crew. Each man involved directly in the recovery went over his part mentally until he felt that he was perfect in his function.

On the morning of December 27, the crew was up early; in fact, it is safe to say that even the men who had been on watch the night before were up. At 3:40 A.M. on the dimly lit flight deck, Commander Donald S. Jones was revving up his helicopter. Beside him was his copilot, Lieutenant Commander Carl J. Frank. His two crewmen were AWC Norval L. Wood and AW2 James B. Dorsey.

In the chopper were the three men of the UDT-12 Team. These included Lieutenant (jg) Richard J. Flanagan, SFC Donald L. Schwab, and Robert H. Coggin.

It was still dark over the Pacific as the chopper

left the deck of The Fighting Lady at 3:45 A.M. High in the dark sky above, Apollo VIII was heading toward reentry and the *Yorktown*.

As the sun began to appear on the horizon, a complete calm fell over the crew. Then suddenly a bright light appeared in the sky. Apollo VIII was reentering the atmosphere. As the capsule fell closer to the sea, the crew could see the drama unfold before their eyes. Soon the chutes opened, and at 4:51 A.M. the capsule hit the water just two-and-one-half miles off the port quarter. This was the closest a capsule had ever come to a recovery ship. It almost landed on the flight deck. Cheers went up everywhere as the men realized the capsule had made a safe splash-down.

In the air, the chopper was heading toward the point of splash-down. It was Chief Wood who first spotted the capsule. Inside, the astronauts had confirmed that they were all right, and that everything was "AOK."

At 5:35 A.M. Bob Coggin entered the warm water and attached the sea anchor. He was followed by Lieutenant Flanagan and Don Schwab. These three men attached and inflated the flotation collar. Through the intercom the astronauts joked with the swimmers. They told them that the moon was not made of Limburger cheese, but it was made of American cheese. They also sent out Christmas greetings to everyone.

Soon all three astronauts were in the helicopter, and were heading toward the ship. At 6:21 A.M. the chopper, piloted by Commander Don Jones, landed aboard The Fighting Lady. The first man to go toward the chopper was John Stonesifer, the senior member of the NASA recovery team. Soon after, the three astronauts emerged from the chopper to the cheers of the hundreds of people aboard the *Yorktown*. As they walked down the red carpet, they were welcomed aboard by Captain Fifield. After a few brief words, the three men went below for the briefing.

As the rest of the world watched the activities below decks, the unsung heroes of the *Yorktown* successfully brought the Apollo VIII capsule aboard. By 7:18 A.M. the *Yorktown* had completed her job. Both astronauts and capsule were safely aboard the ship.

Many of the crew mailed letters that day. One member, Melvin L. Bien, saved his letter with the postmark that showed he had been aboard for the historic mission, the last Pacific mission for an aging lady.

That evening the crew cut the large cake that had been baked for the occasion. Everyone was given a piece, and by 10:00 P.M. the entire 540 pound cake was gone. The next day Frank Borman, James Lovell, and William Anders left the *Yorktown* for Hawaii, and a place in the history of man.

Chapter XI

The Apollo VIII mission was over, and it had been a huge success for mankind and for the United States. America now had a strong lead in the race to the moon. With the *Yorktown's* part of the mission over, Captain Fifield made plans for the trip to the East Coast.

Word had been given in September, 1968, that the *Yorktown* was going to be changing her home port from Long Beach, California to Norfolk, Virginia. Most of the crew preferred the Long Beach area and some asked for transfers to ships that were going to stay on the West Coast.

In late January, 1969, the *Yorktown* set sail for the East Coast. Many of the people in the Long Beach area would miss this lady of the seas. She had become a favorite of the local citizens, especially the children. The ship had held open house regularly, which enabled children, clubs, community leaders, and tourists to visit aboard a carrier. The crew had donated money for worthy causes in the Long Beach area, even while at sea off the coast of Korea and Vietnam. She would be missed by the citizens of Long Beach.

As The Fighting Lady sailed south toward South America, Captain Fifield read departing messages he had received on behalf of the ship and crew. Some of these messages called the *Yorktown* "The Queen of the Pacific." She had spent twenty-seven years and three wars in the Pacific, leading in every phase of carrier aviation both in peace and in war. From Marcus Island in August, 1943 to Apollo VIII in December, 1968, she had been the leader. Captain Fifield read with pride these letters honoring The Fighting Lady.

Five days out the ship crossed the equator, and as with every crossing the crew had a ceremony. In naval tradition, everyone who has crossed the equator is a "shellback," and those who have not are "polywogs." It was during this time that the polywogs become shellbacks, with a little fun in the process.

The shellbacks accompanied by Davy Jones, King Neptune and his royal court held the ceremonies on the flight deck. The polywogs on this day lose all rank and are the lowest form of life possible. A seaman, if he is a shellback, has rank over a polywog captain. The polywogs are forced to perform unusual but harmless feats. Liquids are poured over the heads of the unfortunate polywogs, and by the end of the ceremonies the polywogs are a mess. With the closing of the ceremonies they become full-fledged shellbacks. It is all done in fun, and no hard feelings are felt afterwards.

On January 31, the crew got sight of Valparaiso, Chile. As the *Yorktown* entered the harbor, she fired a twenty-one gun salute to the president of Chile, followed by a thirteen gun salute to the commandant of the First Naval Zone. The shore batteries on Valparaiso answered the salutes, which made for a most impressive arrival.

The dock facilities at Valparaiso could not accommodate the huge carrier, so Captain Fifield anchored about a mile from shore. With a fifteen-minute trip by boat, the crew could be ashore. The *Yorktown* welcomed aboard distinguished guests from Valparaiso and the neighboring villages. Also present for the VIP tour were members of the Chilean navy and the press. To show their appreciation for these tours, the Chilean Navy gave tours to over 120 crew members of the *Yorktown*. The Fighting Lady then unloaded over five tons of "Handclasp" material to be given to the needy by the U.S. Naval Mission. These items included clothing, medicines, soap and sporting goods, and were all donated by U.S. manufacturers in a gesture of friendship.

For the next two days, over 11,000 Chileans toured the huge carrier. Almost all of the visitors were impressed by the size of the *Yorktown*, and enjoyed looking at the displays on the hangar deck. The crew had made new friends, and the citizens of Valparaiso left knowing the Americans were indeed their friends.

The *Yorktown* left the coast of Chile and sailed

south. On February 7, she was near historic Cape Horn. At 9:30 P.M. on February 7, she crossed from the Pacific into the Atlantic, thus ending twenty-seven years of service in the Pacific. Crew members on the flight deck watched as the shore line passed on the left. This was the farthest south that the *Yorktown* had ever been. She was now only 490 miles from Antarctica, and the weather was cold. In 1943, the *Yorktown* had entered the Pacific by going through the Panama Canal, but because of her angled deck she now had to pass through Cape Horn. The canal had become obsolete for modern warships and tankers. They had outgrown the canal.

The ship was now sailing north, and one of the sports that a few of the daring members of the crew played was to stand on the front of the flight deck and lean into the wind. This left the person leaning slightly over the front of the flight deck with only the forward motion of the ship to keep him from falling off the bow.

On February 14, the ship entered Guanabara Bay at Rio de Janeiro, Brazil. The crew spent three days touring the city, and enjoying the carnival which had just started. As the crew toured the city, the citizens of Rio toured the ship. Before the *Yorktown* left the bay, the crew unloaded over seven tons of Handclasp material to be given out later by the U.S. Naval Mission there.

Aboard for the cruise to Norfolk, Virginia were three members of the Navy League. These men were retired businessmen, who enjoyed helping the navy. The three were Carl Wilson, Robert Wilson, and Troy Ziglar. Troy had played a vital role in providing the *Yorktown* with its television system, the first of its kind in the world. This system consisted of broadcasting equipment, miles of cables, expensive electronic equipment, and eighty television sets. He and many civilian technicians had installed the system free.

At last, the *Yorktown* arrived at Norfolk, Virginia, and in March many of the crew left for other ships. George Morgan left to go aboard the *Bon Homme Richard*. Later he went aboard the nuclear carrier *Enterprise*. George later stated, after retiring from the navy, that his tour of duty aboard the *Yorktown* was his finest. Also leaving in March was Melvin L. Bien, Jr. He, too, had the same feelings. He stated that the two carriers he served on after the *Yorktown* lacked the warmth and feeling he had felt aboard the CVS-10. The Fighting Lady had always been good at making friends. To thousands of men she was not only a piece of war machinery; she seemed to have a spirit, a spirit that was soon to play a most important part in the life of The Fighting Lady.

On August 5, Captain William F. Charles took command of the *Yorktown*. He would take her into the reserve fleet. After twenty-seven years of duty, she was going to be retired. Retirement sounds good to a man, but for a ship it is the end.

On June 27, 1970, The Fighting Lady was stricken from the United States Navy. She was stripped of her equipment, and her hull began to rust. As the years passed, rust, dirt, and pieces of left-over material from the dock workers were all that remained on the once-proud carrier. Ahead of the

298

Yorktown, tied to the pier at the Military Ocean Terminal in Bayonne, New Jersey, was the *Essex*. A winning bid of $1,600,000 had just been submitted for the *Essex*. She would soon be cut up as scrap. Other ships had already been scrapped or were scheduled to be scrapped. The *Bunker Hill, Ticonderoga, Wasp, Hornet*, and other famous carriers of World War II would soon be no more. The *Yorktown* awaited her fate also.

Not too far away in New York City, a lone man was beginning to turn wheels. This man, James T. Bryan, Jr., had taken it upon himself to try to save the *Yorktown*. He made phone calls, wrote letters, and had personal talks with others to try to save the old carrier. Somewhere along the line he succeeded. The state of South Carolina agreed to buy the *Yorktown* for its new tourist attraction in Charleston, called Patriots Point.

On June 9, the *Yorktown* was towed through the bay, past the *Essex*. She had beaten the *Essex* for the last time; only this time there was no crew aboard to cheer the victory, and it was doubtful that any crew would have cheered. The carrier *Essex* was doomed, and quite possibly the rest of the *Essex* class; only the spirit that The Fighting Lady had somehow given to this small group of men had enabled her to survive.

Aboard for the ceremonies, as the *Yorktown* began her journey, were several plank owners: Joe Sharkey, Bill Schaffer, Ed Sarksiion, and Jim Bryan. Joe had seen to it that the *Yorktown* had received a new paint job before she left on her journey. As she was towed through the harbor, the men got aboard a police launch to watch their Lady being towed past the Statue of Liberty toward Charleston, South Carolina.

On June 15, the *Yorktown* entered Charleston Harbor. As she entered the harbor under tow, Jim Bryan was there on a Coast Guard boat with Harold Syfrett and Bob Alexander, the first Protestant chaplain aboard the *Yorktown*. Over 500 small craft greeted her in the harbor. Horns blew and fire boats sent streams of water high into the air. The Fighting Lady was getting an unrehearsed, heroine's welcome. As the tugs nudged her into her permanent berth, all of Charleston, South Carolina was turned out. People were lined up ten deep on the famous Battery, and traffic on the Cooper River bridge was at a standstill for over an hour as over 500 cars packed onto the bridge. For this many people to greet a ship that many of them had never seen before was a great tribute to the *Yorktown*.

Word got around across the country that the *Yorktown* had been saved from the scrapper's torch. Old shipmates began sending in money and souvenirs, and offering their services to help put the ship in first-class shape again.

Smoke Strean, who was the commander of the first nuclear-powered naval task force in history, found a TBF. Others joined in, helping to pay for this plane and the others that would follow.

Names of World War II crew members began to fill the association's list. Dick Tripp, Don Seaman, James Pfister, Joe Kristufek, and others were named as representatives of their region or squadron. Admirals, captains, and others began helping, until the

U.S.S. *Yorktown* CV-10 Association had a most impressive list of members. It is, even now, by far the largest World War II association in existence. Jim Bryan had had a dream, and it had come true.

For the past several years, the *Yorktown* has been the center of many reunions for the association. In 1978, the guest of honor was President Gerald R. Ford. He was made an honorary member, and his old ship, the *Monterey*, was commemorated in a memento room aboard the *Yorktown*. The *Saratoga* also acquired a room. Other carriers now have their reunions aboard the *Yorktown*. She is a symbol of all World War II carriers and the men who served aboard them.

Located on the hangar deck are plaques honoring men who served aboard the *Yorktown* from 1943 to 1970. These plaques were donated by friends and family. The wall that these plaques hang on separates a theater from the rest of the hangar deck. In this theater visitors can see the movie The Fighting Lady, as well as other movies about carrier life. The name of this theater is The Smokey Stover, Yorktown, Memorial Theater. Thirty-five years after he went down over Truk, Smokey is still a part of the spirit that enabled the *Yorktown* to become the museum she is today. She is proud. She is spirited. She is The Fighting Lady.

APPENDIX A

Below is a list of raids in which the U.S.S. *Yorktown*, CV-10 participated from April 15, 1943 until August 15, 1945:

Attack on Marcus Island, August 31, 1943
*Attack on Wake Island, October 5-6, 1943
Attack on and support of invasion force,
  *Gilbert Islands, November 19-27, 1943
Attack on Marshall Islands, December 4-5, 1943
Attack on and support of invasion force,
  *Marshall Islands, January 29-February 4, 1944
Attack on Truk, February 16-17, 1944
Attack on Marianas Island, February 21-22, 1944
*Attack on Palau Island, March 29-31, 1944
Attack on Woleai Island, April 1, 1944
Attack on Truk Island, April 29-30, 1944
*Attack on and support of invasion force
  Hollandia, New Guinea, April 21-27, 1944
Attack on Guam, June 11-13, 1944
Attack on Bonin Islands, June 15-16, 1944
Defense of Marianas Island and attack on
  Japanese fleet units, June 19-20, 1944
*Attack on and support of invasion force,
  Marianas Island, June 30-July 21, 1944
Attack on Yap Island, Ingulu Atoll, and
  Ulithi Atoll July 25-28, 1944
Attack of Philippine shipping, November 11-15
  1944
*Attack on Central Philippine airfields,
  November 19, 1944
Attack on Luzon airfields in support of
  Occupation of Mindoro, December 14-16, 1944

*Asterisk designates stars that are worn on the Asiatic-Pacific ribbon.

Attack on Luzon and Formosa airfields,
  January 3–9, 1945
*Attack on shipping in South China Sea and
  airfields along French Indo-China coast,
  Canton-Hong Kong area, and Formosa,
  January 10–16, 1945
Attack on shipping and airfields at
  Formosa and Nansei Shoto, January 21–22,
  1945
Attack on Tokyo Bay area airfields
  and aircraft factories, February 16–17, 1945
*Attack on Chichi Jima, Bonin Islands
  February 18, 1945
Attack on and support of invasion force
  Iwo Jima, Valcano Islands, February 20–22,
  1945
Attack on Tokyo Bay area, February 25, 1945
Attack on Kyushu and Shikoku, Japan,
  March 18–19 and 29, 1945
Defense of invasion force Okinawa
  Nansei Shoto and attack on Japanese
  Task Force, April 7, 1945
*Attack on Islands of the Nansei
  Shoto, southern Kyushu, Shikoku,
  and western Honshu in support of
  invasion force, Okinawa, April 24–May 11,
  1945, and May 24–June 13, 1945
Attack on Tokyo area airfields, July 10, 1945
Attack on southern Hokkaido airfields, installa-
  tions, and shipping, July 14–15, 1945
*Attack on Tokyo area airfields and combatant
  shipping at Yokosuka, July 18, 1945
Attack on Kure Naval Base and adjoining air-
  fields, July 24–25, 1945
Attack on Tokyo area airfields and Shipping at
  Maizuru Naval Base, western Honshu, July 30,
  1945
Attack on northern Honshu airfields, August
  9–10, 1945

Attack on Tokyo area airfields, August 13 and 15, 1945

APPENDIX B

Below are some facts concerning the U.S.S. *Yorktown*, CV-10 from December 1, 1941 until October 21, 1945.

Built by: Newport News Shipbuilding & Drydock Co., at Newport News, Virginia
Keel laid: December 1, 1941
Ship launched: January 21, 1943
Ship commissioned: April 15, 1943

Overall length: 880 feet
Overall beam: 147 feet
Maximum draft: 29.6 feet
Speed: Over thirty knots
Horsepower: 150,000

Nautical miles traveled to October 21, 1945: 235,360
Gallons of fuel oil used: 40,315,765
Gallons of fresh water made daily: 86,000
Times ship was fueled: 121
Total number of destroyers fueled: 271
Total number of meals served: Over 8,500,000

Number of five-inch guns: 12
Number of 40-mm. guns: 72
Number of 20-mm. guns: 65

Total number of sorties over enemy targets: 11,346
Total number of aircraft landings on board: 31,170
Total tons of bombs dropped over enemy targets: 3,640
Total number of rockets fired on enemy targets: 6,814

Total number of enemy aircraft shot down by ship's aircraft: 458

Total number of enemy shot down by ship's guns: 14

Total number of enemy aircraft destroyed on ground: 695

Total number of enemy aircraft probably destroyed: 1,191

Total number of enemy aircraft destroyed or damaged: 2,358

Total number of our aircraft lost due to combat: 131

Total number of our aircraft lost operationally: 73

Total number of our aircraft lost, all causes: 204

Total number of enemy ships sunk: 119

Total tonnage of enemy ships sunk: 244,770

Total number of enemy ships damaged: 329

Total tonnage of enemy ships damaged: 820,693

Total number of five-inch shells fired: 15,184

Total number of 40-mm. shells fired: 167,630

Total number of 20-mm. shells fired: 472,757

Total number of officers, ship's company: 150

Total number of enlisted men, ship's company: 2,550

Total number of officers, air group: 175

Total number of enlisted men, air group: 130

Total number of officers, flag: 35

Total number of enlisted men, flag: 65

Total number of officers and enlisted men on board: 3,105

There was a ratio of 1 to 11.5 aircraft lost. For every plane lost on the *Yorktown* there were 11.5 enemy planes either lost or damaged.

The *Yorktown* averaged five ships sunk every month for two years.

The *Yorktown*, while sinking 119 enemy ships, was only hit one time herself by enemy action, and this hit was not serious.

The *Yorktown* was the first *Essex* class carrier to fly her planes into combat, beating the *Essex* by a few minutes. Pilots of Air Group Eighty-eight aboard the *Yorktown* were the last Americans to fight in World War II.

The *Yorktown* had a total of four captains; three of those became rear admirals during World War II.

The *Yorktown* had two nicknames: "The Lucky Y," because of her skill in remaining unharmed, and "The Fighting Lady," because of her combat record and willingness to fight the enemy and destroy him.

APPENDIX C

The following letters were copied from the book, *Into the Wind*, a pictorial book about the *Yorktown*, CV-10 during World War II. From these two letters one can see the respect given to this ship by men who had never been aboard her, yet were touched by her actions.

U.S. Benevolence
September 1st, 1946

Sir:

I should like to try to thank you and your officers on my own behalf and also for the British staff and patients in Shinagowa Hospital, Tokyo, for the wonderful relief work accomplished on and after August 27th, 1945.

We had been living in suspense in the hospital having no reliable news until we saw your carrier's planes that morning . . . then we knew we were all right!

It is impossible to describe the feelings of relief and happiness that ran through the hospital. Staff and patients alike were delirious with joy. We appreciated our bombs but were even more thrilled by the sight of pilots waving to us from planes flying so low.

Few of us bothered to go to bed that night. It is safe to say that none slept.

Pieces of parachute will be most treasured mementos in many homes all over the world for we had a most cosmopolitan population.

I have been asked to thank you also on behalf of the Dutch patients.

I deeply regret that owing to a present disability I cannot come aboard to pay my respects and to thank you and your officers personally, but hope to be able to do so in the near future.

                                    I am, Sir,
The Captain, Officers,   Your obedient servant,
and Men, U.S.S. *Yorktown*   H. H. Cleave,
                              Surgeon Comdr. R.N.
        Senior Allied Medical Officer in Shinagowa
                              Hospital, Toyko

The following letter was received from Major E. J. Currah, liberated British P.O.W.

I should feel grateful if you would kindly convey my thanks to the Captain, Officers, and Ship's Company of the "Fighting Lady" for their extreme kindness to the Prisoners of War at 20-D Camp Sumidagawa, Tokyo. We had been relegated to oblivion for many moons in this remote camp but strangely enough we were picked up very early by your aviators who literally inundated us with gifts. Be this an everlasting tribute to your pilots and observers. When they first spotted us excitement was unbounded, and when they zoomed low over our heads tears of joy welled into many eyes, but, when it rained parcels we just had to go to the ground. It was terrific. It was a great day for us and an unforgettable one. We feel proud that our first real inkling of the end should emanate from men of such a great ship with such a glorious record. Men who had gallantly fought them bit by bit to our very doorstep. Each and everyone of us will forever-more associate liberty and freedom with the U.S.S. *Yorktown*. You have carved a niche in our memories and usurped a big spot in our hearts.

To these two groups of men, the *Yorktown* was the first contact with the outside world. It was through the *Yorktown* that they learned that the war was over, and that the Americans had won. The *Yorktown*, as always, was first!

APPENDIX D

Below is a short history of the U.S.S. *Yorktown*, CV-10; The Fighting Lady.

April, 1943–July, 1943—Training

July, 1943–September, 1945
Engaged in World War II and was awarded the Presidential Unit Citation, fifteen battle stars, and other awards for operating against the Japanese in the Pacific Theater.

September, 1945–January, 1947
Engaged principally in returning veterans home from Pacific bases. Decommissioned and placed in Reserve Fleet on January 9, 1947.

January, 1947–December, 1952
In the Reserve Fleet. Removed from the Reserve Fleet and recommissioned on December 15, 1952.

December, 1952–June, 1970
Engaged in the Korean War for which she was awarded the Korean Service Medal and the United Nations Service Medal. Engaged in the Vietnam War for which she received the Armed Forces Expeditionary Medal and the Vietnam Service Medal. She also picked up the Astronauts following the successful Apollo 8 space mission, the first time man had ever orbited the moon.

June, 1970–June, 1975
In the Reserve Fleet.

June 9, 1975
Under tow from Bayonne, New Jersey to Charleston, South Carolina.

June 15, 1975
Moored at Patriots Point.

October 13, 1975
Dedicated on the 200th birthday of the U.S. Navy as the first ship in the Naval and Maritime Museum.

January 3, 1976
Opened to the public as the country's only WWII Aircraft Memorial Museum.

APPENDIX E

While the *Yorktown* was busy at sea fighting the war that won her the right to use the title The Fighting Lady, several members of the crew decided that the carrier should have a real lady to represent her. They wrote a letter to the editors of *Life* magazine asking them for their help in finding a live "Miss Fighting Lady." Below is a copy of that letter as it appeared in *Life* magazine on May 21, 1945.

"MISS FIGHTING LADY"
Sirs:

We the undersigned, members of the crew of the U.S. Navy aircraft carrier known as "The Fighting Lady," are in fervent hopes of finding a typical American girl to be chosen by the crew as the official pin-up of this ship, this girl to have the title of Miss Fighting Lady.

We will accept pictures submitted by, or for, any American girl. These pictures will be judged by a committee selected from various divisions aboard the ship. Those pictures chosen by the committee as most promising will be brought before the entire crew for a final vote.

Upon the ship's arrival in the U.S. and if security reasons permit, we hope to be allowed to give a ball in honor of the girl chosen as Miss Fighting Lady, at which time we will pay our respects to our queen of the Fleet.

We will appreciate sincerely whatever *Life* may do to aid us in our efforts to find this girl.

PhM3c Sam S. Pearl	SC1 Joseph W. Berg
S1c John Kenneth Thomas	HA1c Charles E. Starks
S1c R. P. Kitchen	BM1c John B. Parrott
Mus2c E. L. Dunning	F1c Windell E. Lawson
EM3c James F. McKee	CPL. Hewey J. Doyle, USMC
MaM1c H. E. Bolden	F1c Louis E. Bowman
S1c Joseph F. Braun	QM2c Luther Dick
GM3c Robert H. Davis	MM1c Ray Prensser

Out of the more than 1,200 photographs that were sent to the committee for the beauty contest, the winner was finally selected. She was Betty Jo Copeland of Fort Worth, Texas.

She received the word that she had won on October 20, 1945, when she received a telephone call from an officer aboard the *Yorktown*. She later flew to San Francisco to be presented the title of Miss Fighting Lady.

Betty Jo was 5 feet 5 inches tall, weighed 125 pounds, had naturally curly light-brown hair and brown eyes. She was an all-around athlete, a gin-rummy addict, a dabbler at painting, an avid reader of books-of-the-month, an amateur pianist, and an accomplished dancer.

Captain Boone presented her with a watch, which had the following inscription: "Miss Fighting Lady," followed by the words "Presented by the U.S.S. *Yorktown*." At the dance, Chaplain Moody introduced her to her dance partners. These were men who had been fortunate enough to win a drawing which entitled them to dance with her.

The U.S.S. *Yorktown*, CV-10, The Fighting Lady, now had a pin-up to represent her on the land as she had represented her country at sea. She had both a beauty and a lady in Betty Jo Copeland, Miss Fighting Lady.

APPENDIX F

Below is a list of the Commanding Officers aboard the U.S.S. *Yorktown* (CV-10) (CVA-10) (CVS-10).

Joseph J. Clark, Captain USN (April 4, 1943–February 10, 1944)

Ralph E. Jennings, Captain USN (February 10, 1944–September 29, 1944)

Thomas S. Combs, Captain USN (September 29, 1944–April 23, 1945)

Walter F. Boone, Captain USN (April 23, 1945–November 19, 1945)

Maurice E. Browder, Captain USN (November 19, 1945–July 16, 1946)

Charles T. Fitzgerald, Commander USN (July 16, 1946–December 26, 1946)

Malcom C. Reeves Commander USN (December 26, 1946– January 9, 1947)

William M. Nation, Captain USN (December 15, 1952–August 3, 1953)

Arnold W. McKechnie, Captain USN (August 3, 1953–August 5, 1954)

Gerald L. Huff, Captain USN (August 5, 1954–July 15, 1955)

Emmett O'Beirne, Captain USN (July 15, 1955–September 14, 1956)

Edward E. Colestock, Captain USN (September 14, 1956–September 28, 1957)

James O. Cobb, Captain USN (September 28, 1957–August 19, 1958)

Porter F. Bedell, Captain USN (August 19, 1958–June 6, 1959)

Louis H. Bauer, Captain USN (June 6, 1959–May 19, 1960)

Charles E. Gibson, Captain USN (May 19, 1960–June 10, 1961)

William G. Privette, Jr., Captain USN (June 10, 1961–June 14, 1962)

Waller G. Moore, Captain USN (June 14, 1962–June 28, 1963)

James P. Lynch, Captain USN (June 28, 1963–June 22, 1964)

Raymond S. Osterhoudt, Captain USN (June 22, 1964–June 11, 1965)

James B. Cain, Captain USN (June 11, 1965–May 7, 1966)

William M. McCulley, Jr., Captain USN (May 7, 1966–July 20, 1967)

William L. Bennett, Captain, USN (July 20, 1967–July 26, 1968)

John C. Fifield, Captain USN (July 26, 1968–August 5, 1969)

William F. Charles, Captain USN (August 5, 1969–June 27, 1970)

The following poem was written by *New York Times* war correspondent, George F. Horne. It has been taken from the book *Into the Wind*.

SAGA OF THE YORKTOWN

Men have sung the songs of battle
In the deathless lore of war,
Of fighting men and wanderers of the sea;
Of Brandywine and Lexington
And sad Corregidor,
Of Dewey and of Lafayette and Lee.

There's the famous Lost Battalion
And the Flying Dutchman tale;
There's the valor of the gallant Light Brigade;
There's the hole of Black Calcutta;
There were deeds in days of sail,
And the words they wrote in history never fade.

You can have your Ancient Mariners
And Flying Dutchie Men.
The cloud-hauled ghostly galleons of yore,
For I sing another saga

314

Of the missing See-V-Ten,
And the legendary company she bore.

She was built of steel and timber,
Of lives, of blood and tears,
And she sailed unfinished out of Norfolk's ken.
Heading straight for the Pacific
With an Indian terrific
Belching smoke and oaths and orders to his men.

She was seen not long thereafter
In the River of the Pearl,
Where her fly-men tried their wings above the foam;
Then she slipped off down the channel
With her petticoats aswirl,
Just like any trollop running off from home.

In the years that followed after
She was seen around the ocean,
At Marcus, Wake and many another isle;
And they say the men on board her
Had a funny sort of notion
They were going to turn back homeward after awhile.

There are mystics in Hawaii
Who stir fortune-teller brew
And deal with ghosts and spirits on the sky,
And they claim that during Kona
When the wind is wet with dew
They can hear the "York" men puffing through
    the sky.

And beyond on the horizon
They can see a form ride low,
And hear the wheezy grinding of her gears,
But no answer greets their hail
From the old men at the rail,
And when the dawn comes up she disappears.

There were yellow men on Kwajalein,
And monkeys up at Truk,
Who saw the ship's old bird men through the flak,
As they winged through any weather

Babbling strange words all together:
"Tally Ho Ack! Tally Ack Ack! Tally Ack!"

They were bearded, gaunt and shaggy
And their whiskers rode the breeze
Like the brooms of ancient witches 'cross the moon:
All their fly suits whipped in tatters
As they'd slap their bony knees
Crying: "Yoicks! We're going to 'Frisco
   pretty soon."

But they never came to 'Frisco,
Though their wives and sweethearts wait,
Old and feeble, staunch and faithful to the last.
You can see them peering daily
Out beyond the Golden Gate
Where the ships of all the nations flicker past.

But not the phantom carrier,
Not the See-V-Ten
Who scuds the far blue reaches with her crew;
Though some prophets swear they'll see her
Creeping homeward once again,
Probably in 1952.

PRESIDENTIAL UNIT CITATION

Only six of the twenty-three fleet carriers engaged in combat in World War II received the Presidential Unit Citation. The U.S.S. *Yorktown* CV-10 was one of those carriers.

The President of the United States takes pleasure in presenting the Presidential Unit Citation to the
U.S.S. *YORKTOWN*
and her attached air groups participating in the following operations:

August 31, 1943, Marcus: October 5–6, 1943, Wake; November 19 to December 5, 1943, Gilberts; January 29 to February 23, 1944, Marshalls, Truk, Marianas; March 29 to April 30, 1944, Palau, Hollandia, Truk: AG-5 (VF-5, VB-5, VT-5).

June 11 to July 28, 1944, Marianas, Bonins, Yap:

AG-1 (VF-1, VB-1, VT-1, Part of VFN-77).

November 11 to 19, 1944, Luzon; December 14 to 16, Luzon; January 3 to 22, 1945, Philippines, Formosa, China Sea, Ryukyus: AG-3 (VF-3, VB-3, VT-3).

February 16 to 25, 1945, Japan, Bonins: AG-3 (VF-3, VBF-3, VB-3, VT-3).

March 18 to June 9, 1945, Ryukyus, Japan: AG-9 (2) (VF-9, VBF-9, VB-9, VT-9).

July 10 to August 15, 1945, Japan: AG-88 (VF-88, VBF-88, VB-88, VT-88). for services set forth in the following.

CITATION:

For extraordinary heroism in action against enemy Japanese forces in the air, at sea and on shore in the Pacific War Area from August 31, 1943, to August 15, 1945. Spearheading our concentrated carrier-warfare in forward areas, the U.S.S. *Yorktown* and her air groups struck crushing blows toward annihilating the enemy's fighting strength; they provided air cover for our amphibious forces; they fiercely countered the enemy's savage aerial attacks and destroyed his planes; and they inflicted terrific losses on the Japanese in Fleet and merchant marine units sunk or damaged. Daring and dependable in combat, the *YORKTOWN* with her gallant officers and men rendered loyal service in achieving the ultimate defeat of the Japanese Empire.

For the President,
James Forrestal
Secretary of the Navy

THE FIGHTING LADY

Below are some of the statistics of the *Yorktown* during World War II.

Total number of sorties over enemy targets: 11,346
Total number of five-inch shells fired: 15,184
Total number of 40-mm shells fired: 167,630
Total number of 20-mm shells fired: 472,757
Total number of rockets fired on enemy targets: 6,814
Total tons of bombs dropped over enemy targets: 3,640
Total number of aircraft landings on board: 31,170
Total number of enemy aircraft destroyed or damaged:
   2,358
Total number of American aircraft lost due to combat:
   131
Total number of ships sunk: 119
Total number of ships damaged: 329
Total tonnage of enemy ships sunk or damaged:
   1,065,463
Total number of officers and men on board: 3,105
Total times the Yorktown was hit by enemy action: 1
*Total times the Yorktown was inoperable due to enemy
   action*: 0

The *Yorktown* was a flagship during most of her World War II career.

BIBLIOGRAPHY

Baldwin, Hanson W. *Sea Fights and Shipwrecks*. New York: Modern Literary Editions Publishing Company, 1955.

Bryan, J., III *Aircraft Carrier*. New York: Ballantine Books, Inc., 1966.

Frank, Pat, and Harrington, Joseph D. *Rendezvous at Midway*. New York: Paperback Library, Inc., 1968.

Friedman, Norman *U.S.S. Yorktown CV-10*. Annapolis: Leeward Publications, 1977.

Hoehling, A. A. *The FRANKLIN Comes Home*. New York: Manor Books, 1976.

Hoyt, Edwin P. *The Death of the PRINCETON*. New York: Lancer Books, 1972.

Into The Wind, U.S.S. YORKTOWN CV-10, World War II. 1945

Loomis, Robert D. *Great American Fighter Pilots of World War II*. New York: Random House, 1961.

Macintyre, Donald *Aircraft Carrier*. New York: Ballantine Books, Inc., 1968.

Polmar, Norman *Aircraft Carriers*. Garden City, N.Y.: Doubleday & Co., 1968.

Reynolds, Clark G. *The Saga of Smokey Stover*. Charleston, S.C. Tradd Street Press, 1978.

Roscoe, Theodore *On The Seas and in The Skies*. New York: Hawthorne Books, Inc., 1970.

Steinberg, Rafael *Island Fighting*. New York: Time-Life Books, Inc., 1978.

U.S.S. Yorktown CV-10 Association, Inc. Newsletters.

U.S.S. YORKTOWN CVS-10, "The Fighting Lady." 1969.

Winter, Richard *From the Devil's Triangle To The Devil's Jaw*. New York: Bantam Books, Inc., 1977.

World Book Encyclopedia. Chicago: Field Enterprises, Volume 18, 1957.